SIR PHILIP SIDNEY

Selected Poetry and Prose

Edited by T. W. CRAIK, M.A., PH.D.

Lecturer in English
in the University of Leicester

METHUEN & CO LTD
11 NEW FETTER LANE LONDON EC4

This edition first published 1965
Introduction and Notes © T. W. Craik 1965
Printed in Great Britain by
Richard Clay (The Chaucer Press), Ltd.,
Bungay, Suffolk

Contents

Contents

Preface

My object in this volume is to put forward a selection of poems and prose passages from Sir Philip Sidney's most characteristic original works, that is, *The Defence of Poesy, Astrophel and Stella,* and *Arcadia.* I hope that the reader who first makes Sidney's acquaintance in this selection will read on where I have to leave off: Sidney is an author of remarkably even quality, and there are plenty of good things left for the seeker.

I have taken care to include what I regard as Sidney's best things, and have not excluded the most frequently anthologized poems. I have also, where possible, chosen extracts which throw light on each other.

The order of presentation is (with the exception of some of the miscellaneous poems at the end) the approximate order of composition. The reader should, however, bear in mind that the revised *Arcadia* contains matter from the original version which preceded most of Sidney's other extant poetry and prose. The Chronology, it must be added, depends partly on conjectures based upon Sidney's known opportunities for writing and upon such internal evidence as the works themselves afford.

It will be seen that the extracts from *Arcadia* do not go beyond the Third Book. This is because I regard Sidney's elaborate revision not as misplaced ingenuity but as a transformation for the better: more strange, but also more rich, than the original version. I regret its incompleteness as much as I regret the incompleteness of *The Faerie Queene* and *Don Juan.* Although in reading through *Arcadia* we have to make do with the original version's concluding books (which themselves contain many beauties: the final trial scene would undoubtedly have been transferred, much as it stands, to the revised version), in selection we may end with the Third Book, which is almost wholly Sidney's latest work. In selecting from these first three books of *Arcadia,* my principle has been, first, to include those passages which I could not spare, and second, to provide a continuous narrative, in the text where possible, and where impossible, in the notes.

The text of the prose is based on Feuillerat's reprints of the Elizabethan editions (see Short Bibliography). *The Defence of Poesy* is presented in an eclectic text: I have in general followed the words of Ponsonby's (1595) edition, but I have followed the paragraphing of Olney's (also 1595: called *An Apology for Poetry*) and admitted its readings where they are evidently superior. The text of *Arcadia* is from the edition of 1590, with emendations from that of 1593, collated with the Old *Arcadia* when Sidney has transferred a passage from this to the revised version. For the text of *Astrophel and Stella* and the other poems, including those which appear in *Arcadia*, I have used Professor Ringler's excellent edition (see Short Bibliography) and accepted his readings almost without exception. Spelling has throughout been modernized (except when an important established Elizabethan spelling occurs, such as 'burthen', 'murther', 'perfittest', and the like); and the punctuation has been modified in the direction of modernism, but not thoroughly modernized, as this would make Sidney's long sentences harder, not easier, to follow. When a sentence remains difficult for the modern reader it is explained in the notes.

The notes are critical and explanatory in character. As I have said, they fill in the gaps in the story of *Arcadia* and explain the references to other chapters of it. Not every allusion is explained: I have assumed, for example, that an encyclopaedia such as *Smith's Classical Dictionary* or the *Encyclopaedia Britannica* will be at hand for any reader who wishes information about Lucretius or Boccaccio. My notes (in which I am often indebted to the valuable work of previous editors cited in the Short Bibliography) attempt to supply as much explanation and commentary as will encourage an appreciative reading of Sidney; but that appreciation will finally rest on the reader's own efforts, not on mine.

                                                        T. W. CRAIK

Chronology of Sidney's Life and Works

1554   Philip Sidney born (30 November) at Penshurst, Kent; eldest son of Sir Henry Sidney and his wife Mary (daughter of John Dudley, Duke of Northumberland; sister of Robert Dudley, Earl of Leicester).

      Lyly born. Fulke Greville born.

1555   *Latimer and Ridley burnt.*

1556   *Cranmer burnt.*

1557   *Songs and Sonnets ('Tottel's Miscellany': poems of Wyatt, Surrey, and others) published.*

1558   *Queen Mary died. Queen Elizabeth I.*

1559   *Book of Common Prayer (1549, revised 1552) revised and reissued.*

1560   Sir Henry Sidney becomes Lord President of the Marches of Wales; lives at Ludlow Castle with his family.

1561   *Castiglione's* The Courtier *(Hoby's translation) published.*

1563   *Foxe's* Acts and Monuments *('The Book of Martyrs') published.*

1564   Sidney entered at Shrewsbury School, with Greville.

      Shakespeare, Marlowe, Galileo born. Calvin, Michelangelo died.

1565   Sir Henry Sidney becomes Lord Deputy of Ireland.

1568   Sidney entered at Christ Church, Oxford.

1569   *Heliodorus's* Aethiopian History *(Underdowne's translation) published.*

1570   *Queen Elizabeth excommunicated by the Pope.*

1571   Sidney leaves Oxford (without taking his degree) and becomes a courtier.

1572   Sidney gets leave of Queen Elizabeth to travel abroad to learn languages. Goes to Paris (May) and witnesses the Saint Bartholomew's Day massacre of the Protestants (began 24 August). Leaves Paris.

1573   Sidney at Frankfort (March); meets Hubert Languet (aged 54, French scholar and Protestant) and follows him to Vienna. Goes to Italy (October).

1574   Sidney in Italy, Poland, Vienna.

1575   Sidney returns to England (May). Accompanies Queen Elizabeth's progresses to Kenilworth (Earl of Leicester) and Chartley (Earl of Essex).

1576   Sidney joins his father in Ireland.

> *Frobisher's first voyage to America. First public theatre built in London.*

1577   Sidney sent as ambassador to greet the new Elector Palatine and the new Emperor of Germany, and to help organize a league of Protestant princes (March). Visits William of Orange. Returns to England (June), visits his sister Mary (1561–1626; married in April to Earl of Pembroke) at Wilton, and probably begins *Arcadia*.

1578   Sidney at Court; defends his father's Irish policy; studies the Dutch war of independence from Spain; meets Spenser; writes a masque (*The Lady of May*) for performance before Queen Elizabeth on her visit to Wanstead (Earl of Leicester).

> *Lyly's* Euphues *published.*

1579   Sidney called a puppy by Earl of Oxford (leader of the party which favoured the Queen's proposed marriage with Alençon, which Leicester opposed); gives him the lie and challenges him to a duel, which Queen Elizabeth forbids. Studies the use of Latin metres for English poetry, with Spenser, Dyer, and Harvey.

> *Spenser's* Shepherds' Calendar *dedicated to Sidney.*
> *Gosson's* School of Abuse *dedicated to Sidney.*

1580   Sidney offends Queen Elizabeth by writing to dissuade her from marrying Alençon (January); leaves Court, and stays at Wilton with his sister (March–August). Joins her in translating the Psalms into English verse, probably completes *Arcadia* and perhaps writes *Defence of Poesy*.

Drake returns from his voyage round the world.

1581   Sidney becomes M.P. for Kent. Takes leading part in a Court tournament to honour French state visitors.

1582   Sidney in London and (in summer) at Ludlow; probably writes *Astrophel and Stella*.

1583   Sidney knighted (January). Marries Frances Walsingham (aged 15, daughter of Sir Francis Walsingham, statesman).

1584   Sidney begins translating Du Plessis Mornay's (Protestant) *La Vérité de la Religion Chrestienne;* probably also revising *Arcadia*. Interested in Raleigh's Virginian expedition. Ambassador to France. Daughter born.

1585   Sidney appointed joint Master of Ordnance. Attempts to join Drake's expedition against the Spaniards; is recalled by Queen Elizabeth, sent on Leicester's military expedition to Netherlands, and (November) made Governor of Flushing.

1586   Sidney wounded at Zutphen (22 September), and dies of his wound (17 October); his embalmed body sent to England.

1587   Sidney given a public funeral in St Paul's Cathedral (16 February). His translation of Du Plessis Mornay (completed by Golding) published.

Mary Queen of Scots executed.

1588   *Spanish Armada defeated.*

1590   Sidney's revised *Arcadia* (Books I–III) published.

Marlowe's Tamburlaine (*both parts*) *published. Spenser's* Faerie Queene (*Books I–III*) *published.*

1591   Sidney's *Astrophel and Stella* published (three unauthorized editions).

Ariosto's Orlando Furioso (*Harington's translation*) *published.*

1593   Sidney's revised *Arcadia* (Books I–III, 'augmented and ended' with the conclusion of the Old *Arcadia*, making five books in all) published.

Marlowe died. Shakespeare's Venus and Adonis *published.*

1595   Sidney's *The Defence of Poesy* published (two editions, one called *An Apology for Poetry*).

1596   Spenser's Faerie Queene (*Books I–VI*) *published.*

1598   Sidney's *Arcadia* (as in 1593) published 'with sundry new additions by the same author', *i.e.*, *Certain Sonnets*, *The Defence of Poesy*, *Astrophel and Stella*, and *The Lady of May*. Thirteen other editions appeared from 1599 to 1674.

INTRODUCTION

SIDNEY IN HIS TIME

Sir Philip Sidney was not quite thirty-three years old when he died. In his short life he had shown himself the embodiment of the renaissance ideal of a gentleman: like Hamlet, he was courtier, soldier, and scholar; and when Spenser drew Sir Calidore, the champion of Courtesy, in Book VI of his *Faerie Queene*, he took Sidney as his model.

The renaissance ideal was not mere virtuosity, but virtue, and Sidney used his various talents in the service of his country and his God. The sixteenth century was a period of conflict. The fighting in the Netherlands, in which Sidney died, was part of the nationalistic and religious warfare which had, for England, its climax in the defeat of the Spanish Armada. In his infancy the Protestant martyrs had been burned in England, and before he was eighteen years old he had witnessed the massacre of the Protestants in Paris. As a diplomat, Sidney laboured for the formation of an alliance of Protestant princes; as a propagandist, he translated Du Plessis Mornay's treatise as *A Work concerning the Trueness of the Christian Religion*; and for a private work of devotion he versified the Psalms. It is most important to recognize that, for all the fancy and charm of his works, Sidney was essentially a serious-minded man. He had all a young man's earnestness as well as a young man's brilliance, and he learned the lessons which his times taught him.

Seriousness and idealism were the basis of Sidney's life and writings. His life-long friend and first biographer, Sir Fulke Greville, testifies

> that though I lived with him and knew him from a child, yet I never knew him other than a man: with such staidness of mind, lovely and familiar gravity, as carried grace and reverence above

I

greater years. His talk ever of knowledge, and his very play tending to enrich his mind.

Like Milton's, Sidney's early years were a preparation for future tasks; but whereas Milton was a poet by design and a controversialist and public servant through force of circumstance, Sidney's writings were the overflow from a mind engaged on the duties of a courtier and statesman. His descent, on both sides, pre-ordained such a career for him, but his high principles led him to this career not as a means of self-advancement but as a means of self-fulfilment. He got neither wealth nor power from his service at Court; he knew the hostility of faction, and wrote defences of his father's and his uncle's policies against their detractors; he was made uneasy and impatient by Queen Elizabeth's political manoeuvrings, her reluctance to oppose Spain openly, and her flirtations with French alliance and French marriage. What he felt he declared: as Greville says, 'his heart and tongue went both one way'. For writing the Queen a long memorandum dissuading her from marrying the Duke of Alençon, he incurred her anger and his own banishment from Court. Earlier, she had forced him to endure without retaliation an insult from the Earl of Oxford, who supported the French marriage. Later, she prevented his sailing with Drake's expedition against the Spaniards, an attempt on his part to find the opportunity for courageous action. All this must have bitterly chafed Sidney's impetuous character: the young man who gave the Earl of Oxford the lie and challenged him to a duel, and who threatened to thrust his dagger into his father's secretary if he let private letters be seen, was a man of strong passions, however much he might subordinate them to moral principles. His poems to 'Stella' likewise show powerful feelings which it cost him an effort to subdue; and if, as seems possible, he could not afford to marry anyone when 'Stella' was married by her relations to the wealthy Lord Rich, it must have increased his frustration at Court, the materialism of which is condemned by Spenser in *Colin Clout's Come Home Again* and *Mother Hubberd's Tale* and by Raleigh in *The Lie*. Though he served the Queen faithfully, and took pleasure in some aspects of Court life (his style always kindles when he writes of tournaments, pageantry, and the splendour of art), his writings show him creating an ideal world in which courage and goodness can have their full scope: and even in *Arcadia*, as we shall see, there is folly, selfishness, and treason.

Sidney, as befitted a renaissance gentleman, spoke lightly of his writings. In the introduction to *The Defence of Poesy* he confesses that in his youth and idleness he has 'slipped into the title of a poet', and calls poetry his 'unelected vocation'. In Sonnet XC of *Astrophel and Stella*, protesting that his poetry proceeds wholly from Stella's beauty and his love, he denies that he writes for fame, and goes so far as to declare

> In truth I swear, I wish not there should be
> Grav'd in mine epitaph a poet's name.

The dedication of *Arcadia*, his 'toyful book' as he called it in a letter to his brother, is worth quoting in full, as an example of Sidney's lightness of touch:

TO MY DEAR LADY AND SISTER, THE COUNTESS OF PEMBROKE

Here now have you (most dear, and most worthy to be most dear Lady) this idle work of mine: which I fear (like the spider's web) will be thought fitter to be swept away than worn to any other purpose. For my part, in very truth (as the cruel fathers among the Greeks were wont to do to the babes they would not foster) I could well find in my heart to cast out in some desert of forgetfulness this child which I am loth to father. But you desired me to do it, and your desire to my heart is an absolute commandment. Now it is done, only for you, only to you: if you keep it to yourself, or to such friends who will weigh errors in the balance of good will, I hope, for the father's sake, it will be pardoned, perchance made much of, though in itself it have deformities. For indeed for severer eyes it is not, being but a trifle, and that triflingly handled. Your dear self can best witness the manner, being done in loose sheets of paper, most of it in your presence, the rest by sheets sent unto you as fast as they were done. In sum, a young head, not so well stayed as I would it were (and shall be when God will), having many many fancies begotten in it, if it had not been in some way delivered, would have grown a monster, and more sorry might I be that they came in than that they got out. But his chief safety shall be the not walking abroad; and his chief protection the bearing the livery of your name, which (if much good will do not deceive me) is worthy to be a sanctuary for a greater offender. This say I, because I know the virtue so; and this say I, because it may be ever so; or to say better, because it will be ever so. Read it then at your idle times, and the follies your good judgement will find in it blame not, but laugh at. And so, looking for no better stuff than in an haberdasher's shop glasses or feathers, you will continue to love the writer, who doth exceedingly love you; and most most heartily prays you may long live to be a principal ornament to the family of the Sidneys.

> Your loving brother
> Philip Sidney.

But though it is true that Sidney's works were in fact his recreations (as Charles Lamb said of *his*), it is clear that he bestowed much care on them, not only in their style but also in their substance. He never, of course, wrote for money like Greene and Nashe, nor in hopes of recommending himself to office like Lyly and Spenser, though he was as poor for a gentleman as they were for commoners; his works circulated only in manuscripts (some of which would be copied at his expense for presentation to friends). But his own standards of morality and artistry were very high, as his *Defence of Poesy* shows; and though his *Arcadia* is not didactic, as is *The Faerie Queene*, in which Spenser openly instructs his reader, its effect, like the aim of Spenser's allegory, is 'to fashion a gentleman or noble person in virtuous and gentle discipline'. Greville thus sums up his friend's work:

> But the truth is, his end was not writing, even while he wrote; nor his knowledge moulded for tables or schools [for councils or academies]; but both his wit and understanding bent upon his heart, to make himself and others, not in words or opinion, but in life and action, good and great.

THE DEFENCE OF POESY

Sidney was a generous patron of the arts, and many books were dedicated to him. Among these was Stephen Gosson's *The School of Abuse: containing a pleasant invective against Poets, Pipers, Players, Jesters, and such like Caterpillars of a Commonwealth* (1579). This dedication was a sincere blunder, not an ironical gesture of provocation, and it shows that Sidney was then better known as a Protestant than as a poet. Gosson himself, from being a poet and playwright, had turned Puritan; and his chief argument was that poems, and especially plays (enticing spectators into the corrupting new playhouses), were undermining the nation's virtue and making Englishmen effeminate and licentious, 'rocking us asleep in all ungodliness'. To this he added the general charge that fiction was nothing but lying, and he took his stand upon the authority of Plato, who had argued that poets should be banished from an ideal commonwealth.

What acknowledgement (if any) Sidney sent Gosson is unknown. In a letter to Gabriel Harvey, Spenser (by that time acquainted with Sidney, and writing from Leicester House) tells him,

> New books I hear of none, but only one that writing a certain book called *The School of Abuse*, and dedicating it to Master Sidney, was for his labour scorned: if at least it be in the goodness of that nature to scorn.

The Defence of Poesy is in part a reply to Gosson's book, but it is not a point-by-point refutation in the manner dear to sixteenth-century controversialists. Sidney does not quote Gosson, nor even refer to him or his book, but instead defends poetry against all possible objections. He is not taking sides in what presently became a pamphlet war between the opponents and apologists of the stage, but seems rather to recognize beneath Gosson's charges the traditional objection to poetry as a worldly distraction from the higher claims of the spirit (Chaucer, it will be remembered, added a retraction of most of his secular poetry to the end of *The Parson's Tale*). It is true that in the course of his argument Sidney catalogues the several species of poetry – the pastoral, elegiac, iambic, satiric, comic, tragic, lyric, and heroic – and shows that none of these is necessarily bad in itself; it is true that he brilliantly rebuts the charges that poetry is full of lies ('The poet nothing affirms, and therefore never lieth. . . . What child is there, that coming to a play, and seeing *Thebes* written in great letters upon an old door, doth believe that it is Thebes?') and that poetry is corrupting ('But what! shall the abuse of a thing make the right use odious? . . . Whatsoever being abused doth most harm, being rightly used doth most good.'); but at its most characteristic, *The Defence of Poesy* is less a defence than a glorification.

Here Sidney's moral and artistic idealism comes into play. Poetry is the exercise not merely of craft ('It is not rhyming and versing that maketh a poet') but of the imagination. The poet is a maker, a creator. He outgoes Nature herself. 'Her world is brazen, the poets only deliver a golden.' Far from slavishly imitating the natural world, he transcends it, for what he really imitates is not the actual but the ideal. Sidney thus uses Platonism against Plato; but he is far from merely scoring a debater's point, for he immediately proceeds to state the value of such creation. By showing his readers perfection, the poet can make them see their goal; he can give them models to imitate (like Sidney's own Pyrocles and Musidorus, Philoclea and Pamela); and by delighting them with his pictures and stories, he can lead them towards knowledge and goodness.

On such a subject as this, Sidney is very properly eloquent, but he never falls into the error, very common among orators of his period who were intoxicated with Ciceronian rhetoric, of inflating his style: he warned his brother that Ciceronianism was 'the chief abuse of Oxford' in putting style above matter, and in *The Defence of Poesy* he mocks those who 'cast sugar and spice upon every dish that is served to the table, like those Indians, not content to wear earrings at the fit and natural place of the ears, but they will thrust jewels through their nose and lips, because they will be sure to be fine'. (In this devastating use of comparisons, Sidney anticipates a later critic, Dr Johnson.) He writes fluently and vivaciously, and his control of tone is so excellent that he can move easily from jest to earnest and back again. The course of his essay is also well controlled without losing spontaneity in formality, and he manages to bring in not only his exalted tribute to poetic imagination (which is given in this Selection, because of its importance to all Sidney's writings) but also a spirited review of the state of English literature when he composed the *Defence*. As will be seen from the Chronology which precedes this Introduction, Sidney was writing before the great Elizabethan works of Spenser, Marlowe, and Shakespeare (poetry which stood in need of no defence) appeared, and we may be reasonably sure that *The Faerie Queene* would have converted him to the 'old rustic language' which he could not approve in *The Shepherds' Calendar*, and that for the sake of Shakespeare's richer and deeper unity he would have condoned his defiance of the unities of time and place or his mingling of kings and clowns. He knew poetry when he saw it, whatever guise it happened to be wearing:

> Certainly I must confess mine own barbarousness, I never heard the old song of Percy and Douglas, that I found not my heart moved more than with a trumpet; and yet it is sung but by some blind crowder [fiddler], with no rougher voice than rude style: which being so evil apparelled in the dust and cobwebs of that uncivil age, what would it work, trimmed in the gorgeous eloquence of Pindar?

We may feel that a pindaric version might be more gorgeous, but it would not be nearly so much like *Chevy Chase*, and dissent from Sidney's preference for classical form, but we can see that his taste was not confined to the antique and to imitations of the antique. His own epic and sonnets show that, indebted though he was to ancient and modern Europe, he wished to grow his foreign plants in English soil.

ASTROPHEL AND STELLA

Sidney did not introduce the sonnet into England. That had been done by Sir Thomas Wyatt (1503–42), most of whose poems were collected for printing in 1557 and had been circulating in manuscript since the time of their composition. *Astrophel and Stella* is, however, the first English sonnet-sequence. It had many imitators, the best of which – Daniel's, Drayton's, and Shakespeare's – are far from being mere imitations. But it has never been superseded, and has fascinated generations of readers as the record of 'a transcendent passion pervading and illuminating action, pursuits, studies, feats of arms, the opinions of contemporaries and his judgement of them' (Lamb).

How far it is the record of a passion which Sidney really felt, and the product of an actual situation, is a question much discussed and incapable of a final definite solution. Stella is Sidney's name for Penelope Devereux, daughter of the Earl of Essex. Her dying father had proposed a marriage between her and Sidney in 1576 (she being then thirteen years old), but nothing was concluded, and there is little probability (despite biographers' wishful conjecture) that they had ever met. Penelope, who had seemingly lived with her aunt and uncle the Earl and Countess of Huntingdon since her widowed mother was married again in 1578 (to the Earl of Leicester, Sidney's uncle), was brought to Court in January 1581 by her aunt. In March her aunt and uncle were negotiating her marriage with Lord Rich, who was nearly twenty-one and had just inherited his father's estates and title. The marriage took place early in November. It seems to have been an unhappy one, and, seven years and four children later, Lady Rich became the mistress of Sir Charles Blount,[1] whom she married in 1605, immediately after her husband finally divorced her.

Stella is identified as Penelope in three sonnets in which Sidney puns upon her married name Rich (XXIV; XXXV; and XXXVII, not selected, in which he says that Stella, rich in all beauty and virtue, 'Hath no misfortune but that Rich she is'); and in the Eighth Song Stella's 'yoke' can only be her marriage. Sonnet LXXVIII, the portrait of a jealous husband, concludes with a threat to make him a cuckold, and in the Fourth and Eighth Songs Astrophel entreats Stella to lie with him. The inescapable conclusion is that Sidney is expressing an adulterous love for Penelope Rich, and that *Astrophel and Stella* is a tribute to her beauty and (when Stella refuses Astrophel at the dictate of 'tyrant honour') to her virtue. A further conclusion from this is that for a time at least he felt such a passion, for, if not, he would have been making a wholly unjustifiable use of her name and

---

[1] It is often stated that she and Blount were in love, and practically engaged, before her marriage, but Ringler (*Poems*, p. 446, note 1) has shown that this was never affirmed by either of them, being first alleged in 1668 upon no authority.

character.[1] But to suppose, as we surely must, that the feelings he expresses are genuine, does not oblige us to take *Astrophel and Stella* for a faithful record of fact. Many of the incidents described, such as Astrophel's abstraction at the tournament (Sonnet LIII) or Stella's noonday riding or her taking boat upon the Thames (Sonnets XXII and CIII), are probably happy inventions making a skilful use of ordinary incidents to show the lover's feelings; and the same may be said of the dramatically conceived sequence in which Astrophel rides to visit Stella, sees her house with rapture, and then suffers her displeasure (Sonnets LXXXIV, LXXXV, and LXXXVI).

It is as poetry, not as autobiography, that we read *Astrophel and Stella*, and we may sympathize with Professor C. S. Lewis when he censures 'the perverse demand for story', and stresses the importance of 'lyrical meditation'. Though occasionally two or three sonnets form a group, and the general arrangement of the sonnets has been made with skill, presumably by the author, the sonnet is essentially a single poem complete in itself.[2] It is indeed notable that Sidney prefers the couplet ending, which gives finality, often epigrammatic, to the poem:

> Dumb swans, not chatt'ring pies, do lovers prove:
> They love indeed, who quake to say they love. (LIV)

The end of a sonnet often justifies the means. Thus, Sonnet XVII, a fanciful mythological compliment identifying Cupid's bow with Stella's eyebrows and his arrows with her looks, ends with the pregnant phrase 'and I was in his way'; and in Sonnet LII, which

---

[1] No other sonnet-sequence is addressed to an identifiable married woman. This, with the attacks on Lord Rich, disposes of the view that these sonnets are mere court-compliment. It should, however, be noticed that the poems implying that Stella is married, though they are important, are not numerous. Many of the others might just as aptly have been addressed to the proud beauty of medieval and Petrarchan convention by her humble adorer.

[2] For this reason I have not scrupled to represent *Astrophel and Stella* by about half the sonnets and less than half the songs. The songs have been grouped together. In the first authorized edition they are interspersed among the sonnets, but I very much doubt whether Sidney himself so placed them, and in selection there seemed no virtue in following this arrangement.

recounts a suit at law between Virtue and Love, the poet proposes an ingenious settlement:

> Well, Love, since this demur our suit doth stay,
> Let Virtue have that Stella's self; yet thus,
> That Virtue but that body grant to us.

This is consciously shocking and witty, and anticipates Donne. Like *The Defence of Poesy*, Sidney's poems combine grace and strength. They are, almost without exception, lucidly argued, generally with a turn of direction at the sestet's commencement, though this is never allowed to become a mechanical formula. The dramatic Sonnet XLVII, 'What, have I thus betray'd my liberty?', with its turn and counterturn, is very lively, as its fluctuating mood requires: there is just a hint of rueful humour in the lover's recognition of his helplessness. However, the search for humour, irony, and detachment should not be pressed too far. It has been argued that Sidney deliberately wrote some sonnets of inferior quality, and placed them early in the sequence to contrast with more passionate and dramatic sonnets later; Sonnet VII (on Stella's eyes) and Sonnet IX ('Queen Virtue's Court, which some call Stella's face'), with the sonnets mentioning Cupid and Venus, according to this interpretation,

> do not so much show Sidney's immaturity as a poet as Astrophel's immaturity as a lover. Shakespeare, in the same way, showed the element of unreality in Romeo's love for Rosaline, Juliet's predecessor, by the conventional conceits he employs.[1]

But in *Romeo and Juliet* we have Mercutio and Friar Laurence, not to mention Romeo himself and the whole dramatic action, to help us put the hero's love for Rosaline in perspective. In *Astrophel and Stella* there are no such independent points of reference. Every reader who identified Penelope Rich with Stella must have identified Sidney himself with Astrophel[2] (by which name, in-

---

[1] Muir, *Sir Philip Sidney*, p. 30. His treatment of Sonnet XXXI as an ironical poem is discussed in the note to it.

[2] The name should, strictly speaking, be Astrophil (i.e., star-lover; Stella being the star), and is so given in Ringler's edition. Since, however, the spelling Astrophel has the support of most early texts and of long tradition, it seems best to continue to use it.

deed, he is called in more than one elegy), and assumed that in all his sonnets he was doing his best. The sonnet was still too new a form in England for a poet to use it otherwise than seriously: and though he derides Petrarch's mere imitators, Sidney himself is sincerely Petrarchan at heart. The modern reader who finds his conceits extravagant and artificial at first must bear in mind the Elizabethan delight in extravagance and artifice, and may compare the disguised Pyrocles's item-by-item inventory of Philoclea's beauties (*Arcadia*, Book II, Chapter 11), or Sidney's own description of Philoclea and Pyrocles sitting on the river bank as 'making the green bank the situation, and the river the prospect, of the most beautiful buildings of Nature' (Book II, Chapter 17), or his statement when Cecropia whips Philoclea that 'weeping Cupid told his weeping mother that he was sorry he was not deaf, as well as blind, that he might never know so lamentable a work' (Book III, Chapter 20). Nor are the most elaborate conceits found only among the sonnets which are placed near the beginning of the sequence: the very last (Sonnet CVIII, not in this Selection) begins

> When Sorrow, using mine own fire's might,
> Melts down his lead into my boiling breast.

Sidney's poetry is orderly, subtle, and ingenious. The ingenuity appears in the conceits and in the unexpected but wholly satisfying development of the ideas. Such surprises are the more effective within the formal structure of the sonnet, with its pattern of rhymes, to which Sidney often adds a further pattern by his balanced rhetoric: for example, his repeated concession 'It is most true' in Sonnet V (where, however, he does not overwork the device, but varies it by cutting down his phrase in the sestet to 'True', thereby preparing for the concentration of the last line), or the eloquent repetitions of Sonnet LXIV. This is orderliness without rigidity. The subtlety of Sidney's poetry is seen not only in all these features but also in the variety of his style: he can begin a sonnet as colloquially and abruptly as Donne:

> As good to write, as for to lie and groan
> (Sonnet XL)

or he can be as lyrically eloquent as Spenser:

> Come Sleep, O Sleep, the certain knot of peace,
> The baiting-place of wit, the balm of woe,
> The poor man's wealth, the prisoner's release,
> Th'indifferent judge between the high and low.
>   (Sonnet XXXIX)

Nowhere is he more lyrical than in the songs, where he fits the form to the mood. The rhythmical exhilaration of the First Song, with its animated questions and its emphatic refrain 'To you, to you, all song of praise is due', is countered by the sober trochaic movement of 'In a grove most rich of shade'.

ARCADIA

Whereas Sidney's sonnets and lyrics recommend themselves at first sight by their concentration, his long epic romance *Arcadia* is not immediately tempting to a modern reader. Yet it was attractive to its first readers:

> Here are amorous courting (he was young in years), sage counselling (he was ripe in judgement), valorous fighting (his sovereign profession was arms), and delightful pastime by way of pastoral exercises.

Gabriel Harvey's summary gives a very fair idea of the book's contents, and implies that they were all close to Sidney's own heart. Sidney is one of those authors who have put a great part of themselves into their work: reading *Arcadia*, we continually feel ourselves in direct touch with his mind. The book, indeed, was written as a present for his sister, and sent to her in instalments, as he states in the dedication; and though in the revised version he has omitted all direct address to the 'fair ladies' who were its first readers, much of the original intimacy, the assumption of shared interests and shared principles, is communicated. That he revised the book (and appears to have suspended the revision only when he went on his fatal campaign to the Netherlands) suggests that he still needed it as an outlet for his romantic imagination and moral idealism. It is tempting to speculate whether Arcadia was to Sidney and his sister what Gondal and Angria were to the Brontës; certainly it was very much what Faerie Land was to Spenser.

In its epic character, like Spenser's *Faerie Queene*, the book reflects its period. As Spenser had taken Ariosto's *Orlando Furioso* for his model, so Sidney in the same neo-classical spirit went to the *Arcadia* (1501) of Sannazaro for his idealized pastoral world where shepherd boys pipe as though they should never be old, and to the *Aethiopian History* (fourth century A.D.) of Heliodorus for his complex plotting and abundance of adventurous incident. Heliodorus's work, to which Sidney approvingly refers in *The Defence of Poesy*, was a prose epic; Sannazaro's was an alternation of a prose story with poetic eclogues, twelve in number to correspond with the twelve books of an epic poem. Sidney divided his *Arcadia* into five 'books or acts' (as he called them) corresponding with the five acts of a classical drama, with eclogues between the books corresponding with the choric songs. This was the form of the first (completed) *Arcadia*, called hereafter the Old *Arcadia*, which still survives in nine manuscripts and has been printed as the fourth volume of Feuillerat's edition of Sidney's *Works*.

The story concerns the aged King of Arcadia, Basilius; his young and beautiful wife Gynecia;[1] their two daughters, Pamela and Philoclea; and two young princes, Musidorus of Thessalia and Pyrocles of Macedonia. Basilius, needlessly desiring to know his future, has consulted an oracle and received a riddling and ominous reply:

> Thy elder care shall from thy careful face
> By princely mean be stol'n, and yet not lost;
> Thy younger shall with nature's bliss embrace
> An uncouth love, which nature hateth most;
> Thou with thy wife adultery shalt commit,
> And in thy throne a foreign state shall sit;
> All this on thee this fatal year shall hit.[2]

[1] Pronounce the 'g' hard. 'Pamela' is stressed on the second syllable, not on the first as nowadays.

[2] *Uncouth:* strange. *State:* ruler. This is the oracle as given in the Old *Arcadia*. In the revision it is slightly expanded.

In unkingly fear, and a foolish effort to fly his fate, he removes his family to the country, where he lives in a lodge with Gynecia and Philoclea, placing Pamela for her still greater safety in another lodge under the eye of a shepherd unworthily promoted for the purpose, the bumptious Dametas, who with his ill-natured wife Miso and his stupid daughter Mopsa provides the broader comedy of the book. The young princes arrive, fall in love with the daughters, and disguise themselves; Pyrocles, who loves Philoclea, disguises himself as an Amazon and is received into Basilius's lodge; Musidorus, who loves Pamela, disguises himself as a shepherd and takes service with Dametas. They soon show their valour, Pyrocles saving Philoclea from a lion, and Musidorus Pamela from a bear, and both defending Basilius's lodge against a crowd of rebels. Meanwhile the situation becomes further involved when the disguised Pyrocles is loved by Basilius, who takes him for a woman, and by Gynecia, who recognizes him for a man. To escape them both he agrees severally to meet them in a dark cavern, where they both go, and unwittingly fulfil the fifth line of the prophecy, while he himself visits Philoclea and fulfils the third and fourth lines. At the same time Musidorus contrives to elope with Pamela, fulfilling the first two lines, for they are captured before leaving the land. The last part of the prophecy comes to pass when Basilius drinks a love-potion prepared by Gynecia for Pyrocles, and falls into a deathlike trance; his queen is brought to trial for causing his death, and the princes for stealing his daughters; and the judge, who sits in Basilius's throne, is the visiting King of Macedonia, the father of Pyrocles and uncle of Musidorus. All the accused are condemned to death, but upon Basilius's sudden recovery there is a general pardon and reconciliation.

A few years after he had composed *Arcadia* Sidney began to rewrite it. The central story (with slight modifications) remained the same, but the book's content was enlarged and its form altered. Whereas the Old *Arcadia* presented the events in chronological order, the new *Arcadia* began not with Basilius and the oracle but with the shipwreck of the two princes not far from Arcadia, the previous actions being retrospectively revealed by dialogue. This method reflects Sidney's respect for Horace, who had prescribed that an epic should begin not at the beginning but in the middle of the action.[1] By adopting it, he allowed himself to describe many new previous adventures of Musidorus and Pyrocles. He also added greatly to the main action. The most important addition is the capture of the princesses and the disguised Pyrocles by Cecropia and their imprisonment in her castle. Every reader who enjoys *Arcadia* must be thankful that Sidney lived to bring this episode within sight of its conclusion (for, with Cecropia dead and Amphialus dying, and Musidorus at liberty, the rescue of the prisoners is certain).

The imprisonment is an episode, in the strict sense of the word, for it has no bearing on the central story of love at cross purposes; but it shows, by its length and by the seriousness with which Sidney works it out, that when he came to revise *Arcadia* he was becoming less interested in the merely romantic complications of his story, and more interested in its opportunities of displaying heroic action and heroic character. Heroism, as he recognizes, is shown not only in deeds of valour, like killing lions and bears and routing rebels; it is shown in fortitude of suffering. The stoical character of Pamela, who elsewhere is less endearing than her wholly delightful sister, is brought out especially well in her sublime contempt for her wicked aunt's utmost power. Her noble prayer, which was used by Charles I in prison, is essentially serious; it shows Sidney's own religious spirit underlying his superficially pagan-antique romance, and it suits the tragic note which he sounds in this episode. His treatment of the princesses' cousin Amphialus, on whose account (though not at his desire nor with his consent) they suffer, is worth special attention. Instead of making him a villain, and crudely contrasting his desire for Philoclea with Pyrocles's, Sidney makes him one of the most moving figures in the book. He is a princely man, valiant and sensitive, who is driven to a tragic end by an irresistible passion (his love for Philoclea) and by treacherous circumstances (his mother's

---

[1] In his *Art of Poetry*. Thus, Virgil's Aeneas recounts the sack of Troy to Dido in Book II. Spenser begins *The Faerie Queene* not with Gloriana's feast, at which the knights embark on their quests (*cf.* his letter to Raleigh, usually appended to *The Faerie Queene*), but with the Red-Cross Knight and Una taking shelter in the Wood of Error.

capture of the princesses, which makes him a rebel to his king and an unwitting tormentor of his beloved). His suicide is a dramatic scene, with an elaborate speech in Sidney's grandest manner; but his real death takes place when he hears himself accused of cruelty, first by the haughty Pamela and then by her sister:

> Amazed with this speech [of Pamela's], he turned his eye, full of humble sorrowfulness, to Philoclea. 'And is this (most excellent Lady) your doom of me also?' She, sweet lady, sat weeping: for as her most noble kinsman she had ever favoured him, and loved his love, though she could not be in love with his person; and now partly unkindness of his wrong, partly pity of his case, made her sweet mind yield some tears before she could answer; and her answer was no other, but that she had the same cause as her sister had. He replied no further, but delivering from his heart two or three untaught sighs, rose, and with most low reverence went out of their chamber.
>
> (Book III, Chapter 24)

Amphialus is profoundly pathetic because a romance destined to end happily for the princesses and their lovers is destined to end unhappily for him.[1] Sidney's management of tone during the imprisonment is very skilful, for he must do justice to the prisoners' grief and at the same time keep his reader assured of their approaching release. The dialogue between the sorrowing Pyrocles and the at-first-unrecognized Philoclea in the preceding chapter (Book III, Chapter 23) even contains touches of high comedy; these touches enrich the prevailing mood without threatening it.

The whole enterprise of writing *Arcadia*, indeed, demanded remarkable literary tact. The central plot, improperly handled, could easily have become both ridiculous and indecent. That it is neither is a tribute to Sidney's personality. Consider his treatment of the incident where the disguised Pyrocles watches the princesses bathing in the river (Book II, Chapter 11). The young man – who was not too high-minded to admire Philoclea's legs as she ran away from the lion – frankly confesses his delight in her naked beauty, in a poem which anticipates the erotic spirit of Marlowe's *Hero and Leander*, and which shows that Sidney himself was no puritan. Yet there is no disagreeable suggestion that

[1] At least in thwarting his love for Philoclea. But see note, pp. 240–1.

Pyrocles is spying on the girls. It is a stroke of luck, not a calculated opportunity: Sidney makes it clear that Pyrocles has followed them in the hope of speaking to Philoclea without the suspicious Gynecia's presence, and that when they are bathing he has never an eye for Pamela. Moreover, the situation is not used by Sidney as an end in itself, but is made to lead naturally on to Pyrocles's encounter with Amphialus.

This incident well illustrates Sidney's manner of handling the story. The book never actually stands still, but it is always ready to pause for an episodic digression (there are numerous subsidiary stories, any one of which would be matter for a whole romance, branching off from the main stem) or for a lyrical interlude. Sidney's style itself is a leisurely one. This does not mean that it is loose or flaccid – on the contrary, his long sentences are firmly shaped – but that he makes perpetual use of parenthesis, circumlocution, personification, and the extended simile. This ornate style is particularly the mark of the revised *Arcadia*, and there are readers who prefer the less elaborate expression and the simpler narrative construction of the earlier version.[1] However, the heightened style suits Sidney's whole idealistic approach to his heroes and heroines, who are perfect in their virtue and beauty, though very capable of human emotions.

MISCELLANEOUS POEMS

The revised *Arcadia* ends abruptly, in the middle of a sentence in Book III. It was first published as a fragment, and was later completed by adding the rest of the story from the Old *Arcadia*. This composite version included, besides the poems written for both versions, one ('The lad Philisides') which was not, probably because that poem used an English setting incongruous with the place-names of Arcadia and its neighbours. It is printed in this

[1] For the passage quoted on p. 11, the Old *Arcadia* has 'sitting down together upon the green bank hard by the river'. The earlier version was not written in a conspicuously different style from the later, however, as may be seen from Musidorus's dialogue with Pyrocles in Book I, Chapter 12, which more or less directly follows the text of the Old *Arcadia*.

Selection, together with other poems from *Arcadia* which do not occur within the selected narrative, and with a few separate lyrics and sonnets which do not form a part of any larger work of Sidney's. The two sonnets with which this Selection concludes have sometimes been printed at the end of *Astrophel and Stella* by nineteenth-century editors, but they were not so placed in any early edition, nor intended by Sidney himself to conclude his sequence of sonnets. The second of them, nevertheless, seems an appropriate final piece, for in it he not merely repudiates worldly love but embraces divine love. If, as Sidney's latest editor thinks, this sonnet was written before *Astrophel and Stella*,[1] this only shows how firmly fixed was its theme in Sidney's mind. It is echoed in his last words to his brother:

> Love my memory, cherish my friends; their faith to me may assure you they are honest. But above all, govern your will and affections by the will and word of your creator, in me beholding the end of this world, with all her vanities.

[1] Ringler, *Poems*, p. 434.

From
THE DEFENCE OF POESY

When the right virtuous Edward Wotton and I were at the
Emperor's Court together, we gave ourselves to learn horsemanship of John Pietro Pugliano, one that with great commendation had the place of an esquire in his stable. And he,
according to the fertileness of the Italian wit, did not only   5
afford us the demonstration of his practice, but sought to enrich
our minds with the contemplations therein which he thought
most precious. But with none I remember mine ears were at any
time more loaden, than when (either angered with slow pay-
ment, or moved with our learner-like admiration) he exercised   10
his speech in the praise of his faculty. He said soldiers were
the noblest estate of mankind, and horsemen the noblest of
soldiers. He said they were the masters of war, and ornaments of peace; speedy goers, and strong abiders; triumphers
both in camps and courts. Nay, to so unbelieved a point he   15
proceeded, as that no earthly thing bred such wonder to a
prince as to be a good horseman. Skill of government was but a
pedanteria in comparison. Then would he add certain praises, by
telling what a peerless beast the horse was; the only serviceable
courtier without flattery, the beast of most beauty, faithfulness, 20
courage, and such more, that if I had not been a piece of a
logician before I came to him, I think he would have persuaded me to have wished myself a horse. But thus much at
least with his no few words he drave into me, that self-love is
better than any gilding to make that seem gorgeous wherein   25
ourselves be parties.

Wherein, if Pugliano's strong affection and weak arguments

7. *contemplations:* principles.
12. *estate:* class.
14. *abiders:* defenders.
27. *affection:* prejudice.

NOTES: p. 213

19

will not satisfy you, I will give you a nearer example of myself, who (I know not by what mischance) in these my not old years and idlest times having slipped into the title of a poet, am pro- 30 voked to say something unto you in the defence of that my unelected vocation, which if I handle with more good will than good reasons, bear with me, since the scholar is to be pardoned that followeth the steps of his master. And yet I must say that, as I have more just cause to make a pitiful defence of poor 35 Poetry, which from almost the highest estimation of learning is fallen to be the laughing-stock of children, so have I need to bring some more available proofs; since the former is by no man barred of his deserved credit, the silly latter hath had even the names of philosophers used to the defacing of it, with great 40 danger of civil war among the Muses.

And first, truly, to all them that professing learning inveigh against Poetry may justly be objected, that they go very near to ungratefulness, to seek to deface that which, in the noblest nations and languages that are known, hath been the first light- 45 giver to ignorance, and first nurse, whose milk by little and little enabled them to feed afterwards of tougher knowledges. And will they now play the hedgehog that, being received into the den, drave out his host? or rather the vipers, that with their birth kill their parents? Let learned Greece in any of her 50 manifold sciences be able to show me one book before Musaeus, Homer, and Hesiod, all three nothing else but poets. Nay, let any history be brought that can say any writers were there before them, if they were not men of the same skill, as Orpheus, Linus, and some other are named: who, having been the first of 55 that country that made pens deliverers of their knowledge to their posterity, may justly challenge to be called their fathers in learning; for not only in time they had this priority (although in itself antiquity be venerable) but went before them, as causes

34. *his master:* Pugliano.
38. *available:* serviceable.
38. *the former:* horsemanship.
39. *the silly latter:* poor Poetry.
54. *men of the same skill:* poets also.

to draw with their charming sweetness the wild untamed 60
wits to an admiration of knowledge. So as Amphion was said
to move stones with his poetry to build Thebes; and Orpheus
to be listened to by beasts, indeed stony and beastly people. So
among the Romans were Livius Andronicus, and Ennius. So
in the Italian language the first that made it aspire to be a 65
treasure-house of science were the poets Dante, Boccace, and
Petrarch. So in our English were Gower and Chaucer, after
whom, encouraged and delighted with their excellent fore-
going, others have followed, to beautify our mother tongue,
as well in the same kind as in other arts.   70

This did so notably show itself, that the philosophers of
Greece durst not a long time appear to the world but under the
mask of poets. So Thales, Empedocles, and Parmenides sang
their natural philosophy in verses; so did Pythagoras and
Phocylides their moral counsels; so did Tyrtaeus in war 75
matters, and Solon in matters of policy: or rather, they, being
poets, did exercise their delightful vein in those points of
highest knowledge, which before them lay hidden to the
world. For that wise Solon was directly a poet it is manifest,
having written in verse the notable fable of the Atlantic Island, 80
which was continued by Plato. And truly, even Plato, whosoever well considereth shall find that in the body of his work,
though the inside and strength were Philosophy, the skin as it
were and beauty depended most of Poetry: for all stands upon
dialogues, wherein he feigns many honest burgesses of Athens 85
to speak of such matters, that, if they had been set on the rack,
they would never have confessed them; besides his poetical
describing the circumstances of their meetings, as the well
ordering of a banquet, the delicacy of a walk, with interlacing
mere tales, as Gyges' Ring and others, which who knows not to 90
be flowers of poetry did never walk into Apollo's garden.

63. *beastly:* beast-like, uncivilized.
66. *science:* knowledge.
66. *Boccace:* Boccaccio.
68–69. *fore-going:* example.
74. *natural philosophy:* scientific studies.
80. *Atlantic Island:* Atlantis, a fictitious utopian kingdom.

NOTES: p. 213

B

And even historiographers (although their lips sound of things done, and verity be written in their foreheads) have been glad to borrow both fashion and perchance weight of the poets. So Herodotus entitled his history by the name of the nine 95 Muses; and both he and all the rest that followed him either stole or usurped of Poetry their passionate describing of passions, the many particularities of battles, which no man could affirm, or, if that be denied me, long orations put in the mouths of great kings and captains, which it is certain they 100 never pronounced. So that, truly, neither philosopher nor historiographer could at the first have entered into the gates of popular judgements, if they had not taken a great passport of Poetry, which in all nations at this day where learning flourisheth not, is plain to be seen, in all which they have some 105 feeling of Poetry. In Turkey, besides their law-giving divines, they have no other writers but poets. In our neighbour country Ireland, where truly learning goes very bare, yet are their poets held in a devout reverence. Even among the most barbarous and simple Indians, where no writing is, yet have 110 they their poets, who make and sing songs, which they call Areytos, both of their ancestors' deeds and praises of their gods: a sufficient probability that if ever learning come among them, it must be by having their hard dull wits softened and sharpened with the sweet delights of Poetry. For until they find 115 a pleasure in the exercise of the mind, great promises of much knowledge will little persuade them that know not the fruits of knowledge. In Wales, the true remnant of the ancient Britons, as there are good authorities to show the long time they had poets, which they called bards, so through all the conquests of 120 Romans, Saxons, Danes, and Normans, some of whom did seek to ruin all memory of learning from among them, yet do their poets even to this day last; so as it is not more notable in the soon beginning than in long continuing. But since the authors of most of our sciences were the Romans, and before 125

94. *fashion:* form.
94. *weight:* substance.
103. *popular judgements:* the people's understanding.

NOTES: p. 213

them the Greeks, let us a little stand upon their authorities, but even so far as to see what names they have given unto this now scorned skill.

Among the Romans a poet was called *Vates*, which is as much as a diviner, foreseer, or prophet, as by his conjoined words 130 *vaticinium* and *vaticinari* is manifest: so heavenly a title did that excellent people bestow upon this heart-ravishing knowledge. And so far were they carried into the admiration thereof, that they thought in the chanceable hitting upon any such verses great foretokens of their following fortunes were placed. Where- 135 upon grew the word of *Sortes Virgilianae*, when, by sudden opening Virgil's book, they lighted upon some verse of his, as it is reported by many, whereof the histories of the emperors' lives are full, as of Albinus, the governor of our island, who in his childhood met with this verse, 140

Arma amens capio nec sat rationis in armis;

and in his age performed it: although it were a very vain and godless superstition, as also it was to think that spirits were commanded by such verses – whereupon this word charms, derived of *carmina*, cometh – so yet serveth it to show the 145 great reverence those wits were held in. And altogether not without ground, since both the Oracles of Delphos and Sibylla's prophecies were wholly delivered in verses. For that same exquisite observing of number and measure in the words, and that high flying liberty of conceit proper to the poet, did 150 seem to have some divine force in it.

And may not I presume a little farther, to show the reason-ableness of this word *Vates*, and say that the holy David's Psalms are a divine poem? If I do, I shall not do it without the testimony of great learned men, both ancient and modern. 155 But even the name Psalms will speak for me, which, being interpreted, is nothing but Songs; then that it is fully written

126. *stand upon:* consider.
127. *but even:* just.
131. *vaticinium:* 'a prophecy'.
131. *vaticinari:* 'to prophesy'.
145. *carmina:* 'songs', 'poems'.

NOTES: p. 213

in metre, as all learned Hebricians agree, although the rules be not yet fully found; lastly and principally, his handling his prophecy, which is merely poetical. For what else is the awak- 160 ing his musical instruments, the often and free changing of persons, his notable *prosopopeias*, when he maketh you, as it were, see God coming in his majesty, his telling of the beasts' joyfulness, and hills' leaping, but a heavenly poesy, wherein almost he showeth himself a passionate lover of that unspeak- 165 able and everlasting beauty to be seen by the eyes of the mind, only cleared by faith? But truly now having named him, I fear me I seem to profane that holy name, applying it to Poetry, which is among us thrown down to so ridiculous an estimation: but they that with quiet judgements will look a little 170 deeper into it, shall find the end and working of it such, as, being rightly applied, deserveth not to be scourged out of the Church of God.

But now, let us see how the Greeks named it, and how they deemed of it. The Greeks named him ποιητήν, which name hath, 175 as the most excellent, gone through other languages. It cometh of this word ποιεῖν, which is to make: wherein, I know not whether by luck or wisdom, we Englishmen have met with the Greeks in calling him a maker: which name, how high and incomparable a title it is, I had rather were known by marking 180 the scope of other sciences than by my partial allegation.

There is no art delivered unto mankind that hath not the works of Nature for his principal object, without which they could not consist, and on which they so depend, as they become actors and players, as it were, of what Nature will have 185 set forth. So doth the astronomer look upon the stars, and, by that he seeth, setteth down what order Nature hath taken

160. *merely:* wholly.
161–2. *changing of persons:* introduction of dialogue.
162. *prosopopeias:* personifications of inanimate objects.
164. *poesy:* poetry.
175. ποιητήν: *poieten* (accusative of *poietes*), 'a poet'.
177. ποιεῖν: *poiein,* 'to make'.
178. *have met with:* agree with.
181. *partial:* prejudiced.

NOTES: pp. 213–14

therein. So do the geometrician and arithmetician in their diverse sorts of quantities. So doth the musician in times tell you which by nature agree, which not. The natural philosopher 190 thereon hath his name, and the moral philosopher standeth upon the natural virtues, vices, or passions of man; and 'follow Nature' (saith he) 'therein, and thou shalt not err'. The lawyer saith what men have determined; the historian what men have done. The grammarian speaketh only of the rules of 195 speech; and the rhetorician and logician, considering what in Nature will soonest prove and persuade, thereon give artificial rules, which still are compassed within the circle of a question according to the proposed matter. The physician weigheth the nature of man's body, and the nature of things helpful or 200 hurtful unto it. And the metaphysic, though it be in the second and abstract notions, and therefore be counted supernatural, yet doth he indeed build upon the depth of Nature. Only the poet, disdaining to be tied to any such subjection, lifted up with vigour of his own invention, doth grow in effect into another 205 Nature, in making things either better than Nature bringeth forth, or, quite anew, forms such as never were in Nature, as the Heroes, Demigods, Cyclops, Chimeras, Furies, and such like: so as he goeth hand in hand with Nature, not enclosed within the narrow warrant of her gifts, but freely ranging within the 210 zodiac of his own wit.

Nature never set forth the earth in so rich tapestry as divers poets have done, neither with so pleasant rivers, fruitful trees, sweet-smelling flowers, nor whatsoever else may make the too much loved earth more lovely. Her world is brazen, the poets 215 only deliver a golden. But let those things alone, and go to man (for whom as the other things are, so it seemeth in him her uttermost cunning is employed), and know whether she have brought forth so true a lover as Theagenes, so constant a friend as Pylades, so valiant a man as Orlando, so right a prince as 220 Xenophon's Cyrus, so excellent a man every way as Virgil's Aeneas. Neither let this be jestingly conceived, because the

201. *metaphysic:* metaphysician.
222. *jestingly conceived:* taken in jest.

NOTES: p. 214

works of the one be essential, the other in imitation or fiction; for every understanding knoweth the skill of each artificer standeth in that Idea or foreconceit of the work, and not in the work itself. And that the poet hath that Idea is manifest, by delivering them forth in such excellency as he hath imagined them. Which delivering forth also is not wholly imaginative, as we are wont to say by them that build castles in the air: but so far substantially it worketh, not only to make a Cyrus, which had been but a particular excellency, as Nature might have done, but to bestow a Cyrus upon the world to make many Cyruses, if they will learn aright why and how that maker made him.

Neither let it be deemed too saucy a comparison to balance the highest point of man's wit with the efficacy of Nature; but rather give right honour to the heavenly Maker of that maker, who, having made man to his own likeness, set him beyond and over all the works of that second nature: which in nothing he showeth so much as in Poetry, when with the force of a divine breath he bringeth things forth surpassing her doings, with no small argument to the incredulous of that first accursed fall of Adam, since our erected wit maketh us know what perfection is, and yet our infected will keepeth us from reaching unto it. But these arguments will by few be understood, and by fewer granted. Thus much (I hope) will be given me, that the Greeks with some probability of reason gave him the name above all names of learning. Now let us go to a more ordinary opening of him, that the truth may be the more palpable: and so I hope, though we get not so unmatched a praise as the etymology of his names will grant, yet his very description, which no man will deny, shall not justly be barred from a principal commendation.

Poesy therefore is an art of imitation, for so Aristotle termeth it in the word μιμεσις, that is to say, a representing, counterfeit-

223. *the one:* Nature.
223. *the other:* the poet.
233. *that maker:* Xenophon.
237. *that maker:* the poet.
248. *opening:* exposition.
254. *μιμεσις:* mimesis, 'imitation'.

ing, or figuring forth: to speak metaphorically, a speaking 255 picture; with this end, to teach and delight. Of this have been three general kinds.

The chief, both in antiquity and excellency, were they that did imitate the unconceivable excellencies of God. Such were David in his Psalms; Solomon in his Song of Songs, in his 260 Ecclesiastes, and Proverbs; Moses and Deborah in their Hymns; and the writer of Job; which, beside other, the learned Emanuel Tremellius and Franciscus Junius do entitle the poetical part of the Scripture. Against these none will speak that hath the Holy Ghost in due holy reverence. In this kind, 265 though in a full wrong divinity, were Orpheus, Amphion, Homer in his Hymns, and many other, both Greeks and Romans. And this poesy must be used by whosoever will follow St James's counsel in singing psalms when they are merry, and I know is used with the fruit of comfort by some, 270 when, in sorrowful pangs of their death-bringing sins, they find the consolation of the never-leaving goodness.

The second kind is of them that deal with matters philosophical: either moral, as Tyrtaeus, Phocylides, and Cato; or natural, as Lucretius, and Virgil's Georgics; or astronomical, as 275 Manilius and Pontanus; or historical, as Lucan; which who mislike, the fault is in their judgements quite out of taste, and not in the sweet food of sweetly uttered knowledge.

But because this second sort is wrapped within the fold of the proposed subject, and takes not the course of his own inven- 280 tion, whether they properly be poets or no let grammarians dispute; and go to the third, indeed right poets, of whom chiefly this question ariseth; betwixt whom and these second is such a kind of difference as betwixt the meaner sort of painters, who counterfeit only such faces as are set before them, and the 285 more excellent, who, having no law but wit, bestow that in colours upon you which is fittest for the eye to see: as the constant though lamenting look of Lucretia, when she punished in herself another's fault; wherein he painteth not Lucretia whom he never saw, but painteth the outward beauty of such a 290 virtue. For these third be they which most properly do imitate to teach and delight, and to imitate borrow nothing of what is, hath been, or shall be; but range, only reined with learned discretion, into the divine consideration of what may be, and should be. These be they that, as the first and most noble sort 295 may justly be termed *Vates*, so these are waited on in the excellentest languages and best understandings, with the foredescribed name of Poets; for these indeed do merely make to imitate, and imitate both to delight and teach, and delight to move men to take that goodness in hand, which without delight 300 they would fly as from a stranger, and teach, to make them know that goodness whereunto they are moved; which being the noblest scope to which ever any learning was directed, yet want there not idle tongues to bark at them.

These be subdivided into sundry more special denomina- 305 tions. The most notable be the Heroic, Lyric, Tragic, Comic, Satiric, Iambic, Elegiac, Pastoral, and certain others, some of these being termed according to the matter they deal with, some by the sorts of verses they liked best to write in; for indeed the greatest part of poets have apparelled their poetical inventions 310 in that numbrous kind of writing which is called verse; indeed but apparelled, verse being but an ornament and no cause to Poetry, since there have been many most excellent poets that never versified, and now swarm many versifiers that need never answer to the name of poets. For Xenophon, who did imitate so 315 excellently as to give us *effigiem iusti imperii*, 'the portraiture of a just Empire', under the name of Cyrus (as Cicero saith of him), made therein an absolute heroical poem; so did Heliodorus in his sugared invention of that picture of love in Theagenes and Chariclea; and yet both these wrote in prose: which I speak to 320 show that it is not rhyming and versing that maketh a poet, no more than a long gown maketh an advocate, who though he pleaded in armour should be an advocate and no soldier. But it

298. *make:* compose poetry.
303. *scope:* end, aim.
308. *these:* these poets.
311. *numbrous:* metrical.
312. *cause:* essential part.

is that feigning notable images of virtues, vices, or what else, with that delightful teaching, which must be the right describ- 325 ing note to know a poet by; although indeed the Senate of Poets hath chosen verse as their fittest raiment, meaning, as in matter they passed all in all, so in manner to go beyond them: not speaking (table talk fashion or like men in a dream) words as they chanceably fall from the mouth, but peizing each syllable 330 of each word by just proportion, according to the dignity of the subject.

Now therefore it shall not be amiss first to weigh this latter sort of Poetry by his works, and then by his parts; and if in neither of these anatomies he be condemnable, I hope we shall 335 obtain a more favourable sentence. This purifying of wit, this enriching of memory, enabling of judgement, and enlarging of conceit, which commonly we call learning, under what name soever it come forth, or to what immediate end soever it be directed, the final end is to lead and draw us to as high a per- 340 fection as our degenerate souls, made worse by their clayey lodgings, can be capable of. This, according to the inclination of man, bred many formed impressions. For some that thought this felicity principally to be gotten by knowledge, and no knowledge to be so high and heavenly as acquaintance with the 345 stars, gave themselves to Astronomy; others, persuading themselves to be demigods if they knew the causes of things, became natural and supernatural philosophers; some an admirable delight drew to Music; and some the certainty of demonstration to the Mathematics. But all, one and other, having this 350 scope – to know, and by knowledge to lift up the mind from the dungeon of the body to the enjoying his own divine essence. But when by the balance of experience it was found that the astronomer looking to the stars might fall into a ditch, that the inquiring philosopher might be blind in himself, and the 355

330 *peizing:* weighing.
336. *wit:* intelligence.
337. *enabling:* strengthening.
338. *conceit:* imagination.
355. *blind in himself:* ignorant of his own nature.

NOTES: p. 215

mathematician might draw forth a straight line with a crooked
heart, then, lo, did proof, the overruler of opinions, make
manifest that all these are but serving sciences, which, as they
have each a private end in themselves, so yet are they all
directed to the highest end of the mistress knowledge, by the 360
Greeks called ἀρχιτεκτονικη, which stands (as I think) in the
knowledge of a man's self, in the ethic and politic consideration,
with the end of well doing and not of well knowing only; even
as the saddler's next end is to make a good saddle, but his
farther end to serve a nobler faculty, which is horsemanship; 365
so the horseman's to soldiery, and the soldier not only to have
the skill, but to perform the practice of a soldier. So that, the
ending end of all earthly learning being virtuous action, those
skills that most serve to bring forth that, have a most just title to
be princes over all the rest. Wherein we can show the poet is 370
worthy to have it before any other competitors: among whom
principally to challenge it step forth the moral philosophers,
whom me thinks I see coming towards me with a sullen
gravity, as though they could not abide vice by daylight,
rudely clothed for to witness outwardly their contempt of out- 375
ward things, with books in their hands against glory, whereto
they set their names, sophistically speaking against subtlety,
and angry with any man in whom they see the foul fault of
anger. These men casting largesse as they go of definitions,
divisions, and distinctions, with a scornful interrogative do 380
soberly ask whether it be possible to find any path so ready to
lead a man to virtue as that which teacheth what virtue is, and
teacheth it not only by delivering forth his very being, his
causes, and effects, but also by making known his enemy Vice,
which must be destroyed, and his cumbersome servant Passion, 385
which must be mastered; by showing the generalities that contains it, and the specialities that are derived from it; lastly, by

357. *proof:* experience.
361. ἀρχιτεκτονικη: *architektonike,* 'the master-knowledge.'
364. *next end:* immediate object.
368. *ending end:* ultimate object.
386. *generalities:* its collective genus.
387. *specialities:* its various species.

NOTES: p. 215

plain setting down, how it extendeth itself out of the limits of a man's own little world to the government of families, and maintaining of public societies. 390

The historian scarcely gives leisure to the moralist to say so much, but that he, loaden with old mouse-eaten records, authorizing himself (for the most part) upon other histories, whose greatest authorities are built upon the notable foundation of hearsay; having much ado to accord differing writers 395 and to pick truth out of partiality; better acquainted with a thousand years ago than with the present age, and yet better knowing how this world goes than how his own wit runs; curious for antiquities and inquisitive of novelties; a wonder to young folks and a tyrant in table talk; denieth, in a great chafe, 400 that any man for teaching of virtue, and virtuous actions, is comparable to him. 'I am *Testis temporum, lux veritatis, vita memoriae, magistra vitae, nuntia vetustatis*. The philosopher' (saith he) 'teacheth a disputative virtue, but I do an active. His virtue is excellent in the dangerless Academy of Plato, but 405 mine showeth forth her honourable face in the battles of Marathon, Pharsalia, Poitiers, and Agincourt. He teacheth virtue by certain abstract considerations, but I only bid you follow the footing of them that have gone before you. Old-aged experience goeth beyond the fine-witted philosopher, but I 410 give the experience of many ages. Lastly, if he make the songbook, I put the learner's hand to the lute; and if he be the guide, I am the light.'

Then would he allege you innumerable examples, confirming story by story how much the wisest senators and princes have 415 been directed by the credit of history, as Brutus, Alphonsus of Aragon, and who not, if need be? At length the long line of their disputation makes a point in this, that the one giveth the precept, and the other the example.

Now, whom shall we find (since the question standeth for 420 the highest form in the school of learning) to be Moderator? Truly, as me seemeth, the poet; and if not a Moderator, even

400. *chafe:* passion.
418. *makes a point:* ends.

NOTES: p. 215

the man that ought to carry the title from them both, and much more from all other serving sciences. Therefore compare we the poet with the historian, and with the moral philosopher; 425 and, if he go beyond them both, no other human skill can match him. For as for the divine, with all reverence it is ever to be excepted, not only for having his scope as far beyond any of these as eternity exceedeth a moment, but even for passing each of these in themselves. And for the lawyer, though *Jus* be 430 the daughter of Justice, the chief of virtues, yet because he seeks to make men good rather *formidine poenae* than *virtutis amore*, or, to say righter, doth not endeavour to make men good, but that their evil hurt not others, having no care, so he be a good citizen, how bad a man he be: therefore, as our wickedness 435 maketh him necessary, and necessity maketh him honourable, so is he not in the deepest truth to stand in rank with these who all endeavour to take naughtiness away, and plant goodness even in the secretest cabinet of our souls. And these four are all that any way deal in the consideration of men's manners, which 440 being the supreme knowledge, they that best breed it deserve the best commendation.

The philosopher therefore and the historian are they which would win the goal, the one by precept, the other by example. But both, not having both, do both halt. For the philosopher, 445 setting down with thorny arguments the bare rule, is so hard of utterance, and so misty to be conceived, that one that hath no other guide but him shall wade in him till he be old before he shall find sufficient cause to be honest: for his knowledge standeth so upon the abstract and general, that happy is that 450 man who may understand him, and more happy that can apply what he doth understand. On the other side, the historian, wanting the precept, is so tied, not to what should be but to what is, to the particular truth of things and not to the general

424–5. *compare we:* let us compare.
427. *the divine:* divinity.
430. *Jus:* 'Law'.
439. *cabinet:* room.
445. *halt:* limp.

NOTES: p. 215

reason of things, that his example draweth no necessary con- 455
sequence, and therefore a less fruitful doctrine.

Now doth the peerless poet perform both: for whatsoever
the philosopher saith should be done, he giveth a perfect picture
of it in some one by whom he presupposeth it was done; so as
he coupleth the general notion with the particular example. A 460
perfect picture I say, for he yieldeth to the powers of the
mind an image of that whereof the philosopher bestoweth but
a wordish description: which doth neither strike, pierce, nor
possess the sight of the soul so much as that other doth.

For as in outward things, to a man that had never seen an 465
elephant or a rhinoceros, who should tell him most exquisitely
all their shapes, colour, bigness, and particular marks, or of a
gorgeous palace the architecture, with declaring the full
beauties might well make the hearer able to repeat, as it were
by rote, all he had heard, yet should never satisfy his inward 470
conceit with being witness to itself of a true lively knowledge:
but the same man, as soon as he might see those beasts well
painted, or that house well in model, should straightways
grow, without need of any description, to a judicial compre-
hending of them: so no doubt the philosopher with his learned 475
definitions, be it of virtues, vices, matters of public policy or
private government, replenisheth the memory with many
infallible grounds of wisdom, which, notwithstanding, lie
dark before the imaginative and judging power, if they be
not illuminated or figured forth by the speaking picture of 480
Poesy.

*

Now, to that which commonly is attributed to the praise of
History, in respect of the notable learning is got by marking
the success, as though therein a man should see virtue exalted
and vice punished: truly that commendation is peculiar to 485
Poetry, and far off from History. For indeed Poetry ever sets
Virtue so out in her best colours, making Fortune her well-

471. *lively:* lifelike.
482. *to that:* as to that.
484. *success:* outcome.

NOTES: p. 215

waiting handmaid, that one must needs be enamoured of her. Well may you see Ulysses in a storm, and in other hard plights; but they are but exercises of patience and magnanimity, to make them shine the more in the near-following prosperity. And of the contrary part, if evil men come to the stage, they ever go out (as the tragedy writer answered to one that misliked the show of such persons) so manacled as they little animate folks to follow them. But the historian, being captived to the truth of a foolish world, is many times a terror from well-doing, and an encouragement to unbridled wickedness.

For see we not valiant Miltiades rot in his fetters? The just Phocion and the accomplished Socrates put to death like traitors? The cruel Severus live prosperously? The excellent Severus miserably murdered? Sylla and Marius dying in their beds? Pompey and Cicero slain then when they would have thought exile a happiness? See we not virtuous Cato driven to kill himself, and rebel Caesar so advanced that his name yet, after 1600 years, lasteth in the highest honour? . . . I conclude, therefore, that [Poetry] excelleth History, not only in furnishing the mind with knowledge, but in setting it forward to that which deserves to be called and accounted good: which setting forward, and moving to well doing, indeed setteth the laurel crown upon the poet as victorious, not only of the historian, but over the philosopher, howsoever in teaching it may be questionable.

For suppose it be granted (that which I suppose with great reason may be denied) that the philosopher, in respect of his methodical proceeding, doth teach more perfectly than the poet, yet do I think that no man is so much φιλοφιλοσοφος as to compare the philosopher, in moving, with the poet.

And that moving is of a higher degree than teaching, it may by this appear, that it is well-nigh both the cause and the effect of teaching. For who will be taught, if he be not moved with desire to be taught? and what so much good doth that teaching

490. *exercises:* trials.
516. φιλοφιλοσοφος: *philophilosophos* (humorous coinage), 'a lover of philosophers.'

NOTES: p. 215

bring forth (I speak still of moral doctrine) as that it moveth one to do that which it doth teach? For, as Aristotle saith, it is not γνοσις but πραξις must be the fruit. And how πραξις cannot be, without being moved to practise, it is no hard matter 525 to consider.

The philosopher showeth you the way, he informeth you of the particularities, as well of the tediousness of the way, as of the pleasant lodging you shall have when your journey is ended, as of the many by-turnings that may divert you from 530 your way. But this is to no man but to him that will read him, and read him with attentive studious painfulness; which constant desire whosoever hath in him, hath already passed half the hardness of the way, and therefore is beholding to the philosopher but for the other half. Nay truly, learned men have 535 learnedly thought that where once reason hath so much overmastered passion as that the mind hath a free desire to do well, the inward light each mind hath in itself is as good as a philosopher's book; since in nature we know it is well to do well, and what is well and what is evil, although not in the 540 words of art which philosophers bestow upon us. For out of natural conceit the philosophers drew it; but to be moved to do that which we know, or to be moved with desire to know, *Hoc opus, hic labor est.*

Now therein of all sciences (I speak still of human, and 545 according to the human conceit) is our poet the monarch. For he doth not only show the way, but giveth so sweet a prospect into the way, as will entice any man to enter into it. Nay, he doth, as if your journey should lie through a fair vineyard, at the first give you a cluster of grapes, that, full of that taste, you 550 may long to pass further. He beginneth not with obscure definitions, which must blur the margent with interpretations, and load the memory with doubtfulness; but he cometh to you

524. γνοσις: *gnosis*, 'knowledge'.
524. πραξις: *praxis*, 'action'.
534. *beholding:* indebted.
541-2. *out of natural conceit:* from common sense.
552. *margent:* margin.

NOTES: p. 215

with words set in delightful proportion, either accompanied
with, or prepared for, the well enchanting skill of music; and 555
with a tale forsooth he cometh unto you, with a tale which
holdeth children from play, and old men from the chimney
corner. And, pretending no more, doth intend the winning of
the mind from wickedness to virtue: even as the child is often
brought to take most wholesome things by hiding them in such 560
other as have a pleasant taste: which, if one should begin to tell
them the nature of the aloes or rhubarb they should receive,
would sooner take their physic at their ears than at their mouth.
So is it in men (most of which be childish in the best things,
till they be cradled in their graves): glad they will be to hear 565
the tales of Hercules, Achilles, Cyrus, and Aeneas; and, hearing
them, must needs hear the right description of wisdom, valour,
and justice; which, if they had been barely, that is to say
philosophically, set out, they would swear they be brought to
school again.   570

*

Since then Poetry is of all human learning the most ancient and
of most fatherly antiquity, as from whence other learnings
have taken their beginnings; since it is so universal that no
learned nation doth despise it, nor so barbarous nation is without it; since both Roman and Greek gave divine names unto it, 575
the one of prophesying, the other of making, and that indeed
that name of making is fit for him, considering that where all
other arts retain themselves within their subject, and receive, as
it were, their being from it, the poet only bringeth his own
stuff, and doth not learn a conceit out of a matter, but maketh 580
matter for a conceit; since neither his description nor his end
containeth any evil, the thing described cannot be evil; since
his effects be so good as to teach goodness and to delight the
learners of it; since therein (namely in moral doctrine, the chief
of all knowledges) he doth not only far pass the historian, but, 585
for instructing, is wellnigh comparable to the philosopher,
and, for moving, leaveth him behind him; since the Holy
Scripture (wherein there is no uncleanness) hath whole parts in

it poetical, and that even our Saviour Christ vouchsafed to use the flowers of it; since all his kinds are not only in their united 590 forms but in their severed dissections fully commendable: I think (and think I think rightly) the laurel crown appointed for triumphing captains doth worthily (of all other learnings) honour the poet's triumph.

NOTES: p. 216

Sonnets and Songs from
ASTROPHEL AND STELLA

I

Loving in truth, and fain in verse my love to show,
That the dear She might take some pleasure of my pain,
Pleasure might cause her read, reading might make her know,
Knowledge might pity win, and pity grace obtain,
    I sought fit words to paint the blackest face of woe,   5
Studying inventions fine, her wits to entertain,
Oft turning others' leaves, to see if thence would flow
Some fresh and fruitful showers upon my sun-burn'd brain.
    But words came halting forth, wanting Invention's stay,
Invention, Nature's child, fled stepdame Study's blows,   10
And others' feet still seem'd but strangers in my way.
Thus great with child to speak, and helpless in my throes,
    Biting my truand pen, beating myself for spite,
    'Fool,' said my Muse to me, 'look in thy heart and write.'

II

Not at first sight, nor with a dribbed shot,
    Love gave the wound which while I breathe will bleed;
    But known worth did in mine of time proceed
Till by degrees it had full conquest got.

    4. *grace:* favour, love.
    6. *studying:* devising.
    9. *halting:* limping.
    9. *stay:* support.
    11. *still:* always.
    12. *great with child to speak:* anxious to deliver my feelings.
    13. *truand:* idle.

    II. 1. *dribbed:* random.
        3. *mine:* tunnel under the walls of a besieged town.
        3. *of time:* slowly.

NOTES: p. 216

I saw and lik'd, I lik'd but loved not,   5
  I lov'd, but straight did not what Love decreed:
  At length to Love's decrees I, forc'd, agreed,
Yet with repining at so partial lot.
  Now even that footstep of lost liberty
Is gone, and now, like slave-born Muscovite,   10
I call it praise to suffer tyranny;
And now employ the remnant of my wit
  To make myself believe that all is well,
  While with a feeling skill I paint my hell.

III

Let dainty wits cry on the Sisters nine,
That bravely maskt, their fancies may be told;
Or Pindar's apes flaunt they in phrases fine,
Enam'lling with pied flowers their thoughts of gold;
  Or else let them in statelier glory shine,   5
Ennobling new-found tropes with problems old;
Or with strange similes enrich each line,
Of herbs or beasts, which Ind or Afric hold.
  For me, in sooth, no Muse but one I know;
  Phrases and problems from my reach do grow,   10
And strange things cost too dear for my poor sprites.
  How then? even thus: in Stella's face I read
  What Love and Beauty be, then all my deed
But copying is, what in her Nature writes.

        8. *partial lot:* unjust fate.
        9. *footstep:* trace.
    III. 1. *Sisters nine:* the Muses
         2. *bravely maskt:* finely covered.
         3. *apes:* imitators.
         6. *tropes:* rhetorical devices.
         6. *problems:* ingenious questions.

NOTES: p. 216

IV

Virtue, alas, now let me take some rest;
Thou set'st a bate between my will and wit.
If vain Love have my simple soul opprest,
Leave what thou lik'st not, deal not thou with it.
 Thy sceptre use in some old Cato's breast,   5
Churches or schools are for thy seat more fit:
I do confess – pardon a fault confest –
My mouth too tender is for thy hard bit.
 But if that needs thou wilt usurping be
 The little reason that is left in me,   10
And still th'effect of thy persuasions prove,
 I swear my heart such one shall show to thee,
 That shrines in flesh so true a deity,
That, Virtue, thou thyself shalt be in love.

V

It is most true, that eyes are form'd to serve
The inward light, and that the heavenly part
Ought to be king, from whose rules who do swerve,
Rebels to nature, strive for their own smart.
 It is most true, what we call Cupid's dart   5
An image is, which for ourselves we carve,
And, fools, adore in temple of our heart,
Till that good god make church and churchman starve.
 True, that true beauty virtue is indeed,
Whereof this beauty can be but a shade,   10
Which elements with mortal mixture breed:
True, that on earth we are but pilgrims made,
 And should in soul up to our country move:
 True, and yet true that I must Stella love.

IV. 2. *set'st a bate:* sowest discord.
 6. *schools:* schools of philosophy.
 11. *prove:* try.

V. 2. *inward light; heavenly part:* reason.
 13. *our country:* heaven.

NOTES: pp. 216–17

VII

When Nature made her chief work, Stella's eyes,
In colour black why wrapt she beams so bright?
Would she in beamy black, like painter wise,
Frame daintiest lustre mixt of shades and light?
    Or did she else that sober hue devise, 5
In object best to knit and strength our sight,
Lest if no veil those brave gleams did disguise,
They sunlike should more dazzle than delight?
    Or would she her miraculous power show,
That, whereas black seems Beauty's contrary, 10
She even in black doth make all beauties flow?
Both so and thus: she, minding Love should be
    Plac'd ever there, gave him this mourning weed
    To honour all their deaths who for her bleed.

IX

Queen Virtue's Court, which some call Stella's face,
    Prepar'd by Nature's chiefest furniture,
    Hath his front built of alabaster pure;
Gold is the covering of that stately place.
The door by which sometimes comes forth her Grace 5
    Red porphyr is, which lock of pearl makes sure,
    Whose porches rich (which name of cheeks endure)
Marble mixt red and white do interlace.
    The windows now, through which this heavenly guest
Looks over the world, and can find nothing such 10
Which dare claim from those lights the name of best,
Of touch they are that without touch doth touch,

VII. 3. *beamy:* shining.
    6. *in object best . . . our sight:* with the good purpose of concentrating and strengthening our sight.
    12. *minding:* remembering that.

IX. 2. *by Nature's chiefest furniture:* of Nature's richest materials.
    3. *front:* front (of house), forehead.
    6. *porphyr:* porphyry, a hard ornamental rock.
    8. *marble:* (here plural).

NOTES: p. 217

Which Cupid's self from Beauty's mine did draw:
Of touch they are, and poor I am their straw.

X

Reason, in faith thou art well serv'd, that still
Wouldst brabbling be with Sense and Love in me:
I rather wisht thee climb the Muses' hill,
Or reach the fruit of Nature's choicest tree,
    Or seek heav'n's course or heav'n's inside to see: 5
Why shouldst thou toil our thorny soil to till?
Leave sense, and those which sense's objects be:
Deal thou with powers of thoughts, leave love to will.
    But thou wouldst needs fight both with Love and Sense,
With sword of wit giving wounds of dispraise,   10
Till downright blows did foil thy cunning fence:
For, soon as they strake thee with Stella's rays,
    Reason, thou kneel'dst, and offer'd'st straight to prove
    By reason good, good reason her to love.

XII

Cupid, because thou shin'st in Stella's eyes,
    That from her locks, thy day-nets, none scapes free,
    That those lips swell, so full of thee they be,
That her sweet breath makes oft thy flames to rise,
That in her breast thy pap well sugar'd lies,   5

13. *draw:* quarry.

X. 2. *brabbling:* brawling.
    3. *climb the Muses' hill:* write poetry.
    4. *reach the fruit . . . choicest tree:* acquire learning.
    5. *heav'n's course:* (by astronomy).
    5. *heav'n's inside:* (by divinity).
    6. *our thorny soil to till:* to work in human feelings.
    7. *those:* those things.

XII. 2–6, 8. *that:* because.
    5. *pap:* baby's food.

NOTES: pp. 217–18

That her grace gracious makes thy wrongs, that she,
  What words soe'er she speaks, persuades for thee,
That her clear voice lifts thy fame to the skies:
  Thou countest Stella thine, like those whose powers
Having got up a breach by fighting well,   10
Cry 'Victory, this fair day all is ours!'
O no, her heart is such a citadel,
  So fortified with wit, stor'd with disdain,
  That to win it, is all the skill and pain.

XIV

Alas, have I not pain enough, my friend,
  Upon whose breast a fiercer gripe doth tire
  Than did on him who first stale down the fire,
While Love on me doth all his quiver spend,
But with your rhubarb words you must contend   5
  To grieve me worse, in saying that desire
  Doth plunge my well-form'd soul even in the mire
Of sinful thoughts, which do in ruin end?
  If that be sin which doth the manners frame,
Well stay'd with truth in word and faith of deed,   10
Ready of wit, and fearing nought but shame;
  If that be sin which in fixt hearts doth breed
  A loathing of all loose unchastity,
  Then love is sin, and let me sinful be.

6. *that her grace . . . thy wrongs:* because Stella's charm excuses the
    injuries done by Cupid (to her lover).
9. *powers:* army, soldiers.
XIV. 2. *gripe:* vulture.
   2. *tire upon:* tear with the beak.
   3. *stale:* stole.
   5. *rhubarb:* bitter.
   9. *the manners frame:* form right conduct.

NOTES: p. 218

XV

You that do search for every purling spring
　　Which from the ribs of old Parnassus flows,
　　And every flower, not sweet perhaps, which grows
Near thereabout, into your poesy wring;
You that do dictionary's method bring　　　　　　5
　　Into your rhymes, running in rattling rows;
　　You that poor Petrarch's long-deceased woes
With new-born sighs and denizen'd wit do sing;
　　You take wrong ways, those far-fet helps be such
　　As do bewray a want of inward touch,　　　　10
And sure at length stol'n goods do come to light.
　　But if, both for your love and skill, your name
　　You seek to nurse at fullest breasts of Fame,
Stella behold, and then begin to indite.

XVI

In nature apt to like, when I did see
　　Beauties which were of many carats fine,
　　My boiling sprites did thither soon incline,
And, Love, I thought that I was full of thee:
But finding not those restless flames in me　　5
　　Which others said did make their souls to pine,
　　I thought those babes of some pin's hurt did whine,
By my love judging what Love's pain might be.
　　But while I thus with this young lion play'd,
Mine eyes (shall I say curst or blest?) beheld　　10
Stella: now she is nam'd, need more be said?
In her sight I a lesson new have spell'd.
　　I now have learn'd love right, and learn'd even so
　　As who by being poison'd doth poison know.

XV.　4. *poesy:* poetry.
　　　9. *far-fet:* far-fatched, imported.
　　10. *bewray:* reveal, expose.
　　10. *inward touch:* natural ability.
　　14. *indite:* compose.
XVI. 3. *sprites:* feelings.

NOTES: p. 218

XVII

His mother dear Cupid offended late,
  Because that Mars, grown slacker in her love,
  With pricking shot he did not throughly move
To keep the pace of their first loving state.
The boy refus'd for fear of Mars's hate,   5
  Who threaten'd stripes if he his wrath did prove;
  But she in chafe him from her lap did shove,
Brake bow, brake shafts, while Cupid weeping sate;
  Till that his grandam Nature, pitying it,
Of Stella's brows made him two better bows,   10
And in her eyes of arrows infinite.
O how for joy he leaps, O how he crows!
  And straight therewith, like wags new got to play,
  Falls to shrewd turns, and I was in his way.

XVIII

With what sharp checks I in myself am shent
  When into Reason's audit I do go,
  And by just counts myself a bankrout know
Of all those goods which heav'n to me hath lent;

XVII.   3. *throughly:* thoroughly, in mind and body.
        4. *to keep the pace of their first loving state:* to continue as active
              in love as he was at first.
        6. *stripes:* blows.
        6. *prove:* try.
        7. *in chafe:* in heat of anger.
        9. *it:* him.
       11. *infinite:* an infinite quantity.
       13. *wags:* boys.
       14. *falls to shrewd turns:* begins his naughty tricks.
XVIII. 1. *checks:* reproaches.
        1. *shent:* blamed.
        2. *audit:* examination of accounts.
        3. *bankrout:* bankrupt.

NOTES: p. 218

Unable quite to pay even Nature's rent,   5
    Which unto it by birthright I do owe;
    And, which is worse, no good excuse can show,
But that my wealth I have most idly spent.
    My youth doth waste, my knowledge brings forth toys,
My wit doth strive those passions to defend   10
Which, for reward, spoil it with vain annoys.
I see my course to lose myself doth bend:
    I see, and yet no greater sorrow take
    Than that I lose no more for Stella's sake.

XIX

On Cupid's bow how are my heart-strings bent,
    That see my wrack, and yet embrace the same!
    When most I glory, then I feel most shame;
I willing run, yet while I run repent.
My best wits still their own disgrace invent: 5
    My very ink turns straight to Stella's name;
    And yet my words, as them my pen doth frame,
Avise themselves that they are vainly spent.
    For though she pass all things, yet what is all
That unto me, who fare like him that both   10
Looks to the skies and in a ditch doth fall?
O let me prop my mind, yet in his growth,
    And not in nature for best fruits unfit.
    'Scholar,' saith Love, 'bend hitherward your wit.'

XX

Fly, fly, my friends! I have my death wound – fly!
See there that boy, that murth'ring boy I say,
Who, like a thief, hid in dark bush doth lie,
Till bloody bullet get him wrongful prey.

          5. *pay Nature's rent:* keep alive.
          9. *toys:* trifles (his poems).
          11. *vain annoys:* useless griefs.
          12. *lose:* destroy, ruin.
     XIX. 8. *avise themselves:* assure themselves.
          9. *pass:* surpass.
     XX. 2. *murth'ring:* murdering.
NOTES: pp. 218–19

So tyran he no fitter place could spy,   5
Nor so fair level in so secret stay,
As that sweet black which veils the heav'nly eye:
There himself with his shot he close doth lay.
  Poor passenger, pass now thereby I did,
And stay'd, pleas'd with the prospect of the place,   10
While that black hue from me the bad guest hid.
But straight I saw motions of lightning grace,
  And then descried the glist'ring of his dart:
  But ere I could fly thence, it pierc'd my heart.

XXI

Your words, my friend, (right healthful caustics) blame
  My young mind marr'd, whom Love doth windlass so,
  That mine own writings, like bad servants, show
My wits quick in vain thoughts, in virtue lame:
That Plato I read for nought, but if he tame   5
  Such coltish gyres; that to my birth I owe
  Nobler desires, lest else that friendly foe,
Great expectation, wear a train of shame.
  For since mad March great promise made of me,
If now the May of my years much decline,   10
What can be hop'd my harvest time will be?
Sure you say well; your wisdom's golden mine
  Dig deep with learning's spade, now tell me this:
  Hath this world aught so fair as Stella is?

XXII

In highest way of heav'n the sun did ride,
  Progressing then from fair Twins' golden place,
  Having no scarf of clouds before his face,
But shining forth of heat in his chief pride;

5. *tyran:* tyrant.
6. *level:* aiming-place.
6. *stay:* standing-place.
9. *passenger:* passer-by.
12. *lightning* (adj.): rapid.
XXI. 2. *windlass:* ensnare.
6. *gyres:* gyrations, skittishness.

NOTES: p. 219

When some fair ladies, by hard promise tied,   5
    On horseback met him in his furious race,
    Yet each prepar'd, with fans' well-shading grace,
From that foe's wounds their tender skins to hide.
Stella alone with face unarmed marcht,
    Either to do like him which open shone,   10
    Or careless of the wealth, because her own.
Yet were the hid and meaner beauties parcht,
    Her daintiest bare went free. The cause was this,
    The sun which others burn'd, did her but kiss.

XXIV

Rich fools there be whose base and filthy heart
Lies hatching still the goods wherein they flow,
And damning their own selves to Tantal's smart,
Wealth breeding want, more blest, more wretched grow.
    Yet to those fools heav'n such wit doth impart   5
As what their hands do hold, their heads do know,
And knowing love, and loving lay apart
As sacred things, far from all danger's show.
    But that rich fool who by blind Fortune's lot
The richest gem of love and life enjoys,   10
And can with foul abuse such beauties blot,
Let him, depriv'd of sweet but unfelt joys,
    Exil'd for aye from those high treasures which
    He knows not, grow in only folly rich!

XXVII

Because I oft in dark abstracted guise
    Seem most alone in greatest company,
    With dearth of words, or answers quite awry,
    To them that would make speech of speech arise,

XXII. 13. *daintiest:* most delicate (beauty).
XXIV. 3. *and damning:* and who, condemning.

NOTES: p. 219

They deem, and of their doom the rumour flies,   5
    That poison foul of bubbling pride doth lie
    So in my swelling breast that only I
Fawn on myself, and others do despise.
    Yet pride I think doth not my soul possess,
Which looks too oft in his unflattering glass: 10
But one worse fault, ambition, I confess,
That makes me oft my best friends overpass,
    Unseen, unheard, while thought to highest place
    Bends all his powers, even unto Stella's grace.

XXXI

With how sad steps, O Moon, thou climb'st the skies!
    How silently, and with how wan a face!
    What, may it be that even in heav'nly place
That busy archer his sharp arrows tries?
Sure, if that long-with-love-acquainted eyes   5
    Can judge of love, thou feel'st a lover's case;
    I read it in thy looks: thy languisht grace,
To me that feel the like, thy state descries.
    Then ev'n of fellowship, O Moon, tell me,
Is constant love deem'd there but want of wit?   10
Are beauties there as proud as here they be?
Do they above love to be lov'd, and yet
    Those lovers scorn whom that love doth possess?
    Do they call virtue there ungratefulness?

XXVII. 5. *doom:* judgement, opinion.
    9–10. *yet pride . . . unflattering glass:* my soul looks too often in
        its own unflattering glass to be enslaved by pride.
XXXI. 4. *that busy archer:* Cupid.
    7. *languisht grace:* languishing air.
    10–14. *there:* 'in heav'nly place' (3), 'above' (12).
    13. *whom that love doth possess:* whom love controls.
    14. *Do they call . . . ungratefulness?:* 'Do they call ungratefulness
        there a virtue?' (Lamb).

NOTES: p. 220

XXXIII

I might (unhappy word!), O me, I might,
And then would not, or could not, see my bliss,
Till now, wrapt in a most infernal night,
I find how heav'nly day (wretch!) I did miss.
    Heart, rent thyself, thou dost thyself but right: 5
No lovely Paris made thy Helen his,
No force, no fraud robb'd thee of thy delight,
Nor Fortune of thy fortune author is;
    But to myself myself did give the blow,
While too much wit, forsooth, so troubled me   10
That I respects for both our sakes must show,
And yet could not by rising morn foresee
    How fair a day was near. O punisht eyes,
    That I had been more foolish or more wise!

XXXIV

Come, let me write. And to what end? To ease
    A burthen'd heart. How can words ease, which are
    The glasses of thy daily-vexing care?
Oft cruel fights well pictur'd-forth do please.
Art not asham'd to publish thy disease?   5
    Nay, that may breed my fame, it is so rare.
    But will not wise men think thy words fond ware?
Then be they close, and so none shall displease.
    What idler thing than speak and not be heard?
What harder thing than smart and not to speak?   10
Peace, foolish wit! with wit my wit is marr'd.

XXXII.   5. *rent:* rend.
          10. *wit:* circumspection.
          11. *show respects:* be cautious.
XXXIV.   3. *the glasses of:* mirrors reflecting.
          7. *fond ware:* foolish stuff.
          8. *close:* kept private.
          11. *with wit my wit is marr'd:* my brain is turned with puzzling.

NOTES: p. 220

Thus write I while I doubt to write, and wreak
    My harms on ink's poor loss, perhaps some find
    Stella's great powers that so confuse my mind.

XXXV

What may words say, or what may words not say,
Where Truth itself must speak like Flattery?
Within what bounds can one his liking stay,
Where nature doth with infinite agree?
    What Nestor's counsel can my flames allay,   5
Since Reason's self doth blow the coal in me?
And, ah, what hope that Hope should once see day,
Where Cupid is sworn page to Chastity?
Honour is honour'd that thou dost possess
    Him as thy slave, and now long-needy Fame   10
    Doth even grow rich, naming my Stella's name.
Wit learns in thee perfection to express.
    Not thou by praise, but praise in thee is rais'd.
    It is a praise to praise, when thou art prais'd.

XXXVIII

This night, while Sleep begins with heavy wings
    To hatch mine eyes, and that unbitted thought
    Doth fall to stray, and my chief powers are brought
To leave the sceptre of all subject things,
The first that straight my fancy's error brings   5
    Unto my mind is Stella's image, wrought
    By Love's own self, but with so curious draught
That she, methinks, not only shines but sings.

12. *doubt:* fear.
12. *wreak:* revenge.
XXXV. 3. *his liking stay:* confine his love.
    5. *Nestor's counsel:* advice of aged experience.
XXXVIII. 2. *unbitted:* unbridled.
    3. *doth fall to stray:* begins to stray.
    4. *leave:* relinquish.
    5. *error:* wandering.
    7. *draught:* draughtsmanship.

NOTES: p. 220

I start, look, heark; but what in clos'd-up sense
Was held, in open'd sense it flies away,   10
Leaving me nought but wailing eloquence.
I, seeing better sights in sight's decay,
 Call'd it anew, and wooed Sleep again:
 But him, her host, that unkind guest had slain.

XXXIX

Come Sleep, O Sleep, the certain knot of peace,
The baiting-place of wit, the balm of woe,
The poor man's wealth, the prisoner's release,
Th'indifferent judge between the high and low;
 With shield of proof shield me from out the prease   5
Of those fierce darts Despair at me doth throw.
O make in me those civil wars to cease:
I will good tribute pay, if thou do so.
 Take thou of me smooth pillows, sweetest bed,
A chamber deaf to noise and blind to light,   10
A rosy garland and a weary head:
And if these things, as being thine by right,
 Move not thy heavy grace, thou shalt in me,
 Livelier than elsewhere, Stella's image see.

XL

As good to write, as for to lie and groan.
 O Stella dear, how much thy power hath wrought,
 That hast my mind, none of the basest, brought
My still-kept course, while others sleep, to moan!

  13. *it:* Stella's image.
  14. *him:* Sleep.
  14. *that unkind guest:* Stella's image.
 XXXIX. 2. *baiting-place:* halt where travellers and horses are re-
   freshed.
   5. *of proof:* strong.
   5. *prease:* throng.
  14. *livelier:* more lifelike.

NOTES: pp. 220–1

Alas, if from the height of Virtue's throne 5
Thou canst vouchsafe the influence of a thought
Upon a wretch that long thy grace hath sought,
Weigh then how I by thee am overthrown;
And then think thus: although thy beauty be
Made manifest by such a victory, 10
Yet noblest conquerors do wrecks avoid.
Since then thou hast so far subdued me
That in my heart I offer still to thee,
O do not let thy temple be destroy'd!

XLI

Having this day my horse, my hand, my lance
Guided so well that I obtain'd the prize,
Both by the judgement of the English eyes
And of some sent from that sweet enemy France;
Horsemen my skill in horsemanship advance; 5
Townfolks my strength; a daintier judge applies
His praise to sleight which from good use doth rise;
Some lucky wits impute it but to chance;
Others, because of both sides I do take
My blood from them who did excel in this, 10
Think Nature me a man of arms did make.
How far they shoot awry! The true cause is,
Stella lookt on, and from her heav'nly face
Sent forth the beams which made so fair my race.

XL. 8. *weigh:* consider.
11. *do wrecks avoid:* refrain from laying conquered towns
in ruins.
13. *still:* constantly.
XLI. 5. *advance:* commend.
6. *daintier:* finer, nicer.
7. *sleight:* dexterity.
7. *good use:* good practice.
14. *my race:* the course which I rode.

NOTES: p. 221

C

XLII

O eyes which do the spheres of beauty move,
Whose beams be joys, whose joys all virtues be,
Who, while they make Love conquer, conquer Love;
The schools where Venus hath learn'd chastity:
    O eyes, where humble looks most glorious prove,   5
Only-lov'd tyrants, just in cruelty,
Do not, O do not from poor me remove;
Keep still my zenith, ever shine on me.
    For though I never see them but straightways
My life forgets to nourish languisht sprites,   10
Yet still on me, O eyes, dart down your rays!
And if from majesty of sacred lights
    Oppressing mortal sense my death proceed,
    Wracks triumphs be which Love high-set doth breed.

XLV

Stella oft sees the very face of woe
    Painted in my beclouded stormy face,
    But cannot skill to pity my disgrace,
Not though thereof the cause herself she know:
Yet hearing late a fable which did show   5
    Of lovers never known a grievous case,
    Pity thereof gat in her breast such place
That, from that sea deriv'd, tears' spring did flow.
    Alas, if fancy, drawn by imag'd things,
Though false, yet with free scope, more grace doth breed   10
Than servant's wrack, where new doubts honour brings,
Then think, my dear, that you in me do read
    Of lover's ruin some sad tragedy.
    I am not I: pity the tale of me.

XLV.   3. *cannot skill to:* is unable to.
        3. *disgrace:* wretchedness.
        4. *not though . . . she know:* even though she knows that she
            herself is its cause.
        9. *fancy:* imagination.
        9. *imag'd:* pictured.

NOTES: p. 221

XLVII

What, have I thus betray'd my liberty?
    Can those black beams such burning marks engrave
    In my free side? or am I born a slave,
Whose neck becomes such yoke of tyranny?
Or want I sense to feel my misery?   5
    Or sprite, disdain of such disdain to have?
    Who for long faith, tho' daily help I crave,
May get no alms but scorn of beggary.
    Virtue, awake! Beauty but beauty is.
I may, I must, I can, I will, I do   10
Leave following that which it is gain to miss.
Let her go! Soft, but here she comes! Go to,
    Unkind, I love you not! O me, that eye
    Doth make my heart to give my tongue the lie!

XLIX

I on my horse, and Love on me, doth try
    Our horsemanships, while by strange work I prove
    A horseman to my horse, a horse to Love,
And now man's wrongs in me, poor beast, descry.
The reins wherewith my rider doth me tie   5
    Are humbled thoughts, which bit of reverence move,
    Curb'd in with fear, but with gilt boss above
Of hope, which makes it seem fair to the eye.
    The wand is will; thou, fancy, saddle art,
Girt fast by memory; and while I spur   10
My horse, he spurs with sharp desire my heart.
He sits me fast, however I do stir,
    And now hath made me to his hand so right
    That in the manage myself take delight.

XLVII. 4. *becomes:* befits.
    7. *for:* in return for.
    8. *scorn of beggary:* contempt for my beggarly condition.
XLIX. 4. *and now . . . descry:* and now perceive by my own experience
        (as a horse) the tyranny of man (as a rider).
    9. *wand:* crop.   9. *will:* passion.

NOTES: p. 221

LII

A strife is grown between Virtue and Love,
  While each pretends that Stella must be his:
  Her eyes, her lips, her all, saith Love, do this,
Since they do wear his badge, most firmly prove.
But Virtue thus that title doth disprove: 5
  That Stella (O dear name!) that Stella is
  That virtuous soul, sure heir of heav'nly bliss,
Not this fair outside which our hearts doth move.
  And therefore, though her beauty and her grace
Be Love's indeed, in Stella's self he may   10
By no pretence claim any manner place.
Well, Love, since this demur our suit doth stay,
  Let Virtue have that Stella's self; yet thus,
  That Virtue but that body grant to us.

LIII

In martial sports I had my cunning tried,
  And yet to break more staves did me address,
  While, with the people's shouts, I must confess,
Youth, luck, and praise even fill'd my veins with pride;
When Cupid, having me his slave descried   5
  In Mars's livery prancing in the press,
  'What now, Sir Fool!' said he (I would no less),
'Look here, I say!' I look'd, and Stella spied,
  Who, hard by, made a window send forth light.
My heart then quak'd, then dazzled were mine eyes,   10
One hand forgot to rule, th'other to fight,
Nor trumpet's sound I heard, nor friendly cries;
  My foe came on, and beat the air for me,
  Till that her blush taught me my shame to see.

LII. 2. *pretends:* claims.
    4. *his:* Love's (indirect speech).
    6. *that:* because.
LIII. 6. *press:* crowd (of contenders).
    11. *rule:* guide (the horse).   11. *fight:* grip (the lance).
    13. *beat the air for me:* found nothing to meet his lance.

NOTES: p. 221

LIV

Because I breathe not love to every one,
  Nor do not use set colours for to wear,
  Nor nourish special locks of vowed hair,
Nor give each speech a full point of a groan,
The courtly nymphs, acquainted with the moan   5
  Of them who in their lips Love's standard bear,
  'What, he!' say they of me, 'now I dare swear
He cannot love; no, no, let him alone.'
    And think so still, so Stella know my mind;
Profess indeed I do not Cupid's art;   10
But you, fair maids, at length this true shall find,
That his right badge is but worn in the heart.
  Dumb swans, not chatt'ring pies, do lovers prove:
  They love indeed, who quake to say they love.

LXI

Oft with true sighs, oft with uncalled tears,
Now with slow words, now with dumb eloquence,
I Stella's eyes assail, invade her ears;
But this at last is her sweet-breath'd defence:
  That who indeed in-felt affection bears   5
So captives to his saint both soul and sense
That, wholly hers, all selfness he forbears;
Thence his desires he learns, his life's course thence.
  Now since her chaste mind hates this love in me,
  With chasten'd mind I straight must show that she   10
Shall quickly me from what she hates remove.
  O Doctor Cupid, thou for me reply,
  Driv'n else to grant, by angel's sophistry,
That I love not without I leave to love.

LIV. 4. *full point:* full stop, end.
     10. *profess:* claim proficiency in.
     13. *pies:* magpies.
LXI. 6. *captives:* makes captive.   6. *his saint:* his beloved.
     11. *remove:* turn away.
     14. *leave:* cease.

NOTES: pp. 221–2

LXII

Late tir'd with woe, even ready for to pine
With rage of love, I call'd my love unkind;
She in whose eyes love, though unfelt, doth shine,
Sweet said that I true love in her should find.
    I joy'd; but straight thus water'd was my wine: 5
That love she did, but lov'd a love not blind,
Which would not let me whom she lov'd decline
From nobler course fit for my birth and mind;
    And therefore, by her love's authority,
    Will'd me these tempests of vain love to fly,   10
And anchor fast myself on Virtue's shore.
    Alas, if this the only metal be
    Of love, new-coin'd to help my beggary,
Dear, love me not, that you may love me more.

LXIV

No more, my dear, no more these counsels try;
    O give my passions leave to run their race;
    Let Fortune lay on me her worst disgrace,
Let folk o'ercharg'd with brain against me cry,
Let clouds bedim my face, break in mine eye,   5
    Let me no steps but of lost labour trace,
    Let all the earth with scorn recount my case,
But do not will me from my love to fly.
    I do not envy Aristotle's wit,
Nor do aspire to Caesar's bleeding fame,   10
Nor aught do care though some above me sit,
Nor hope nor wish another course to frame,
    But that which once may win thy cruel heart:
    Thou art my wit, and thou my virtue art.

LXII. 1. *pine:* perish.
2. *rage:* violence.
2. *my love:* my beloved.
6. *a love not blind:* Virtue, not Cupid.
NOTES: p. 222

LXVI

And do I see some cause a hope to feed,
Or doth the tedious burden of long woe
In weaken'd minds quick apprehending breed
Of every image which may comfort show?
    I cannot brag of word, much less of deed;   5
Fortune wheels still with me in one sort slow;
My wealth no more, and no whit less my need;
Desire still on the stilts of fear doth go.
    And yet amid all fears a hope there is,
Stol'n to my heart since last fair night, nay day,   10
Stella's eyes sent to me the beams of bliss,
Looking on me while I lookt other way:
    But when mine eyes back to their heav'n did move,
    They fled with blush which guilty seem'd of love.

LXIX

O joy too high for my low style to show!
    O bliss fit for a nobler state than me!
    Envy, put out thine eyes, lest thou do see
What oceans of delight in me do flow!
My friend, that oft saw through all masks my woe,   5
    Come come, and let me pour myself on thee:
    Gone is the winter of my misery,
My spring appears, O see what here doth grow!
For Stella hath, with words where faith doth shine,
Of her high heart giv'n me the monarchy: 10
I, I, oh I may say that she is mine.
And though she give but thus conditionly
    This realm of bliss, while virtuous course I take,
    No kings be crown'd but they some covenants make.

LXVI. 6. *Fortune wheels still . . . slow:* Fortune's wheel always turns for
      me with an unchanging slowness.
    8. *stilts:* crutches.
LXIX. 2. *nobler state:* greater prince.
    14. *but:* except, unless.

NOTES: p. 222

LXXI

Who will in fairest book of Nature know
   How virtue may best lodg'd in beauty be,
   Let him but learn of Love to read in thee,
Stella, those fair lines which true goodness show.
There shall he find all vices' overthrow,   5
   Not by rude force, but sweetest sov'reignty
   Of reason, from whose light those night-birds fly,
That inward sun in thine eyes shineth so.
   And, not content to be perfection's heir
Thyself, dost strive all minds that way to move   10
Who mark in thee what is in thee most fair.
So while thy beauty draws the heart to love,
   As fast thy virtue bends that love to good.
   But ah, Desire still cries, 'Give me some food!'

LXXII

Desire, though thou my old companion art,
   And oft so clings to my pure love that I
   One from the other scarcely can descry,
While each doth blow the fire of my heart,
Now from thy fellowship I needs must part: 5
   Venus is taught with Dian's wings to fly.
   I must no more in thy sweet passions lie:
Virtue's gold now must head my Cupid's dart.
   Service and honour, wonder with delight,
Fear to offend, will worthy to appear,   10
Care shining in mine eyes, faith in my sprite,
These things are left me by my only Dear;
   But thou, Desire, because thou wouldst have all,
   Now banisht art – but yet, alas, how shall?

LXXI. 7. *those night-birds:* the vices.
LXXII. 10. *will worthy to appear:* the desire to appear worthy.

LXXIII

Love still a boy and oft a wanton is,
School'd only by his mother's tender eye:
What wonder then if he his lesson miss,
When for so soft a rod dear play he try?

    And yet my Star, because a sugar'd kiss   5
In sport I suckt while she asleep did lie,
Doth lour, nay chide, nay threat for only this.
Sweet, it was saucy Love, not humble I.

    But no scuse serves, she makes her wrath appear
    In Beauty's throne; see now, who dares come near 10
Those scarlet judges threat'ning bloody pain?

    O heav'nly fool, thy most kiss-worthy face
    Anger invests with such a lovely grace
That Anger's self I needs must kiss again.

LXXIV

I never drank of Aganippe well,
Nor ever did in shade of Tempe sit,
And Muses scorn with vulgar brains to dwell,
Poor layman I, for sacred rites unfit.

    Some do I hear of poets' fury tell,   5
But (God wot) wot not what they mean by it;
And this I swear by blackest brook of hell,
I am no pick-purse of another's wit.

    How falls it then, that with so smooth an ease
My thoughts I speak, and what I speak doth flow 10
In verse, and that my verse best wits doth please?
Guess we the cause: What, is it thus? Fie, no.

    Or so? Much less. How then? Sure thus it is:
My lips are sweet, inspir'd with Stella's kiss.

LXXIII.   7. *lour:* look angry.
          9. *scuse:* excuse.
        12. *fool:* dear.
LXXIV.   9. *how falls it:* how chances it.
        11. *best wits:* the best (readers') minds.

NOTES: p. 222

LXXVIII

O how the pleasant airs of true love be
 Infected by those vapours which arise
 From out that noisome gulf which gaping lies
Between the jaws of hellish Jealousy!
A monster, others' harm, self-misery,   5
 Beauty's plague, Virtue's scourge, succour of lies,
 Who his own joy to his own hurt applies,
And only cherish doth with injury;
 Who since he hath by Nature's special grace
 So piercing paws as spoil when they embrace,   10
So nimble feet as stir still, though on thorns,
 So many eyes aye seeking their own woe,
 So ample ears as never good news know,
Is it not evil that such a devil wants horns?

LXXXIII

Good brother Philip, I have borne you long.
 I was content you should in favour creep,
 While craftily you seem'd your cut to keep,
As though that fair soft hand did you great wrong:
I bare with envy, yet I bare your song,   5
 When in her neck you did love-ditties peep;
 Nay, more fool I, oft suffer'd you to sleep
In lilies' nest where Love's self lies along.
 What, doth high place ambitious thoughts augment?
Is sauciness reward of courtesy?   10
Cannot such grace your silly self content
But you must needs with those lips billing be,
 And through those lips drink nectar from that tongue?
 Leave that, Sir Phip, lest off your neck be wrung!

LXXVIII. 3. *noisome:* offensive.
    10. *spoil:* destroy.
LXXXIII. 3. *your cut to keep:* to keep your distance, behave yourself.
    8. *lilies' nest:* Stella's bosom.
    10. *is sauciness . . . courtesy?:* is your sauciness the reward of
      her courtesy?

NOTES: p. 223

LXXXIV

Highway, since you my chief Parnassus be,
  And that my Muse, to some ears not unsweet,
  Tempers her words to trampling horses' feet
More oft than to a chamber-melody;
Now, blessed you, bear onward blessed me   5
  To her where I my heart safeliest shall meet:
  My Muse and I must you of duty greet
With thanks and wishes, wishing thankfully.
  Be you still fair, honour'd by public heed,
By no encroachment wrong'd, nor time forgot,   10
Nor blam'd for blood, nor sham'd for sinful deed;
And, that you know I envy you no lot
  Of highest wish, I wish you so much bliss,
  Hundreds of years you Stella's feet may kiss.

LXXXV

I see the house. My heart, thyself contain!
  Beware full sails drown not thy tott'ring barge,
  Lest joy, by nature apt sprites to enlarge,
Thee to thy wrack beyond thy limits strain;
Nor do like lords whose weak confused brain,   5
  Not 'pointing to fit folks each undercharge,
  While every office themselves will discharge,
With doing all leave nothing done but pain.

LXXXIV. 3. *tempers:* tunes.
          11. *blood:* murder.
          11. *sinful deed:* robbery.
          12–13. *lot/Of highest wish:* happiest fate.
LXXXV. 2. *beware:* take care that.
      2. *tott'ring:* tempest-tossed.
      6. *fit folks:* suitable servants.
      8. *leave nothing done but pain:* accomplish nothing but their
          own trouble.

NOTES: p. 223

But give apt servants their due place: let eyes
See beauty's total sum summ'd in her face,   10
Let ears hear speech which wit to wonder ties,
Let breath suck up those sweets, let arms embrace
    The globe of weal, lips Love's indentures make:
    Thou but of all the kingly tribute take.

LXXXVI

Alas, whence came this change of looks? If I
    Have chang'd desert, let mine own conscience be
    A still-felt plague to self-condemning me;
Let woe gripe on my heart, shame load mine eye.
But if all faith like spotless ermine lie   5
    Safe in my soul, which only doth to thee
    As his sole object of felicity
With wings of love in air of wonder fly,
    O ease your hand, treat not so hard your slave:
In justice pains come not till faults do call;   10
Or if I needs, sweet judge, must torments have,
Use something else to chasten me withal
    Than those blest eyes where all my hopes do dwell:
    No doom should make one's heav'n become his hell.

LXXXVII

When I was forc'd from Stella ever dear
(Stella, food of my thoughts, heart of my heart,
Stella, whose eyes make all my tempests clear)
By iron laws of duty to depart,
    Alas, I found that she with me did smart: 5
I saw that tears did in her eyes appear,
I saw that sighs her sweetest lips did part,
And her sad words my sadded sense did hear.

13. *globe of weal:* world of good.
13. *indentures:* contracts.
LXXXVI. 2. *chang'd desert:* lost my worthiness.
    4. *gripe on:* tear at (like a vulture).
LXXXVII. 8. *sadded:* saddened.

NOTES: p. 223

For me, I wept to see pearls scatter'd so,
  I sigh'd her sighs and wailed for her woe,   10
Yet swam in joy, such love in her was seen.
  Thus, while th'effect most bitter was to me,
  And nothing than the cause more sweet could be,
I had been vext, if vext I had not been.

LXXXVIII

Out, traitor Absence, dar'st thou counsel me
From my dear captainess to run away
Because in brave array here marcheth she
That to win me oft shows a present pay?
  Is faith so weak? Or is such force in thee?   5
When sun is hid, can stars such beams display?
Cannot heav'n's food, once felt, keep stomachs free
From base desire on earthly cates to prey?
  Tush, Absence! while thy mists eclipse that light,
  My orphan sense flies to the inward sight,   10
Where memory sets forth the beams of love:
  That, where before heart lov'd and eyes did see,
  In heart both sight and love now coupled be:
United powers make each the stronger prove.

LXXXIX

Now that of absence the most irksome night
  With darkest shade doth overcome my day,
  Since Stella's eyes, wont to give me my day,
Leaving my hemisphere leave me in night,
Each day seems long and longs for long-stay'd night;   5
  The night, as tedious, woos th'approach of day.

12. *th'effect:* Stella's sorrow.
13. *the cause:* Stella's love.
LXXXVIII. 5. *thee:* absence.
8. *cates:* food.

NOTES: p. 223

Tir'd with the dusty toils of busy day,
Languisht with horrors of the silent night,
Suff'ring the evils both of the day and night,
   While no night is more dark than is my day,   10
Nor no day hath less quiet than my night:
   With such bad mixture of my night and day,
That living thus in blackest winter night,
   I feel the flames of hottest summer day.

XC

Stella, think not that I by verse seek fame,
   Who seek, who hope, who love, who live but thee;
   Thine eyes my pride, thy lips my history:
If thou praise not, all other praise is shame.
Nor so ambitious am I as to frame   5
   A nest for my young praise in laurel tree:
   In truth I swear, I wish not there should be
Grav'd in mine epitaph a poet's name.
   Ne if I would, could I just title make
That any laud to me thereof should grow,   10
Without my plumes from others' wings I take:
For nothing from my wit or will doth flow,
   Since all my words thy beauty doth indite,
   And love doth hold my hand and makes me write.

XCII

Be your words made, good Sir, of Indian ware,
   That you allow me them by so small rate?
   Or do you cutted Spartans imitate?
Or do you mean my tender ears to spare,

XC. 11. *without:* unless.
   13. *indite:* dictate.
XCII. 1. *Indian ware:* gold and silver from the American Indies.
   2. *by so small rate:* so few at a time.
   3. *cutted:* laconic.

NOTES: p. 224

That to my questions you so total are? 5
  When I demand of Phoenix Stella's state,
  You say, forsooth, you left her well of late.
O God, think you that satisfies my care?
  I would know whether she did sit or walk,
How cloth'd, how waited on, sigh'd she or smil'd, 10
Whereof, with whom, how often did she talk,
With what pastime time's journey she beguil'd,
  If her lips deign'd to sweeten my poor name.
  Say all, and, all well said, still say the same.

CIII

O happy Thames that didst my Stella bear,
I saw thyself with many a smiling line
Upon thy cheerful face joy's livery wear,
While those fair planets on thy streams did shine.
  The boat for joy could not to dance forbear, 5
While wanton winds, with beauties so divine
Ravisht, stay'd not till in her golden hair
They did themselves (O sweetest prison) twine.
  And fain those Aeol's youths there would their stay
Have made, but forc'd by nature still to fly, 10
First did with puffing kiss those locks display:
She, so dishevell'd, blusht: from window I
  With sight thereof cried out, 'O fair disgrace,
  Let honour's self to thee grant highest place.'

      5. *total:* concise.
CIII. 4. *planets:* Stella's eyes.
      6. *wanton:* playful.
      9. *Aeol's youths:* young sons of Aeolus, god of the winds.
   13. *fair disgrace:* sweet disorder.

NOTES: p. 224

First Song

Doubt you to whom my Muse these notes intendeth,
Which now my breast o'ercharg'd to music lendeth?
    To you, to you, all song of praise is due:
Only in you my song begins and endeth.

Who hath the eyes which marry state with pleasure?   5
Who keeps the key of Nature's chiefest treasure?
    To you, to you, all song of praise is due:
Only for you the heav'n forgat all measure.

Who hath the lips where wit in fairness reigneth?
Who womankind at once both decks and staineth?   10
    To you, to you, all song of praise is due:
Only by you Cupid his crown maintaineth.

Who hath the feet whose step all sweetness planteth?
Who else for whom Fame worthy trumpets wanteth?
    To you, to you, all song of praise is due: 15
Only to you her sceptre Venus granteth.

Who hath the breast whose milk doth passions nourish?
Whose grace is such that when it chides doth cherish?
    To you, to you, all song of praise is due:
Only through you the tree of life doth flourish.   20

Who hath the hand which without stroke subdueth?
Who long-dead beauty with increase reneweth?
    To you, to you, all song of praise is due:
Only at you all envy hopeless rueth.

First Song. 5. *marry state with pleasure:* combine dignity with charm.
      6. *Nature's chiefest treasure:* Stella's heart.
    10. *both decks and staineth:* adorns and bedims.

Who hath the hair which, loosest, fastest tieth?   25
Who makes a man live then glad when he dieth?
  To you, to you, all song of praise is due:
Only of you the flatterer never lieth.

Who hath the voice which soul from senses sunders?
Whose force but yours the bolts of beauty thunders?   30
  To you, to you, all song of praise is due:
Only with you not miracles are wonders.

Doubt you to whom my Muse these notes intendeth,
Which now my breast o'ercharg'd to music lendeth?
  To you, to you, all song of praise is due: 35
Only in you my song begins and endeth.

Second Song

Have I caught my heav'nly jewel
Teaching Sleep most fair to be?
Now will I teach her that she,
When she wakes, is too too cruel.

Since sweet Sleep her eyes hath charmed,   5
The two only darts of Love,
Now will I with that boy prove
Some play, while he is disarmed.

Her tongue waking still refuseth,
Giving frankly niggard No: 10
Now will I attempt to know
What No her tongue sleeping useth.

25. *which, loosest, fastest tieth:* which ties (the lover) most firmly when it is unbound.

26. *live then glad when he dieth:* enjoy the happiness of living when he dies (for love).

32. *not miracles are wonders:* miracles are performed naturally.

Second Song. 7–8. *prove/Some play:* have a contest.
    9. *waking:* awake.   9. *still:* always.
    10. *niggard:* miserly.

NOTES: p. 224

See, the hand which waking guardeth,
Sleeping grants a free resort:
Now will I invade the fort;   15
Cowards Love with loss rewardeth.

But, O fool, think of the danger
Of her just and high disdain!
Now will I, alas, refrain;
Love fears nothing else but anger.   20

Yet those lips so sweetly swelling
Do invite a stealing kiss:
Now will I but venture this;
Who will read must first learn spelling.

Oh, sweet kiss! but ah, she's waking!   25
Louring beauty chastens me:
Now will I away hence flee.
Fool, more fool, for no more taking!

Fourth Song

'Only joy, now here you are,
Fit to hear and ease my care,
Let my whispering voice obtain
Sweet reward for sharpest pain:
Take me to thee, and thee to me.'   5
'No, no, no, no, my dear, let be.'

'Night hath clos'd all in her cloak,
Twinkling stars love-thoughts provoke;
Danger hence good care doth keep,
Jealousy itself doth sleep: 10
Take me to thee, and thee to me.'
'No, no, no, no, my dear, let be.'

26. *louring:* frowning.
Fourth Song. 9. *danger . . . keep:* caution keeps away danger.

NOTES: p. 224

'Better place no wit can find,
Cupid's yoke to loose or bind;
These sweet flowers on fine bed too,   15
Us in their best language woo:
Take me to thee, and thee to me.'
'No, no, no, no, my dear, let be.'

'This small light the moon bestows
Serves thy beams but to disclose,   20
So to raise my hap more high;
Fear not else, none can us spy:
Take me to thee, and thee to me.'
'No, no, no, no, my dear, let be.'

'That you heard was but a mouse,   25
Dumb sleep holdeth all the house;
Yet asleep, methinks, they say,
Young fools, take time while you may.
Take me to thee, and thee to me.'
'No, no, no, no, my dear, let be.'   30

'Niggard Time threats, if we miss
This large offer of our bliss,
Long stay ere he grant the same:
Sweet, then, while each thing doth frame,
Take me to thee, and thee to me.'   35
'No, no, no, no, my dear, let be.'

'Your fair mother is abed,
Candles out, and curtains spread;
She thinks you do letters write;
Write, but first let me indite: 40
Take me to thee, and thee to me.'
'No, no, no, no, my dear, let be.'

28. *time:* opportunity.
32. *large:* generous.
33. *stay:* delay.
34. *frame:* suit.
40. *write, but first let me indite:* let me dictate what you should do.

NOTES: p. 224

'Sweet, alas, why strive you thus?
Concord better fitteth us.
Leave to Mars the force of hands: 45
Your power in your beauty stands.
Take me to thee, and thee to me.'
'No, no, no, no, my dear, let be.'

'Woe to me, and do you swear
Me to hate but I forbear?   50
Cursed be my destines all,
That brought me so high to fall.
Soon with my death I will please thee.'
'No, no, no, no, my dear, let be.'

Eighth Song

In a grove most rich of shade,
Where birds wanton music made,
May, then young, his pied weeds showing,
New-perfum'd with flowers fresh growing,

Astrophel with Stella sweet   5
Did for mutual comfort meet,
Both within themselves oppressed,
But each in the other blessed.

Him great harms had taught much care;
Her fair neck a foul yoke bare: 10
But her sight his cares did banish;
In his sight her yoke did vanish.

50. *but:* unless.
51. *destines:* destinies.

Eighth Song.   2. *wanton:* gay.
3. *pied weeds:* many-coloured dress.
9. *care:* sorrow.
10. *a foul yoke bare:* bore a foul yoke (her marriage).

NOTES: p. 224

Wept they had, alas the while!
But now tears themselves did smile,
While their eyes, by love directed,
Interchangeably reflected.   15

Sigh they did, but now betwixt
Sighs of woe were glad sighs mixt,
With arms crost yet testifying
Restless rest and living dying.   20

Their ears hungry of each word
Which the dear tongue would afford,
But their tongues restrain'd from walking
Till their hearts had ended talking.

But, when their tongues could not speak,   25
Love itself did silence break;
Love did set his lips asunder,
Thus to speak in love and wonder:

'Stella, sovereign of my joy,
Fair triumpher of annoy,   30
Stella, star of heavenly fire,
Stella, lodestar of desire,

'Stella, in whose shining eyes
Are the lights of Cupid's skies,
Whose beams, where they once are darted,   35
Love therewith is straight imparted,

'Stella, whose voice, when it speaks,
Senses all asunder breaks,
Stella, whose voice, when it singeth,
Angels to acquaintance bringeth,   40

19. *yet:* still.
21. *of:* for.
23. *walking:* going, moving.
27. *his:* Astrophel's.
30. *of:* over.

NOTES: p. 224

'Stella, in whose body is
Writ each character of bliss,
Whose face all, all beauty passeth,
Save thy mind, which yet surpasseth:

'Grant, O grant – but speech, alas,   45
Fails me, fearing on to pass! –
Grant – O me! what am I saying?
But no fault there is in praying –

'Grant, O dear, on knees I pray,'
(Knees on ground he then did stay)   50
'That, not I, but, since I love you,
Time and place for me may move you.

'Never season was more fit,
Never room more apt for it;
Smiling air allows my reason;   55
These birds sing, Now use the season.

'This small wind, which so sweet is,
See how it the leaves doth kiss;
Each tree in his best attiring,
Sense of love to love inspiring.   60

'Love makes earth the water drink,
Love to earth makes water sink;
And, if dumb things be so witty,
Shall a heavenly grace want pity?'

42. *character:* letter, sign.
50. *stay:* support.
53. *season:* time.
54. *room:* place.
55. *allows my reason:* proves me right.
56. *use the season:* take time while you may.
63. *witty:* wise.

NOTES: p. 224

There his hands, in their speech, fain   65
Would have made tongue's language plain;
But her hands, his hands repelling,
Gave repulse all grace excelling.

Then she spake; her speech was such,
As not ears but heart did touch: 70
While such wise she love denied,
As yet love she signified.

'Astrophel,' said she, 'my love
Cease in these effects to prove;
Now be still, yet still believe me,   75
Thy grief more than death would grieve me.

'If that any thought in me
Can taste comfort but of thee,
Let me, fed with hellish anguish,
Joyless, hopeless, endless languish.   80

'If those eyes you praised be
Half so dear as you to me,
Let me home return stark blinded
Of those eyes, and blinder minded.

'If to secret of my heart   85
I do any wish impart
Where thou art not foremost placed,
Be both wish and I defaced.

'If more may be said, I say
All my bliss in thee I lay;   90
If thou love, my love, content thee,
For all love, all faith, is meant thee.

68. *gave repulse all grace excelling:* made refusal exceedingly lovely.
70. *such wise:* in such manner.
73. *my love/Cease . . . to prove:* cease to test my love by these doings.
80. *endless:* endlessly.
88. *defaced:* unmade, destroyed.

NOTES: p. 224

'Trust me, while I thee deny,
In myself the smart I try.
Tyrant honour doth thus use thee: 95
Stella's self might not refuse thee.

'Therefore, dear, this no more move,
Lest, though I leave not thy love,
Which too deep in me is framed,
I should blush when thou art named.'   100

Therewithal away she went,
Leaving him so passion-rent
With what she had done and spoken,
That therewith my song is broken.

Eleventh Song

'Who is it that this dark night
Underneath my window plaineth?'
'It is one who from thy sight
Being, ah, exil'd, disdaineth
Every other vulgar light.'   5

'Why alas, and are you he?
Be not yet those fancies changed?'
'Dear, when you find change in me,
Though from me you be estranged,
Let my change to ruin be.'   10

'Well, in absence this will die;
Leave to see and leave to wonder.'
'Absence sure will help, if I
Can learn how myself to sunder
From what in my heart doth lie.'   15

97. *this no more move:* urge this thing no more.
98. *thy love:* my love for you.

Eleventh Song. 5. *vulgar:* ordinary.
    12. *leave:* cease.   12. *wonder:* admire.

NOTES: p. 224

'But time will these thoughts remove;
Time doth work what no man knoweth.'
'Time doth as the subject prove;
With time still th'affection groweth
In the faithful turtle dove.' 20

'What if you new beauties see,
Will not they stir new affection?'
'I will think they pictures be,
Image-like of saints' perfection,
Poorly counterfeiting thee.' 25

'But your reason's purest light
Bids you leave such minds to nourish.'
'Dear, do reason no such spite;
Never doth thy beauty flourish
More than in my reason's sight.' 30

'But the wrongs love bears will make
Love at length leave undertaking.'
'No, the more fools it do shake,
In a ground of so firm making,
Deeper still they drive the stake.' 35

'Peace, I think that some give ear;
Come no more lest I get anger.'
'Bliss, I will my bliss forbear,
Fearing, sweet, you to endanger;
But my soul shall harbour there.' 40

'Well, be gone, be gone I say,
Lest that Argus' eyes perceive you.'
'O unjustest Fortune's sway,
Which can make me thus to leave you,
And from louts to run away.' 45

18. *time doth as the subject prove:* time's effects vary accord-
    ing to what they work on.
27. *minds:* moods, feelings.
32. *undertaking:* striving, attempting.
33. *it do shake:* do shake it.

NOTES: p. 224

From ARCADIA

BOOK I, CHAPTER 12
*Palladius, after long search of Daiphantus, lighteth on an Amazon
Lady. Her habit, song, and who she was. Objections of the one
against women, and love of them. The answers of the other for
them both. Their passionate conclusion in relenting kindness.*

So directed he his course to Laconia, as well among the Helots   5
as Spartans. There indeed he found his fame flourishing, his
monuments engraved in marble, and yet more durably in men's
memories; but the universal lamenting his absented presence,
assured him of his present absence. Thence into the Elean
province, to see whether at the Olympian games (there cele-   10
brated) he might in such concourse bless his eyes with so
desired an encounter: but that huge and sportful assembly
grew to him a tedious loneliness, esteeming nobody found,
since Daiphantus was lost. Afterward he passed through
Achaia and Sicyonia, to the Corinthians, proud of their two   15
seas, to learn whether by the strait of that Isthmus it were
possible to know of his passage. But finding every place more
dumb than other to his demands, and remembering that it was
late-taken love which had wrought this new course, he returned
again (after two months' travel in vain) to make a fresh search   20
in Arcadia; so much the more, as then first he bethought himself of the picture of Philoclea, which (resembling her he had
once loved) might perhaps awake again that sleeping passion.
And having already passed over the greatest part of Arcadia,
one day coming under the side of the pleasant mountain   25
Maenalus, his horse (nothing guilty of his inquisitiveness) with
flat tiring taught him, that discreet stays make speedy journeys.

19. *late-taken:* recently-caught.
27. *flat:* downright, plain.

NOTES: pp. 225–6
78

And therefore lighting down, and unbridling his horse, he himself went to repose himself in a little wood he saw thereby. Where lying under the protection of a shady tree, with intention to make forgetting sleep comfort a sorrowful memory, he saw a sight which persuaded and obtained of his eyes that they would abide yet a while open. It was the appearing of a Lady, who because she walked with her side toward him, he could not perfectly see her face; but so much he might see of her, that was a surety for the rest, that all was excellent.

Well might he perceive the hanging of her hair in fairest quantity, in locks, some curled, and some as it were forgotten, with such a careless care, and an art so hiding art, that she seemed she would lay them for a pattern, whether nature simply, or nature helped by cunning, be the more excellent: the rest whereof was drawn into a coronet of gold richly set with pearl, and so joined all over with gold wires, and covered with feathers of divers colours, that it was not unlike to an helmet, such a glittering show it bare, and so bravely it was held up from the head. Upon her body she ware a doublet of sky-colour satin, covered with plates of gold, and as it were nailed with precious stones, that in it she might seem armed; the nether part of her garment was full of stuff, and cut after such a fashion, that though the length of it reached to the ankles, yet in her going one might sometimes discern the small of her leg, which with the foot was dressed in a short pair of crimson velvet buskins, in some places open (as the ancient manner was) to show the fairness of the skin. Over all this she ware a certain mantle, made in such manner, that coming under her right arm, and covering most of that side, it had no fastening of the left side but only upon the top of the shoulder, where the two ends met, and were closed together with a very rich jewel, the device whereof (as he after saw) was this: a Hercules made in little form, but set with a distaff in his hand as he once was by Omphale's commandment, with a word in Greek, but thus to be interpreted, *Never more valiant*. On the same side,

53. *buskins:* high boots.
61. *word:* motto.

NOTES: p. 226

on her thigh she ware a sword, which as it witnessed her to be
an Amazon, or one following that profession, so it seemed but
a needless weapon, since her other forces were without with-   65
standing. But this Lady walked outright, till he might see her
enter into a fine close arbour: it was of trees whose branches so
lovingly interlaced one the other, that it could resist the
strongest violence of eyesight; but she went into it by a door
she opened; which moved him as warely as he could to follow   70
her, and by and by he might hear her sing this song, with a
voice no less beautiful to his ears, than her goodliness was full
of harmony to his eyes.

> Transform'd in show, but more transform'd in mind,
> I cease to strive, with double conquest foil'd: 75
> For (woe is me) my powers all I find
> With outward force and inward treason spoil'd.
>
> For from without came to mine eyes the blow
> Whereto mine inward thoughts did faintly yield;
> Both these conspir'd poor Reason's overthrow;   80
> False in myself, thus have I lost the field.
>
> Thus are my eyes still captive to one sight;
> Thus all my thoughts are slaves to one thought still;
> Thus Reason to his servants yields his right;
> Thus in my power transformed to your will.   85
>
> What marvel then I take a woman's hue,
> Since what I see, think, know is all but you?

The ditty gave him some suspicion, but the voice gave him
almost assurance, who the singer was. And therefore boldly
thrusting open the door, and entering into the arbour, he per-   90
ceived indeed that it was Pyrocles thus disguised, wherewith,
not receiving so much joy to have found him, as grief so to
have found him, amazedly looking upon him (as Apollo is

65–66. *without withstanding:* irresistible (i.e., in beauty).
66. *outright:* straight forward.
75. *foil'd:* overthrown.
87. *but:* only.
92–93. *so to have found him:* i.e., disguised as a woman.

NOTES: p. 226

painted when he saw Daphne suddenly turned into a laurel), he was not able to bring forth a word. So that Pyrocles (who had as much shame, as Musidorus had sorrow) rising to him, would have formed a substantial excuse; but his insinuation being of blushing, and his division of sighs, his whole oration stood upon a short narration what was the causer of this metamorphosis. But by that time Musidorus had gathered his spirits together, and yet casting a ghastful countenance upon him (as if he would conjure some strange spirit) he thus spake unto him.

'And is it possible, that this is Pyrocles, the only young prince in the world, formed by nature, and framed by education, to the true exercise of virtue? or is it indeed some Amazon that hath counterfeited the face of my friend, in this sort to vex me? for likelier sure I would have thought it, that any outward face might have been disguised, than that the face of so excellent a mind could have been thus blemished. O sweet Pyrocles, separate yourself a little (if it be possible) from yourself, and let your own mind look upon your own proceedings: so shall my words be needless, and you best instructed. See with yourself, how fit it will be for you in this your tender youth, born so great a prince, and of so rare not only expectation but proof, desired of your old father, and wanted of your native country, now so near your home, to divert your thoughts from the way of goodness; to lose, nay to abuse your time. Lastly to overthrow all the excellent things you have done, which have filled the world with your fame; as if you should drown your ship in the long-desired haven, or like an ill player should mar the last act of his tragedy. Remember (for I know you know it) that if we will be men, the reasonable part of our soul is to have absolute commandment; against which if any sensual weakness arise, we are to yield all our sound forces to the overthrowing of so unnatural a rebellion, wherein how can we want courage, since we are to deal against so weak an

97. *insinuation:* introduction of a speech.
98. *division:* topics of a speech.
107. *sort:* manner.

NOTES: p. 226

adversary, that in itself is nothing but weakness? Nay, we are to resolve, that if reason direct it, we must do it, and if we must do it, we will do it; for to say I cannot is childish, and I will 130 not womanish. And see how extremely every way you endanger your mind; for to take this womanish habit, without you frame your behaviour accordingly, is wholly vain: your behaviour can never come kindly from you, but as the mind is proportioned unto it. So that you must resolve, if you will 135 play your part to any purpose, whatsoever peevish imperfections are in that sex, to soften your heart to receive them, the very first down-step to all wickedness: for do not deceive yourself, my dear cousin, there is no man suddenly either excellently good or extremely evil, but grows either as he holds 140 himself up in virtue or lets himself slide to viciousness. And let us see, what power is the author of all these troubles: forsooth love, love, a passion, and the basest and fruitlessest of all passions. Fear breedeth wit; anger is the cradle of courage; joy openeth and enableth the heart; sorrow, as it closeth, so it 145 draweth it inward to look to the correcting of itself; and so all of them generally have power towards some good by the direction of reason. But this bastard love (for indeed the name of love is most unworthily applied to so hateful a humour), as it is engendered betwixt lust and idleness; as the matter it 150 works upon is nothing but a certain base weakness, which some gentle fools call a gentle heart; as his adjoined companions be unquietness, longings, fond comforts, faint discomforts, hopes, jealousies, ungrounded rages, causeless yieldings; so is the highest end it aspires unto, a little pleasure with much pain 155 before, and great repentance after. But that end how endless it runs to infinite evils, were fit enough for the matter we speak of, but not for your ears, in whom indeed there is so true disposition to virtue: yet thus much of his worthy effects in yourself is to be seen, that (besides your breaking laws of hospitality 160

134. *kindly:* naturally.
145. *enableth:* strengthens.
149. *humour:* state of mind.
156. *endless:* endlessly.

NOTES: p. 226

with Kalander and of friendship with me) it utterly subverts
the course of nature, in making reason give place to sense, and
man to woman. And truly I think hereupon it first gat the name
of love: for indeed the true love hath that excellent nature in it,
that it doth transform the very essence of the lover into the 165
thing loved, uniting, and as it were incorporating it with a
secret and inward working. And herein do these kinds of love
imitate the excellent, for as the love of heaven makes one
heavenly, the love of virtue virtuous, so doth the love of the
world make one become worldly, and this effeminate love of a 170
woman doth so womanize a man that (if he yield to it) it will
not only make him an Amazon, but a launder, a distaff-spinner,
or whatsoever vile occupation their idle heads can imagine,
and their weak hands perform. Therefore (to trouble you no
longer with my tedious but loving words) if either you re- 175
member what you are, what you have been, or what you must
be: if you consider what it is that moved you, or by what
kind of creature you are moved, you shall find the cause so
small, the effect so dangerous, yourself so unworthy to run
into the one, or to be driven by the other, that I doubt not I 180
shall quickly have occasion rather to praise you for having
conquered it, than to give you further counsel how to do it.'

But in Pyrocles this speech wrought no more but that he,
who before he was espied was afraid, after (being perceived)
was ashamed, now being hardly rubbed upon left both fear and 185
shame, and was moved to anger. But the exceeding goodwill he
bare to Musidorus striving with it, he thus, partly to satisfy
him, but principally to loose the reins to his own motions,
made him answer. 'Cousin, whatsoever good disposition nature
hath bestowed upon me, or howsoever that disposition hath 190
been by bringing-up confirmed, this must I confess, that I am
not yet come to that degree of wisdom, to think light of the sex
of whom I have my life; since if I be anything (which your
friendship rather finds than I acknowledge), I was, to come to
it, born of a woman, and nursed of a woman. And certainly (for 195

172. *launder:* laundress.
188. *motions:* impulses, feelings.

NOTES: p. 226

this part of your speech doth nearest touch me) it is strange
to see the unmanlike cruelty of mankind; who not content with
their tyrannous ambition to have brought the others' virtuous
patience under them, like childish masters think their masterhood nothing without doing injury to them who (if we will argue 200
by reason) are framed of nature with the same parts of the
mind for the exercise of virtue as we are. And for example,
even this estate of Amazons (which I now for my greatest
honour do seek to counterfeit) doth well witness that, if
generally the sweetness of their disposition did not make them 205
see the vainness of these things which we account glorious,
they neither want valour of mind, nor yet doth their fairness
take away their force. And truly we men, and praisers of men,
should remember that, if we have such excellencies, it is reason
to think them excellent creatures of whom we are: since a kite 210
never brought forth a good flying hawk. But to tell you true,
as I think it superfluous to use any words of such a subject,
which is so praised in itself as it needs no praises; so withal I
fear lest my conceit (not able to reach unto them) bring forth
words which for their unworthiness may be a disgrace to 215
them I so inwardly honour. Let this suffice, that they are
capable of virtue: and virtue (ye yourself say) is to be loved
(and I too, truly); but this I willingly confess, that it likes me
much better when I find virtue in a fair lodging, than when I am
bound to seek it in an ill-favoured creature, like a pearl in a 220
dunghill. As for my fault of being an uncivil guest to Kalander,
if you could feel what an inward guest myself am host unto,
ye would think it very excusable in that I rather perform the
duties of a host than the ceremonies of a guest. And for my
breaking the laws of friendship with you (which I would rather 225
die than effectually do), truly, I could find in my heart to ask
you pardon for it, but that your now handling of me gives me
reason to confirm my former dealing.' And here Pyrocles

207. *fairness:* beauty.
210. *of whom we are:* from whom we have our being.
214. *conceit:* intellect.
222. *an inward guest:* i.e., love.
226. *effectually:* really.

stayed, as to breathe himself, having been transported with a
little vehemency, because it seemed him Musidorus had over- 230
bitterly glanced against the reputation of womankind: but
then quieting his countenance (as well as out of an unquiet
mind it might be) he thus proceeded on: 'And poor love,'
(said he) 'dear cousin, is little beholding unto you, since you
are not contented to spoil it of the honour of the highest power 235
of the mind, which notable men have attributed unto it, but ye
deject it below all other passions, in truth somewhat strangely;
since, if love receive any disgrace, it is by the company of these
passions you prefer before it. For those kinds of bitter objections (as that lust, idleness, and a weak heart should be, as it 240
were, the matter and form of love) rather touch me, dear
Musidorus, than love. But I am good witness of mine own
imperfections, and therefore will not defend myself. But
herein, I must say you deal contrary to yourself: for if I be so
weak, then can you not with reason stir me up as ye did, by 245
remembrance of mine own virtue; or if indeed I be virtuous,
then must ye confess that love hath his working in a virtuous
heart. And so no doubt hath it, whatsoever I be: for if we love
virtue, in whom shall we love it but in a virtuous creature?
without your meaning be, I should love this word *virtue*, 250
where I see it written in a book. Those troublesome effects you
say it breeds be not the faults of love, but of him that loves,
as an unable vessel to bear such a liquor; like evil eyes, not
able to look on the sun; or like a weak brain, soonest overthrown with the best wine. Even that heavenly love you speak 255
of is accompanied in some hearts with hopes, griefs, longings
and despairs. And in that heavenly love since there are two
parts, the one the love itself, th'other the excellency of the
thing loved, I, not able at the first leap to frame both in me, do
now (like a diligent workman) make ready the chief instrument 260
and first part of that great work, which is love itself; which
when I have a while practised in this sort, then you shall see
me turn it to greater matters. And thus gently you may (if it

241. *touch:* apply to.
NOTES: p. 226

D

please you) think of me. Neither doubt ye, because I wear a
woman's apparel, I will be the more womanish, since I assure 265
you (for all my apparel) there is nothing I desire more than
fully to prove myself a man in this enterprise. Much might be
said in my defence, much more for love, and most of all for that
divine creature which hath joined me and love together. But
these disputations are fitter for quiet schools than my troubled 270
brains, which are bent rather in deeds to perform than in words
to defend the noble desire that possesseth me.' 'O Lord,'
(said Musidorus) 'how sharp-witted you are to hurt yourself!'
'No' (answered he); 'but it is the hurt you speak of, which
makes me so sharp-witted.' 'Even so' (said Musidorus) 'as 275
every base occupation makes one sharp in that practice, and
foolish in all the rest.' 'Nay, rather' (answered Pyrocles) 'as
each excellent thing once well learned serves for a measure of
all other knowledges.' 'And is that become' (said Musidorus)
'a measure for other things, which never received measure in 280
itself?' 'It is counted without measure' (answered Pyrocles)
'because the workings of it are without measure: but otherwise,
in nature it hath measure, since it hath an end allotted unto it.'
'The beginning being so excellent, I would gladly know the
end.' 'Enjoying', answered Pyrocles, with a deep sigh. 'O' 285
(said Musidorus) 'now set ye forth the baseness of it: since if it
end in enjoying, it shows all the rest was nothing.' 'Ye mistake
me' (answered Pyrocles); 'I spake of the end to which it is
directed; which end ends not, no sooner than the life.' 'Alas,
let your own brain disenchant you' (said Musidorus). 'My 290
heart is too far possessed' (said Pyrocles). 'But the head gives
you direction.' 'And the heart gives me life', answered Pyrocles.

But Musidorus was so grieved to see his wellbeloved friend
obstinate, as he thought, to his own destruction, that it forced
him with more than accustomed vehemency to speak these 295
words: 'Well, well,' (said he) 'you list to abuse yourself; it

264. *doubt:* fear.
268–9. *that divine creature:* i.e., Philoclea.
281. *counted:* regarded as being.
296. *you list to abuse yourself:* you are wilfully self-deceived.

NOTES: p. 226

was a very white and red virtue which you could pick out of a
painterly gloss of a visage. Confess the truth, and ye shall find
the utmost was but beauty; a thing which, though it be in as
great excellency in yourself as may be in any, yet I am sure you 300
make no further reckoning of it than of an outward fading
benefit Nature bestowed on you. And yet such is your want of
a true-grounded virtue, which must be like itself in all points,
that what you wisely account a trifle in yourself, you fondly
become a slave unto in another. For my part I now protest, I 305
have left nothing unsaid, which my wit could make me know,
or my most entire friendship to you requires of me; I do
now beseech you even for the love betwixt us (if this other
love have left any in you towards me), and for the remembrance
of your old careful father (if you can remember him, that forget 310
yourself), lastly for Pyrocles' own sake (who is now upon the
point of falling or rising), to purge yourself of this vile infec-
tion; otherwise give me leave to leave off this name of friendship, as an idle title of a thing which cannot be where virtue is
abolished.' The length of these speeches before had not so 315
much cloyed Pyrocles, though he were very impatient of long
deliberations, as the last farewell of him he loved as his own
life did wound his soul. For thinking himself afflicted, he was
the apter to conceive unkindness deeply; in so much, that
shaking his head, and delivering some show of tears, he thus 320
uttered his griefs. 'Alas' (said he) 'Prince Musidorus, how
cruelly you deal with me; if you seek the victory, take it; and if
ye list, triumph. Have you all the reason of the world, and with
me remain all the imperfections, yet such as I can no more lay
from me, than the crow can be persuaded by the swan to cast 325
off all his black feathers. But truly, you deal with me like a
physician, that seeing his patient in a pestilent fever, should
chide him instead of ministering help, and bid him be sick no
more; or rather like such a friend, that visiting his friend con-

298. *gloss:* deceptive appearance.
303. *like itself:* consistent.
319. *conceive unkindness deeply:* take unkindness to heart.
323–4. *have; remain:* (subjunctives) let it be granted that you have,
          etc.

demned to perpetual prison, and loaden with grievous fetters, 330
should will him to shake off his fetters, or he would leave him.
I am sick, and sick to the death; I am a prisoner, neither is
there any redress, but by her to whom I am a slave. Now, if you
list, leave him that loves you in the highest degree; but remember ever to carry this with you, that you abandon your 335
friend in his greatest extremity.'

And herewith the deep wound of his love being rubbed
afresh with this new unkindness began (as it were) to bleed
again, in such sort that he was unable to bear it any longer, but
gushing out abundance of tears, and crossing his arms over his 340
woeful heart, as if his tears had been out-flowing blood, his
arms an over-pressing burthen, he sunk down to the ground,
which sudden trance went so to the heart of Musidorus, that
falling down by him and kissing the weeping eyes of his friend,
he besought him not to make account of his speech; which if it 345
had been over-vehement, yet was it to be borne withal, because
it came out of a love much more vehement; that he had not
thought fancy could have received so deep a wound; but now
finding in him the force of it, he would no further contrary it;
but employ all his service to medicine it, in such sort as the 350
nature of it required. But even this kindness made Pyrocles
the more melt in the former unkindness, which his manlike
tears well showed, with a silent look upon Musidorus, as who
should say, And is it possible that Musidorus should threaten
to leave me? And this struck Musidorus' mind and senses so 355
dumb too, that for grief being not able to say anything, they
rested, with their eyes placed one upon another, in such sort as
might well paint out the true passion of unkindness to be
never aright but betwixt them that most dearly love.

And thus remained they a time; till at length Musidorus, 360
embracing him, said, 'And will you thus shake off your friend?'
'It is you that shake me off,' (said Pyrocles) 'being for my

336. *extremity:* need.
346. *borne withal:* forgiven.
348. *fancy:* the imagination.
358. *paint out:* depict.

NOTES: pp. 226–7

unperfectness unworthy of your friendship.' 'But this' (said
Musidorus) 'shows you more unperfect, to be cruel to him that
submits himself unto you; but since you are unperfect' (said 365
he, smiling) 'it is reason you be governed by us wise and
perfect men. And that authority will I begin to take upon me,
with three absolute commandments: the first, that you increase
not your evil with further griefs; the second, that you love her
with all the powers of your mind; and the last commandment 370
shall be, ye command me to do what service I can towards the
attaining of your desires.' Pyrocles' heart was not so oppressed
with the two mighty passions of love and unkindness but that
it yielded to some mirth at this commandment of Musidorus
that he should love; so that, something clearing his face from 375
his former shows of grief, 'Well' (said he) 'dear cousin, I see by
the well choosing of your commandments that you are far
fitter to be a prince than a counsellor: and therefore I am
resolved to employ all my endeavour to obey you; with this
condition, that the commandments ye command me to lay 380
upon you shall only be, that you continue to love me, and look
upon my imperfections with more affection than judgement.'
'Love you?' (said he) 'Alas, how can my heart be separated
from the true embracing of it, without it burst by being too
full of it? But' (said he) 'let us leave off these flowers of new- 385
begun friendship: and now, I pray you, again tell me, but tell
it me fully, omitting no circumstance, the story of your affection's both beginning and proceeding; assuring yourself that
there is nothing so great, which I will fear to do for you, nor
nothing so small, which I will disdain to do for you. Let me 390
therefore receive a clear understanding, which many times we
miss while those things we account small (as a speech, or a
look) are omitted, like as a whole sentence may fail of his
congruity by wanting one particle. Therefore between friends
all must be laid open, nothing being superfluous nor tedious.' 395
'You shall be obeyed' (said Pyrocles); 'and here are we in as

384. *it:* love.
393–4. *fail of his congruity:* lack grammar and sense.

NOTES: p. 227

fit a place for it as may be; for this arbour nobody offers to
come into but myself, I using it as my melancholy retiring-
place, and therefore that respect is borne unto it; yet if by
chance any should come, say that you are a servant sent from 400
the Queen of the Amazons to seek me, and then let me alone
for the rest.' So sat they down, and Pyrocles thus said.

BOOK I, CHAPTER 13
How Pyrocles fell in love with Philoclea. His counsel and course
therein. His disguising into Zelmane. Her meeting with Dametas,
Basilius, the Queen and her daughters, and their speeches. Her
abode there over entreated; and the place thereof described.

'Cousin,' (said he) 'then began the fatal overthrow of all my   5
liberty, when walking among the pictures in Kalander's house,
you yourself delivered unto me what you had understood of
Philoclea, who much resembling (though I must say much
surpassing) the Lady Zelmane, whom so well I loved, there
were mine eyes infected, and at your mouth did I drink my   10
poison. Yet alas, so sweet was it unto me, that I could not be
contented till Kalander had made it more and more strong
with his declaration. Which the more I questioned, the more
pity I conceived of her unworthy fortune; and when with pity
once my heart was made tender, according to the aptness of   15
the humour, it received quickly a cruel impression of that
wonderful passion which to be defined is impossible, because
no words reach to the strange nature of it; they only know it
which inwardly feel it; it is called love. Yet did I not (poor
wretch) at first know my disease, thinking it only such a wonted   20
kind of desire to see rare sights; and my pity to be no other
but the fruits of a gentle nature. But even this arguing with
myself came of further thoughts, and the more I argued, the
more my thoughts increased. Desirous I was to see the place
where she remained, as though the architecture of the lodges   25

397. *offers:* attempts.
401–2. *let me alone for:* leave me to manage.
16. *humour:* mood.

would have been much for my learning; but more desirous to
see herself, to be judge, forsooth, of the painter's cunning. For
thus at the first did I flatter myself, as though my wound had
been no deeper: but when within short time I came to the
degree of uncertain wishes, and that those wishes grew to 30
unquiet longings, when I could fix my thoughts upon nothing,
but that within little varying they should end with Philoclea;
when each thing I saw seemed to figure out some part of my
passions; when even Parthenia's fair face became a lecture to
me of Philoclea's imagined beauty; when I heard no word 35
spoken but that methought it carried the sound of Philoclea's
name: then indeed, then I did yield to the burthen, finding
myself prisoner before I had leisure to arm myself; and that I
might well, like the spaniel, gnaw upon the chain that ties him,
but I should sooner mar my teeth than procure liberty. 40

'Yet I take to witness the eternal spring of virtue, that I had
never read, heard, nor seen anything, I had never any taste of
philosophy, nor inward feeling in myself, which for a while I
did not call to my succour. But (alas) what resistance was
there, when ere long my very reason was (you will say cor- 45
rupted) I must needs confess, conquered; and that methought
even reason did assure me that all eyes did degenerate from
their creation which did not honour such beauty? Nothing, in
truth, could hold any plea with it, but the reverent friendship
I bare unto you. For as it went against my heart to break any 50
way from you, so did I fear more than any assault to break it to
you: finding (as it is indeed) that to a heart fully resolute,
counsel is tedious, but reprehension is loathsome; and that
there is nothing more terrible to a guilty heart, than the eye of
a respected friend. This made me determine with myself 55
(thinking it a less fault in friendship to do a thing without
your knowledge, than against your will) to take this secret
course. Which conceit was most builded up in me, the last day
of my parting and speaking with you; when upon your speech

47–48. *did degenerate from their creation:* had lost their original percep-
tion.
49. *hold any plea with it:* (legal) try its cause.

NOTES: p. 227

with me, and my but naming love, (when else perchance I 60
would have gone further) I saw your voice and countenance so
change, as it assured me my revealing it should but purchase
your grief with my cumber; and therefore (dear Musidorus)
even ran away from thy wellknown chiding. For having
written a letter, which I know not whether you found or no, 65
and taking my chief jewels with me, while you were in the
midst of your sport, I got a time (as a think) unmarked by any,
to steal away, I cared not whither, so I might scape you; and
so came to Ithonia in the province of Messenia; where lying
secret I put this in practice which before I had devised. For 70
remembering by Philanax's letter and Kalander's speech how
obstinately Basilius was determined not to marry his daughters,
and therefore fearing lest any public dealing should rather
increase her captivity than further my love, Love (the refiner of
invention) had put in my head thus to disguise myself, that 75
under that mask I might (if it were possible) get access, and
what access could bring forth commit to fortune and industry;
determining to bear the countenance of an Amazon. Therefore,
in the closest manner I could, naming myself Zelmane for that
dear lady's sake to whose memory I am so much bound, I 80
caused this apparel to be made, and bringing it near the lodges,
which are hard at hand, by night, thus dressed myself, resting
till occasion might make me to be found by them whom I
sought: which the next morning happened as well as my own
plot could have laid it. For after I had run over the whole 85
pedigree of my thoughts, I gave myself to sing a little, which as
you know I ever delighted in, so now especially, whether it be
the nature of this clime to stir up poetical fancies, or rather (as
I think) of love; whose scope being pleasure, will not so much as
utter his griefs but in some form of pleasure.   90

'But I had sung very little, when (as I think, displeased with
my bad music) comes Master Dametas with a hedging bill in

63. *cumber:* embarrassment, distress.
89. *of love:* the nature of love.
89. *scope:* object, aim.
92. *bill:* tool with a long blade and a long handle.

his hand, chafing, and swearing by the pantable of Pallas, and
such other oaths as his rustical bravery could imagine; and
when he saw me, I assure you my beauty was no more behold- 95
ing to him than my harmony; for leaning his hands upon his
bill, and his chin upon his hands, with the voice of one that
playeth Hercules in a play, but never had his fancy in his head,
the first word he spake to me was, "Am not I Dametas? Why,
am not I Dametas?" He needed not name himself; for 100
Kalander's description had set such a note upon him as made
him very notable unto me, and therefore the height of my
thoughts would not descend so much as to make him any
answer, but continued on my inward discourses; which he
(perchance witness of his own unworthiness, and therefore the 105
apter to think himself contemned) took in so heinous manner,
that standing upon his tip-toes, and staring as if he would have
had a mote pulled out of his eye, "Why" (said he) "thou
woman, or boy, or both, whatsoever thou be, I tell thee here is
no place for thee, get thee gone, I tell thee it is the Prince's 110
pleasure, I tell thee it is Dametas' pleasure." I could not choose
but smile at him, seeing him look so like an ape that had newly
taken a purgation; yet taking myself with the manner, spake
these words to myself: "O spirit" (said I) "of mine, how canst
thou receive any mirth in the midst of thine agonies, and 115
thou, mirth, how darest thou enter into a mind so grown of late
thy professed enemy?" "Thy spirit?" (said Dametas); "Dost
thou think me a spirit? I tell thee I am Basilius' officer, and
have charge of him, and his daughters." "O only pearl" (said I,
sobbing); "That so vile an oyster should keep thee!" "By the 120
comb-case of Diana" (sware Dametas) "this woman is mad:
oysters and pearls? Dost thou think I will buy oysters? I tell
thee once again, get thee packing", and with that lifted up his

93. *pantable:* slipper.
94. *bravery:* swaggering.
95–96. *beholding:* indebted.
101, 102. *note; notable;* mark of recognition, recognizable.
106. *contemned:* scorned.
106. *heinous:* hateful, offended.
113. *taking myself with the manner:* catching myself in the act.

bill to hit me with the blunt end of it; but indeed that put me
quite out of my lesson, so that I forgat all Zelmane-ship, and 125
drawing out my sword, the baseness of the villain yet made me
stay my hand; and he (who, as Kalander told me, from his
childhood ever feared the blade of a sword) ran back backward
(with his hands above his head) at least twenty paces, gaping
and staring, with the very grace (I think) of the clowns that 130
by Latona's prayers were turned into frogs. At length staying,
finding himself without the compass of blows, he fell to a fresh
scolding, in such mannerly manner as might well show he had
passed through the discipline of a tavern. But seeing me walk
up and down without marking what he said, he went his way 135
(as I perceived after) to Basilius: for within a while he came
unto me, bearing indeed shows in his countenance of an honest
and well-minded gentleman, and with as much courtesy as
Dametas with rudeness saluting me, "Fair lady," (said he) "it is
nothing strange, that such a solitary place as this should receive 140
solitary persons; but much do I marvel how such a beauty as
yours is should be suffered to be thus alone." I (that now
knew it was my part to play), looking with a grave majesty
upon him, as if I found in myself cause to be reverenced,
"They are never alone" (said I) "that are accompanied with 145
noble thoughts." "But those thoughts" (replied Basilius) "cannot in this your loneliness neither warrant you from suspicion
in others, nor defend you from melancholy in yourself." I then
showing a mislike that he pressed me so far, "I seek no better
warrant" (said I) "than my own conscience, nor no greater 150
pleasures than mine own contentation." "Yet virtue seeks to
satisfy others" (said Basilius). "Those that be good" (said I);
"and they will be satisfied as long as they see no evil." "Yet
will the best in this country" (said Basilius) "suspect so excellent a beauty, being so weakly guarded." "Then are the best 155
but stark naught" (answered I); "for open suspecting others

130. *clowns:* rustics.
132. *without the compass of:* out of reach of.
143. *my part to play:* my cue to speak.
151. *contentation:* contentment.
156. *but stark naught:* downright bad.

NOTES: p. 227

comes of secret condemning themselves. But in my country
(whose manners I am in all places to maintain and reverence)
the general goodness which is nourished in our hearts makes
everyone think the strength of virtue in another, whereof they 160
find the assured foundation in themselves." "Excellent lady,"
(said he) "you praise so greatly, and yet so wisely, your
country, that I must needs desire to know what the nest is out
of which such birds do fly." "You must first deserve it" (said I)
"before you may obtain it." "And by what means" (said 165
Basilius) "shall I deserve to know your estate?" "By letting me
first know yours" (answered I). "To obey you" (said he) "I
will do it, although it were so much more reason yours should
be known first, as you do deserve in all points to be preferred.
Know you, fair lady, that my name is Basilius, unworthily lord 170
of this country: the rest, either fame hath already brought to
your ears, or (if it please you to make this place happy by your
presence) at more leisure you shall understand of me." I that
from the beginning assured myself it was he, but would not
seem I did so, to keep my gravity the better, making a piece of 175
reverence unto him, "Mighty prince," (said I) "let my not
knowing you serve for the excuse of my boldness; and the
little reverence I do you, impute it to the manner of my
country, which is the invincible land of the Amazons: myself
niece to Senicia, Queen thereof, lineally descended of the 180
famous Penthesilea, slain by the bloody hand of Pyrrhus. I
having in this my youth determined to make the world see the
Amazons' excellencies, as well in private as in public virtue,
have passed some dangerous adventures in divers countries,
till the unmerciful sea deprived me of my company: so that 185
shipwreck casting me not far hence, uncertain wandering
brought me to this place." But Basilius (who now began to
taste of that which since he hath swallowed up, as I will tell
you) fell to more cunning intreating my abode than any greedy
host would use to well-paying passengers. I thought nothing 190

185. *company:* followers, attendants.
188. *that which . . . swallowed up:* i.e., love.
190. *passengers:* travellers.

NOTES: p. 228

could shoot righter at the mark of my desires; yet had I learned already so much that it was against my womanhood to be forward in my own wishes. And therefore he (to prove whether intercessions in fitter mouths might better prevail) commanded Dametas to bring forthwith his wife and daughters 195 thither; three ladies, although of divers, yet all of excellent beauty.

'His wife in grave matronlike attire, with countenance and gesture suitable, and of such fairness (being in the strength of her age) as, if her daughters had not been by, might with just 200 price have purchased admiration; but they being there, it was enough that the most dainty eye would think her a worthy mother of such children. The fair Pamela, whose noble heart I find doth greatly disdain that the trust of her virtue is reposed in such a lout's hands as Dametas, had yet, to show an 205 obedience, taken on a shepherdish apparel, which was but of russet cloth cut after their fashion, with a straight body, open-breasted, the nether part full of pleats, with long and wide sleeves: but believe me, she did apparel her apparel, and with the preciousness of her body made it most sumptuous. Her 210 hair at the full length, wound about with gold lace, only by the comparison to show how far her hair doth excel in colour; betwixt her breasts (which sweetly rase up like two fair mountainets in the pleasant vale of Tempe) there hung a very rich diamond set but in a black horn; the word (I have since 215 read) is this, *Yet still myself.* And thus particularly have I described them, because you may know that mine eyes are not so partial but that I marked them too. But when the ornament of the earth, the model of heaven, the triumph of nature, the life of beauty, the queen of love, young Philoclea appeared in 220 her nymph-like apparel, so near nakedness, as one might well discern part of her perfections, and yet so apparelled as did show she kept best store of her beauty to herself; her hair (alas, too poor a word, why should I not rather call them her beams) drawn up into a net, able to have caught Jupiter when he was in 225

207. *body:* part of the dress above the waist.
217. *because:* so that.

NOTES: p. 228

the form of an eagle; her body (O sweet body) covered with a
light taffeta garment, so cut as the wrought smock came
through it in many places, enough to have made your restrained
imagination have thought what was under it; with the cast of
her black eyes, black indeed, whether nature so made them, 230
that we might be the more able to behold and bear their
wonderful shining, or that she (goddess-like) would work this
miracle with herself, in giving blackness the price above all
beauty. Then (I say) indeed methought the lilies grew pale for
envy, the roses methought blushed to see sweeter roses in her 235
cheeks, and the apples methought fell down from the trees to do
homage to the apples of her breast. Then the clouds gave place,
that the heavens might more freely smile upon her: at the least,
the clouds of my thoughts quite vanished; and my sight (then
more clear and forcible than ever) was so fixed there that (I 240
imagine) I stood like a well-wrought image, with some life in
show, but none in practice. And so had I been like enough to
have stayed long time, but that Gynecia stepping between
my sight and the only Philoclea, the change of object made
me recover my senses: so that I could with reasonable good 245
manner receive the salutation of her and of the Princess
Pamela, doing them yet no further reverence than one princess
useth to another. But when I came to the never-enough-
praised Philoclea, I could not but fall down on my knees, and
taking by force her hand, and kissing it (I must confess) with 250
more than womanly ardency, "Divine Lady," (said I) "let not
the world, nor these great princesses, marvel to see me (contrary to my manner) do this especial honour unto you, since all
both men and women do owe this to the perfection of your
beauty." But she blushing (like a fair morning in May) at this 255
my singularity, and causing me to rise, "Noble Lady," (said
she) "it is no marvel to see your judgement much mistaken
in my beauty, since you begin with so great an error as to
do more honour unto me than to them to whom I myself owe

227. *wrought:* embroidered.
233. *price:* prize.
256. *singularity:* special behaviour to her.

NOTES: p. 228

all service." "Rather" (answered I, with a bowed-down coun- 260
tenance) "that shows the power of your beauty, which forced
me to do such an error, if it were an error." "You are so well
acquainted" (said she sweetly, most sweetly smiling) "with
your own beauty, that it makes you easily fall into the discourse
of beauty." "Beauty in me?" (said I, truly sighing) "Alas, if 265
there be any, it is in my eyes, which your blessed presence hath
imparted unto them."

'But then (as I think) Basilius willing her so to do, "Well,"
(said she) "I must needs confess I have heard that it is a great
happiness to be praised of them that are most praiseworthy; 270
and well I find that you are an invincible Amazon, since you
will overcome, though in a wrong matter. But if my beauty be
anything, then let it obtain thus much of you, that you will
remain some while in this company, to ease your own travel
and our solitariness." "First let me die" (said I) "before any 275
word spoken by such a mouth should come in vain."

'And thus with some other words of entertaining was my
staying concluded, and I led among them to the lodge; truly
a place for pleasantness, not unfit to flatter solitariness; for it
being set upon such an unsensible rising of the ground, as you 280
are come to a pretty height before almost you perceive that you
ascend, it gives the eye lordship over a good large circuit,
which according to the nature of the country being diversified
between hills and dales, woods and plains, one place more clear,
another more darksome, it seems a pleasant picture of nature, 285
with lovely lightsomeness and artificial shadows. The lodge is
of a yellow stone, built in the form of a star; having round
about a garden framed into like points; and beyond the garden,
ridings cut out, each answering the angles of the lodge: at the
end of one of them is the other smaller lodge, but of like fashion, 290
where the gracious Pamela liveth; so that the lodge seemeth
not unlike a fair comet, whose tail stretcheth itself to a star of
less greatness.'

266. *in my eyes:* i.e., as containing Philoclea's reflection.
286. *artificial:* such as a painter might have contrived.
289. *ridings:* tracks, green paths.

NOTES: p. 228

BOOK I, CHAPTER 14
The devices of the first banquet to Zelmane. Her crosses in love,
by the love of Basilius and Gynecia. The conclusion between
Musidorus and Zelmane.

'So Gynecia herself bringing me to my lodging, anon after I
was invited and brought down to sup with them in the garden,   5
a place not fairer in natural ornaments than artificial inventions; where, in a banqueting house among certain pleasant
trees, whose heads seemed curled with the wrappings about of
vine branches, the table was set near to an excellent water-
work: for by the casting of the water in most cunning manner,   10
it makes (with the shining of the sun upon it) a perfect rainbow, not more pleasant to the eye than to the mind, so sensibly
to see the proof of the heavenly Iris. There were birds also
made so finely, that they did not only deceive the sight with
their figure, but the hearing with their songs; which the watery 15
instruments did make their gorge deliver. The table at which
we sat was round, which being fast to the floor whereon we sat,
and that divided from the rest of the building, with turning a
vice (which Basilius at first did to make us sport) the table, and
we about the table, did all turn round, by means of water   20
which ran under, and carried it about as a mill. But alas, what
pleasure did it to me to make divers times the full circle round
about? since Philoclea, being also set, was carried still in equal
distance from me, and that only my eyes did overtake her;
which when the table was stayed, and we began to feed, drank   25
much more eagerly of her beauty than my mouth did of any
other liquor. And so was my common sense deceived (being
chiefly bent to her) that as I drank the wine, and withal stale a
look on her, meseemed I tasted her deliciousness. But alas, the
one thirst was much more inflamed than the other quenched.   30
Sometimes my eyes would lay themselves open to receive all the
darts she did throw, sometimes close up with admiration, as if

23. *set:* seated at table.
32. *admiration:* wonder.

NOTES: p. 229

with a contrary fancy they would preserve the riches of that sight they had gotten, or cast my lids as curtains over the image of beauty her presence had painted in them. True it is, that 35 my reason (now grown a servant to passion) did yet often tell his master that he should more moderately use his delight; but he, that of a rebel was become a prince, disdained almost to allow him the place of a counsellor: so that my senses' delights being too strong for any other resolution, I did even loose the reins 40 unto them; hoping that (going for a woman) my looks would pass either unmarked or unsuspected.

'Now thus I had (as methought) well played my first act, assuring myself that under that disguisement I should find opportunity to reveal myself to the owner of my heart. But 45 who would think it possible (though I feel it true) that in almost eight weeks' space I have lived here (having no more company but her parents, and I being familiar, as being a woman, and watchful, as being a lover), yet could never find opportunity to have one minute's leisure of private conference: the cause 50 whereof is as strange as the effects are to me miserable. And (alas) this it is.

'At the first sight that Basilius had of me (I think Cupid having headed his arrows with my misfortune) he was stricken (taking me to be such as I profess) with great affection towards 55 me, which since is grown to such a doting love, that (till I was fain to get this place, sometimes to retire unto freely) I was even choked with his tediousness. You never saw fourscore years dance up and down more lively in a young lover: now as fine in his apparel as if he would make me in love with a cloak; 60 and verse for verse with the sharpest-witted lover in Arcadia. Do you not think that this is a sallet of wormwood, while mine eyes feed upon the ambrosia of Philoclea's beauty!

'But this is not all; no, this is not the worst; for he (good man) were easy enough to be dealt with: but (as I think) love 65

36–37. *his master:* passion.
57. *this place:* the arbour in which they are talking.
62. *sallet:* salad.
63. *ambrosia:* food of the gods.

and mischief, having made a wager which should have most
power in me, have set Gynecia also on such a fire towards me,
as will never (I fear) be quenched but with my destruction. For
she (being a woman of excellent wit, and of strong-working
thoughts), whether she suspected me by my over-vehement 70
shows of affection to Philoclea (which love forced me unwisely
to utter, while hope of my mask foolishly encouraged me), or
that she hath taken some other mark of me that I am not a
woman, or what devil it is hath revealed it unto her, I know
not; but so it is, that all her countenances, words and gestures, 75
are even miserable portraitures of a desperate affection. Where-
by a man may learn that these avoidings of company do but
make the passions more violent when they meet with fit
subjects. Truly it were a notable dumb show of Cupid's kingdom, to see my eyes (languishing with over-vehement longing) 80
direct themselves to Philoclea; and Basilius as busy about me as
a bee, and indeed as cumbersome, making such vehement suits
to me, who neither could if I would, nor would if I could, help
him; while the terrible wit of Gynecia, carried with the bier of
violent love, runs through us all. And so jealous is she of my 85
love to her daughter, that I could never yet begin to open
my mouth to the unevitable Philoclea, but that her unwished
presence gave my tale a conclusion before it had a beginning.

'And surely, if I be not deceived, I see such shows of liking,
and (if I be acquainted with passions) of almost a passionate 90
liking in the heavenly Philoclea towards me, that I may hope
her ears would not abhor my discourse. And for good Basilius,
he thought it best to have lodged us together, but that the
eternal hatefulness of my destiny made Gynecia's jealousy
stop that and all other my blessings. Yet must I confess that 95
one way her love doth me pleasure: for since it was my foolish
fortune, or unfortunate folly, to be known by her, that keeps
her from bewraying me to Basilius. And thus (my Musidorus)
you have my tragedy played unto you by myself, which I pray

79. *dumb show:* symbolic pageant.
98. *bewraying:* exposing.

NOTES: p. 229

the gods may not indeed prove a tragedy.' And therewith he 100
ended, making a full point of a hearty sigh.

Musidorus recommended to his best discourse all which
Pyrocles had told him. But therein he found such intricateness
that he could see no way to lead him out of the maze; yet perceiving his affection so grounded, that striving against it did 105
rather anger than heal the wound, and rather call his friendship in question than give place to any friendly counsel, 'Well,'
(said he) 'dear cousin, since it hath pleased the gods to mingle
your other excellencies with this humour of love, yet happy it
is that your love is employed upon so rare a woman: for 110
certainly, a noble cause doth ease much a grievous case. But as
it stands now, nothing vexeth me as that I cannot see wherein
I can be serviceable unto you.' 'I desire no greater service of
you' (answered Pyrocles) 'than that you remain secretly in this
country, and sometimes come to this place; either late in the 115
night, or early in the morning, where you shall have my key to
enter; because as my fortune either amends or impairs I may
declare it unto you, and have your counsel and furtherance.
And hereby I will of purpose lead her that is the praise and
yet the stain of all womankind, that you may have so good a 120
view as to allow my judgement. And as I can get the most
convenient time, I will come unto you; for though by reason of
yonder wood you cannot see the lodge, it is hard at hand. But
now' (said she) 'it is time for me to leave you, and towards
evening we will walk out of purpose hitherward; therefore 125
keep yourself close in that time.' But Musidorus, bethinking
himself that his horse might happen to bewray them, thought
it best to return for that day to a village not far off, and
dispatching his horse in some sort, the next day early to come
afoot thither, and so to keep that course afterward, which 130
Pyrocles very well liked of. 'Now farewell, dear cousin' (said

101. *full point:* full stop.
102. *recommended to his best discourse:* thoroughly considered.
117. *because:* so that.
126. *close in that time:* concealed in the meantime.
129. *dispatching:* getting rid of.

he) 'from me, no more Pyrocles, nor Daiphantus now, but Zelmane: Zelmane is my name, Zelmane is my title, Zelmane is the only hope of my advancement.' And with that word going out, and seeing that the coast was clear, Zelmane dis- 135 missed Musidorus, who departed as full of care to help his friend as before he was to dissuade him.

BOOK I, CHAPTER 18
Musidorus disguised. His song. His love, the cause thereof. His course therein.

And so many days were spent, and many ways used, while Zelmane was like one that stood in a tree waiting a good occasion to shoot, and Gynecia a blancher which kept the 5 dearest deer from her. But the day being come on which, according to an appointed course, the shepherds were to assemble and make their pastoral sports before Basilius, Zelmane, fearing lest many eyes and coming divers ways might hap to spy Musidorus, went out to warn him thereof. 10

But before she could come to the arbour, she saw walking from her-ward a man in shepherdish apparel, who being in sight of the lodge it might seem he was allowed there. A long cloak he had on, but that cast under his right arm, wherein he held a sheephook so finely wrought that it gave a bravery to 15 poverty; and his raiments, though they were mean, yet received they handsomeness by the grace of the wearer: though he himself went but a kind of languishing pace, with his eyes sometimes cast up to heaven, as though his fancies strave to mount higher, sometimes thrown down to the ground, as if 20 the earth could not bear the burthen of his sorrows; at length, with a lamentable tune, he sung these few verses.

> 5. *blancher:* hunter's assistant engaged to drive and divert the quarry.
>
> 12. *from her-word:* away from her.
>
> 15. *bravery:* splendour.

NOTES: p. 229

Come, shepherd's weeds, become your master's mind:
Yield outward show, what inward change he tries:
Nor be abasht, since such a guest you find   25
Whose strongest hope in your weak comfort lies.
  Come, shepherd's weeds, attend my woeful cries;
Disuse yourselves from sweet Menalcas' voice:
For other be those tunes which sorrow ties
From those clear notes which freely may rejoice.   30
    Then pour out plaint, and in one word say this:
    Helpless his plaint who spoils himself of bliss.

And having ended, he strake himself on the breast, saying,
'O miserable wretch, whither do thy destinies guide thee?'
The voice made Zelmane hasten her pace to overtake him;   35
which having done, she plainly perceived that it was her dear
friend Musidorus; whereat marvelling not a little, she demanded of him, whether the goddess of those woods had such
a power to transform everybody, or whether, as in all enterprises else he had done, he meant thus to match her in this new 40
alteration.
    'Alas,' (said Musidorus) 'what shall I say, who am loth to
say, and yet fain would have said? I find indeed, that all is but
lip-wisdom which wants experience. I now (woe is me) do try
what love can do. O Zelmane, who will resist it must either have 45
no wit, or put out his eyes. Can any man resist his creation?
Certainly by love we are made, and to love we are made. Beasts
only cannot discern beauty, and let them be in the roll of beasts
that do not honour it.' The perfect friendship Zelmane bare
him, and the great pity she (by good trial) had of such cases, 50
could not keep her from smiling at him, remembering how
vehemently he had cried out against the folly of lovers. And
therefore a little to punish him, 'Why, how now, dear cousin'
(said she); 'You that were last day so high in the pulpit against

25. *guest:* wearer.
26. *your weak comfort:* i.e., as a disguise.
40. *her:* Zelmane.
44. *wants:* lacks.

NOTES: p. 229

lovers, are you now become so mean an auditor? Remember 55
that love is a passion, and that a worthy man's reason must ever
have the masterhood.' 'I recant, I recant' (cried Musidorus),
and withal falling down prostrate, 'O thou celestial, or infernal
spirit of Love, or what other heavenly or hellish title thou list
to have (for effects of both I find in myself), have compassion of 60
me, and let thy glory be as great in pardoning them that be
submitted to thee, as in conquering those that were rebellious.'
'No, no,' (said Zelmane) 'I see you well enough: you make but
an interlude of my mishaps, and do but counterfeit thus, to
make me see the deformity of my passions: but take heed that 65
this jest do not one day turn to earnest.' 'Now I beseech thee'
(said Musidorus, taking her fast by the hand) 'even for the
truth of our friendship, of which (if I be not altogether an
unhappy man) thou hast some remembrance, and by those
secret flames which I know have likewise nearly touched thee, 70
make no jest of that which hath so earnestly pierced me
thorough, nor let that be light to thee which is to me so
burdenous that I am not able to bear it.' Musidorus both in
words and behaviour did so lively deliver out his inward grief,
that Zelmane found indeed he was thoroughly wounded: but 75
there rose a new jealousy in her mind, lest it might be with
Philoclea, by whom, as Zelmane thought, in right all hearts and
eyes should be inherited. And therefore desirous to be cleared
of that doubt, Musidorus shortly (as in haste and full of
passionate perplexedness) thus recounted his case unto her. 80

'The day' (said he) 'I parted from you, I being in mind to
return to a town from whence I came hither, my horse, being
before tired, would scarce bear me a mile hence; where being
benighted, the light of a candle I saw a good way off guided me
to a young shepherd's house, by name Menalcas, who seeing 85
me to be a straying stranger, with the right honest hospitality
which seems to be harboured in the Arcadian breasts, and
though not with curious costliness, yet with cleanly sufficiency,

64. *interlude:* stage-play.
70. *nearly:* closely.
88. *curious:* delicate.

entertained me: and having by talk with him found the manner
of the country something more in particular than I had by   90
Kalander's report, I agreed to sojourn with him in secret, which
he faithfully promised to observe. And so hither to your arbour
divers times repaired; and here by your means had the sight
(O that it had never been so, nay, O that it might ever be so!)
of the goddess, who in a definite compass can set forth infinite   95
beauty.' All this while Zelmane was racked with jealousy.
But he went on, 'For' (said he) 'I lying close, and in truth
thinking of you, and saying thus to myself: "O sweet Pyrocles,
how art thou bewitched! Where is thy virtue? Where is the
use of thy reason? How much am I inferior to thee in the state   100
of the mind, and yet know I that all the heavens cannot bring
me to such thralldom" – scarcely, think I, had I spoken this
word, when the ladies came forth; at which sight, I think the
very words returned back again to strike my soul; at least, an
unmeasurable sting I felt in myself, that I had spoken such   105
words.' 'At which sight?' said Zelmane, not able to bear him
any longer. 'O' (said Musidorus) 'I know your suspicion; no,
no, banish all such fear, it was, it is, and must be Pamela.'
'Then all is safe' (said Zelmane); 'proceed, dear Musidorus.'
'I will not' (said he) 'impute it to my late solitary life (which   110
yet is prone to affections), nor to the much thinking of you
(though that called the consideration of love into my mind,
which before I ever neglected), nor to the exaltation of Venus,
nor revenge of Cupid; but even to her, who is the planet, nay
the goddess, against which the only shield must be my   115
sepulchre. When I first saw her, I was presently stricken, and
I (like a foolish child, that when anything hits him, will strike
himself again upon it) would needs look again; as though I
would persuade mine eyes that they were deceived. But alas,
well have I found that love to a yielding heart is a king, but to a   120
resisting is a tyrant. The more with arguments I shaked the
stake which he had planted in the ground of my heart, the

95. *a definite compass:* a limited space (i.e., her own body).
113. *exaltation:* (astrological) height, cf. 114, *planet.*
116. *presently:* instantly.

NOTES: p. 230

deeper still it sank into it. But what mean I to speak of the
causes of my love, which is as impossible to describe as to
measure the backside of heaven? Let this word suffice, I love. 125

'And that you may know I do so, it was I that came in black
armour to defend her picture, where I was both prevented and
beaten by you. And so I that waited here to do you service
have now myself most need of succour.' 'But whereupon got
you yourself this apparel?' said Zelmane. 'I had forgotten to 130
tell you,' (said Musidorus) 'though that were one principal
matter of my speech; so much am I now master of my own
mind. But thus it happened: being returned to Menalcas'
house, full of tormenting desire, after awhile fainting under the
weight, my courage stirred up my wit to seek for some relief, 135
before I yielded to perish. At last this came into my head, that
very evening that I had to no purpose last used my horse and
armour. I told Menalcas that I was a Thessalian gentleman,
who by mischance having killed a great favourite of the prince
of that country, was pursued so cruelly that in no place but 140
either by favour or corruption they would obtain my destruction; and that therefore I was determined (till the fury of my
persecutors might be assuaged) to disguise myself among
the shepherds of Arcadia, and (if it were possible) to be one of
them that were allowed the Prince's presence; because if the 145
worst should fall, that I were discovered, yet having gotten the
acquaintance of the Prince, it might happen to move his heart
to protect me. Menalcas (being of an honest disposition) pitied
my case, which my face through my inward torment made
credible; and so (I giving him largely for it) let me have this 150
raiment, instructing me in all the particularities touching himself (or myself) which I desired to know: yet not trusting so
much to his constancy as that I would lay my life, and life of
my life, upon it, I hired him to go into Thessalia to a friend of

127. *prevented:* forestalled.
132. *so much:* i.e., so little.
150. *giving him largely:* rewarding him well.
152. *myself:* i.e., as 'Menalcas'.
153-4. *life of my life:* love.

NOTES: p. 230

mine, and to deliver him a letter from me; conjuring him to 155
bring me as speedy an answer as he could, because it imported
me greatly to know whether certain of my friends did yet
possess any favour, whose intercessions I might use for my
restitution. He willingly took my letter, which being well sealed
indeed contained other matter. For I wrote to my trusty 160
servant Calodoulos (whom you know) that as soon as he had
delivered the letter he should keep him prisoner in his house,
not suffering him to have conference with anybody, till he knew
my further pleasure; in all other respects that he should use
him as my brother. And thus is Menalcas gone, and I here a 165
poor shepherd: more proud of this estate than of any kingdom;
so manifest it is, that the highest point outward things can
bring one unto is the contentment of the mind; with which no
estate, without which all estates be miserable. Now have I
chosen this day, because (as Menalcas told me) the other 170
shepherds are called to make their sports, and hope that you
will with your credit find means to get me allowed among
them.' 'You need not doubt' (answered Zelmane) 'but that I
will be your good mistress: marry, the best way of dealing must
be by Dametas, who, since his blunt brain hath perceived some 175
favour the Prince doth bear unto me (as without doubt the
most servile flattery is lodged most easily in the grossest
capacity; for their ordinary conceit draweth a yielding to their
greaters, and then have they not wit to discern the right degrees
of duty), is much more serviceable unto me than I can find any 180
cause to wish him. And therefore despair not to win him, for
every present occasion will catch his senses, and his senses are
masters of his silly mind; only reverence him, and reward
him, and with that bridle and saddle you shall well ride him.'
'O heaven and earth!' (said Musidorus) 'To what a pass are our 185
minds brought, that from the right line of virtue are wryed to
these crooked shifts! But O love, it is thou that dost it: thou
changest name upon name; thou disguisest our bodies, and

158. *favour:* i.e., with the King of Thessalia.
177–8. *grossest capacity:* dullest mental power, thickest heads.
186. *wryed:* turned aside.

NOTES: p. 230

disfigurest our minds. But indeed thou hast reason, for though
the ways be foul, the journey's end is most fair and honourable.' 190

BOOK I, CHAPTER 19
*The means of Musidorus his apprentisage unto Dametas. The
preparation and place of the Pastorals. The lion's assault on
Philoclea, and death by Zelmane. The she-bear's on Pamela, and
death by Dorus. The Io Paean of Dametas, and his scape from
the bear. The victors' praises. Whence those beasts were sent.* 5

'No more, sweet Musidorus,' (said Zelmane) 'of these philo-
sophies; for here comes the very person of Dametas.' And so
he did indeed, with a sword by his side, a forest-bill on his
neck, and a chopping-knife under his girdle: in which well-
provided sort he had ever gone, since the fear Zelmane had 10
put him in. But he no sooner saw her, but with head and arms
he laid his reverence afore her; enough to have made any man
forswear all courtesy. And then, in Basilius' name, he did
invite her to walk down to the place where that day they were
to have the Pastorals. 15
But when he spied Musidorus to be none of the shepherds
allowed in that place, he would fain have persuaded himself to
utter some anger, but that he durst not; yet muttering and
champing, as though his cud troubled him, he gave occasion to
Musidorus to come near him, and feign this tale of his own 20
life: that he was a younger brother of the shepherd Menalcas,
by name Dorus, sent by his father in his tender age to Athens,
there to learn some cunning more than ordinary, that he might
be the better liked of the Prince; and that after his father's
death, his brother Menalcas (lately gone thither to fetch him 25
home) was also deceased; where (upon his death) he had
charged him to seek the service of Dametas, and to be wholly
and ever guided by him, as one in whose judgement and
integrity the Prince had a singular confidence. For token
whereof, he gave Dametas a good sum of gold in ready coin, 30

4. *Io Paean:* hymn of praise.
26. *upon his death:* as he lay dying.

NOTES: p. 230

which Menalcas had bequeathed unto him, upon condition he
should receive this poor Dorus into his service, that his mind
and manners might grow the better by his daily example.
Dametas, that of all manners of style could best conceive of
golden eloquence, being withal tickled by Musidorus' praises, 35
had his brain so turned that he became slave to that which he
that sued to be his servant offered to give him; yet, for countenance' sake, he seemed very squeamish, in respect of the
charge he had of the Princess Pamela. But such was the secret
operation of the gold, helped with the persuasion of the Amazon 40
Zelmane (who said it was pity so handsome a young man
should be anywhere else than with so good a master), that in
the end he agreed (if that day he behaved himself so to the
liking of Basilius, as he might be contented) that then he
would receive him into his service. 45

And thus went they to the lodge, where they found Gynecia
and her daughters ready to go to the field, to delight themselves there a while, until the shepherds' coming; whither also
taking Zelmane with them, as they went Dametas told them
of Dorus, and desired he might be accepted there that day, 50
instead of his brother Menalcas. As for Basilius, he stayed
behind to bring the shepherds, with whom he meant to confer,
to breed the better Zelmane's liking (which he only regarded),
while the other beautiful band came into the fair field appointed
for the shepherdish pastimes. It was indeed a place of delight; 55
for thorough the middle of it there ran a sweet brook, which
did both hold the eye open with her azure streams, and yet seek
to close the eye with the purling noise it made upon the pebble
stones it ran over; the field itself being set in some places with
roses, and in all the rest constantly preserving a flourishing 60
green, the roses added such ruddy show unto it, as though the
field were bashful at his own beauty; about it (as if it had been
to enclose a theatre) grew such a sort of trees, as either excel-

36–37. *that which . . . give him:* i.e., the money.
37–38. *countenance':* appearances'.
38. *squeamish:* reluctant.
39. *charge . . . of:* responsibility for.
53. *regarded:* thought of.

lency of fruit, stateliness of growth, continual greenness, or
poetical fancies have made at any time famous. In most part of 65
which there had been framed by art such pleasant arbours, that
(one answering another) they became a gallery aloft from tree to
tree almost round about, which below gave a perfect shadow, a
pleasant refuge then from the choleric look of Phoebus.

In this place while Gynecia walked hard by them, carrying 70
many unquiet contentions about her, the ladies sat them down,
inquiring diverse questions of the shepherd Dorus; who (keeping his eye still upon Pamela) answered with such a trembling
voice and abashed countenance, and oftentimes so far from the
matter, that it was some sport to the young ladies, thinking it 75
want of education which made him so discountenanced with
unwonted presence. But Zelmane that saw in him the glass of
her own misery, taking the hand of Philoclea, and with burning
kisses setting it close to her lips (as if it should stand there like
a hand in the margin of a book, to note some saying worthy to 80
be marked) began to speak these words, 'O love, since thou art
so changeable in men's estates, how art thou so constant in
their torments?', when suddenly there came out of a wood a
monstrous lion, with a she-bear not far from him of little less
fierceness, which (as they guessed) having been hunted in 85
forests far off were by chance come thither, where before such
beasts had never been seen. Then care, not fear – or fear, not for
themselves – altered something the countenances of the two
lovers, but so as any man might perceive was rather an as-
sembling of powers than dismayedness of courage. Philoclea no 90
sooner espied the lion, but that obeying the commandment of
fear, she leapt up and ran to the lodge-ward as fast as her
delicate legs could carry her, while Dorus drew Pamela behind
a tree, where she stood quaking like the partridge on which
the hawk is even ready to seize. But the lion, seeing Philoclea 95
run away, bent his race to her-ward, and was ready to seize
himself on the prey, when Zelmane (to whom danger then

71. *unquiet contentions:* anxious mental struggles.
92. *to the lodge-ward:* towards the lodge.

NOTES: p. 230

was a cause of dreadlessness, all the composition of her
elements being nothing but fiery) with swiftness of desire crost
him, and with force of affection strake him such a blow upon 100
his chine that she opened all his body: wherewith the valiant
beast turning upon her with open jaws, she gave him such a
thrust thorough his breast that all the lion could do was with
his paw to tear off the mantle and sleeve of Zelmane, with a
little scratch rather than a wound, his death-blow having taken 105
away the effect of his force. But therewithal he fell down, and
gave Zelmane leisure to take off his head, to carry it for a
present to her Lady Philoclea: who all this while (not knowing
what was done behind her) kept on her course, like Arethusa
when she ran from Alpheus; her light apparel being carried up 110
with the wind, that much of those beauties she would at another
time have willingly hidden was presented to the sight of the
twice-wounded Zelmane. Which made Zelmane not follow her
over-hastily, lest she should too soon deprive herself of that
pleasure: but carrying the lion's head in her hand, did not 115
fully overtake her till they came to the presence of Basilius.
Neither were they long there, but that Gynecia came thither
also; who had been in such a trance of musing, that Zelmane
was fighting with the lion before she knew of any lion's coming;
but then affection resisting, and the soon ending of the fight 120
preventing all extremity of fear, she marked Zelmane's fighting.
And when the lion's head was off, as Zelmane ran after Philoclea, so she could not find in her heart but run after Zelmane:
so that it was a new sight Fortune had prepared to those
woods, to see these great personages thus run one after the 125
other, each carried forward with an inward violence: Philoclea
with such fear, that she thought she was still in the lion's
mouth, Zelmane with an eager and impatient delight, Gynecia
with wings of love flying she neither knew nor cared to know
whither. But now being all come before Basilius amazed with 130
this sight, and fear having such possession in the fair Philoclea
that her blood durst not yet to come to her face to take away

101. *chine:* backbone.
120. *resisting:* resisting fear (for herself).

NOTES: p. 230

the name of paleness from her most pure whiteness, Zelmane
kneeled down and presented the lion's head unto her. 'Only
Lady' (said she) 'here see you the punishment of that un- 135
natural beast, which, contrary to his own kind, would have
wronged prince's blood, guided with such traitorous eyes as
durst rebel against your beauty.' 'Happy am I and my beauty
both' (answered the sweet Philoclea, then blushing, for fear
had bequeathed his room to his kinsman bashfulness) 'that 140
you, excellent Amazon, were there to teach him good manners.'
'And even thanks to that beauty' (answered Zelmane) 'which
can give an edge to the bluntest swords.' There Philoclea told
her father how it had happened: but as she had turned her eyes
in her tale to Zelmane, she perceived some blood upon 145
Zelmane's shoulder, so that, starting with the lovely grace of
pity, she showed it to her father and mother; who, as the nurse
sometimes with overmuch kissing may forget to give the babe
suck, so had they with too much delighting in beholding and
praising Zelmane left off to mark whether she needed succour. 150
But then they ran both unto her, like a father and mother to
an only child, and (though Zelmane assured them it was
nothing) would needs see it; Gynecia having skill in surgery,
an art in those days much esteemed, because it served to
virtuous courage, which even ladies would (ever with the con- 155
tempt of cowards) seem to cherish. But looking upon it (which
gave more inward-bleeding wounds to Zelmane, for she might
sometimes feel Philoclea's touch, whilst she helped her
mother), she found it was indeed of no importance: yet applied
she a precious balm unto it, of power to heal a greater grief. 160
    But even then, and not before, they remembered Pamela,
and therefore Zelmane (thinking of her friend Dorus) was
running back to be satisfied, when they might all see Pamela
coming between Dorus and Dametas, having in her hand the
paw of a bear, which the shepherd Dorus had newly presented 165
unto her, desiring her to accept it, as of such a beast, which
though she deserved death for her presumption, yet was her
wit to be esteemed, since she could make so sweet a choice.

---

136. *kind:* nature (being the king of beasts).

Dametas for his part came piping and dancing, the merriest man in a parish. But when he came so near as he might be 170 heard of Basilius, he would needs break thorough his ears with this joyful song of their good success.

> Now thanked be the great God Pan
> Which thus preserves my loved life:
> Thanked be I that keep a man   175
> Who ended hath this fearful strife:
> For if my man must praises have,
> What then must I that keep the knave?
>
> For as the Moon the eye doth please
> With gentle beams not hurting sight,   180
> Yet hath Sir Sun the greatest praise,
> Because from him doth come her light:
> So if my man must praises have,
> What then must I that keep the knave?

Being all now come together, and all desirous to know each 185 other's adventures, Pamela's noble heart would needs gratefully make known the valiant mean of her safety: which (directing her speech to her mother) she did in this manner. 'As soon' (said she) 'as ye were all run away, and that I hoped to be in safety, there came out of the same woods a foul horrible 190 bear, which, fearing belike to deal while the lion was present, as soon as he was gone came furiously towards the place where I was, and this young shepherd left alone by me; I truly (not guilty of any wisdom, which since they lay to my charge, because they say it is the best refuge against that beast, but 195 even pure fear bringing forth that effect of wisdom) fell down flat of my face, needing not counterfeit being dead, for indeed I was little better. But this young shepherd, with a wonderful courage, having no other weapon but that knife you see, standing before the place where I lay, so behaved himself that 200 the first sight I had (when I thought myself already near

187. *mean:* instrument (i.e., Dorus).

Charon's ferry) was the shepherd showing me his bloody knife
in token of victory.' 'I pray you,' (said Zelmane, speaking to
Dorus, whose valour she was careful to have manifested) 'in
what sort, so ill-weaponed, could you achieve this enterprise?' 205
'Noble lady,' (said Dorus) 'the manner of these beasts' fighting
with any man, is to stand upon their hinder feet: and so this
did, and being ready to give me a shrewd embracement, I
think the God Pan (ever careful of the chief blessings of
Arcadia) guided my hand so just to the heart of the beast, that 210
neither she could once touch me, nor (which is the only
matter in this worthy remembrance) breed any danger to the
Princess. For my part, I am rather (with all subjected humbleness) to thank her excellencies, since the duty thereunto gave
me heart to save myself, than to receive thanks for a deed 215
which was her only inspiring.' And this Dorus spake, keeping
affection as much as he could back from coming into his eyes
and gestures. But Zelmane (that had the same character in her
heart) could easily decipher it, and therefore to keep him the
longer in speech, desired to understand the conclusion of the 220
matter, and how the honest Dametas was escaped.

'Nay,' (said Pamela) 'none shall take that office from myself,
being so much bound to him as I am for my education.' And
with that word (scorn borrowing the countenance of mirth)
somewhat she smiled, and thus spake on. 'When' (said she) 225
'Dorus made me assuredly perceive that all cause of fear was
passed, the truth is I was ashamed to find myself alone with
this shepherd: and therefore looking about me, if I could see
anybody, at length we both perceived the gentle Dametas,
lying with his head and breast as far as he could thrust himself 230
into a bush; drawing up his legs as close unto him as he could;
for, like a man of a very kind nature, soon to take pity of himself, he was full resolved not to see his own death. And when
this shepherd pushed him, bidding him to be of good cheer, it

204. *have manifested:* cause to be made known.
208. *shrewd:* mischievous, hurtful.
209. *the chief blessings:* i.e., the Princesses.
212. *worthy remembrance:* worth remembering.

was a great while, ere we could persuade him that Dorus was 235
not the bear: so that he was fain to pull him out by the heels,
and show him the beast, as dead as he could wish it; which you
may believe me was a very joyful sight unto him. But then he
forgat all courtesy, for he fell upon the beast, giving it many a
manful wound: swearing by much, it was not well such beasts 240
should be suffered in a commonwealth. And then my governor,
as full of joy as before of fear, came dancing and singing before
us as even now you saw him.' 'Well, well,' (said Basilius) 'I have
not chosen Dametas for his fighting, nor for his discoursing,
but for his plainness and honesty, and therein I know he will 245
not deceive me.'

But then he told Pamela (not so much because she should
know it, as because he would tell it) the wonderful act Zelmane
had performed, which Gynecia likewise spake of, both in such
extremity of praising, as was easy to be seen the construction 250
of their speech might best be made by the grammar rules of
affection. Basilius told with what a gallant grace she ran with
the lion's head in her hand, like another Pallas with the spoils
of Gorgon. Gynecia sware, she saw the very face of the young
Hercules killing the Nemean lion, and all with a grateful assent 255
confirmed the same praises: only poor Dorus (though of equal
desert, yet not proceeding of equal estate) should have been left
forgotten, had not Zelmane again with great admiration begun
to speak of him; asking whether it were the fashion or no in
Arcadia that shepherds should perform such valorous enter- 260
prises. This Basilius (having the quick sense of a lover) took as
though his mistress had given him a secret reprehension that
he had not showed more gratefulness to Dorus; and therefore
(as nimbly as he could) enquired of his estate, adding promise
of great rewards: among the rest, offering to him, if he would 265
exercise his courage in soldiery, he would commit some charge
unto him under his lieutenant Philanax. But Dorus (whose
ambition climbed by another stair), having first answered

250. *construction*: construing, interpretation.
257. *estate*: rank.
258. *admiration*: wonder.

touching his estate, that he was brother to the shepherd
Menalcas, who among other was wont to resort to the Prince's 270
presence, and excused his going to soldiery by the unaptness he
found in himself that way: he told Basilius that his brother in
his last testament had willed him to serve Dametas; and therefore (for due obedience thereunto) he would think his service
greatly rewarded, if he might obtain by that mean to live in the 275
sight of his Prince, and yet practise his own chosen vocation.
Basilius (liking well his goodly shape and handsome manner)
charged Dametas to receive him like a son into his house:
saying that his valour and Dametas' truth would be good
bulwarks against such mischiefs as (he sticked not to say) were 280
threatened to his daughter Pamela.

Dametas, no whit out of countenance with all that had been
said (because he had no worse to fall into than his own),
accepted Dorus: and withal, telling Basilius that some of the
shepherds were come, demanded in what place he would see 285
their sports. Who first curious to know whether it were not
more requisite for Zelmane's hurt to rest than sit up at those
pastimes; and she (that felt no wound but one) earnestly
desiring to have the Pastorals, Basilius commanded it should be
at the gate of the lodge: where the throne of the Prince being, 290
according to the ancient manner, he made Zelmane sit between
him and his wife therein, who thought herself between drowning and burning: and the two young ladies of either side the
throne, and so prepared their eyes and ears to be delighted by
the shepherds. 295

But before all of them were assembled to begin their sports,
there came a fellow, who being out of breath (or seeming so to
be) for haste, with humble hastiness told Basilius that his
mistress, the Lady Cecropia, had sent him to excuse the mischance of her beasts' ranging in that dangerous sort, being 300
happened by the folly of the keeper; who, thinking himself able
to rule them, had carried them abroad, and so was deceived:

> 280. *sticked:* hesitated.
> 283. *no worse:* no worse countenance, face.
> 302. *carried them abroad:* brought them out of doors.

NOTES: p. 231

E

whom yet (if Basilius would punish for it) she was ready to deliver. Basilius made no other answer but that his mistress, if she had any more such beasts, should cause them to be killed: 305 and then he told his wife and Zelmane of it, because they should not fear those woods, as though they harboured such beasts, where the like had never been seen. But Gynecia took a further conceit of it, mistrusting greatly Cecropia, because she had heard much of the devilish wickedness of her heart, and 310 that particularly she did her best to bring up her son Amphialus (being brother's son to Basilius) to aspire to the crown, as next heir male after Basilius; and therefore saw no reason but that she might conjecture it proceeded rather of some mischievous practice than of misfortune. Yet did she only utter her doubt to 315 her daughters, thinking, since the worst was past, she would attend a further occasion, lest overmuch haste might seem to proceed of the ordinary mislike between sisters-in-law: only they marvelled that Basilius looked no further into it; who (good man) thought so much of his late-conceived common- 320 wealth that all other matters were but digressions unto him. But the shepherds were ready, and with well handling themselves, called their senses to attend their pastimes.

BOOK II, CHAPTER 4
Basilius his hawking. Gynecia's hurt by Dametas' overturning her coach. Her jealousy over Zelmane. Philoclea's love-passions, vow of chastity, revocation, lamentation.

But as Dorus was about to tell further, Dametas (who came whistling, and counting upon his fingers how many load of 5 hay his seventeen fat oxen ate up in a year) desired Zelmane from the King that she would come into the lodge, where they stayed for her. 'Alas,' (said Dorus, taking his leave) 'the sum is this, that you may well find you have beaten your sorrow against such a wall, which with the force of rebound may well 10 make your sorrow stronger.' But Zelmane, turning her speech to Dametas, 'I shall grow' (said she) 'skilful in country matters,

320–1. *his late-conceived commonwealth:* i.e., Zelmane.

NOTES: p. 231

if I have often conference with your servant.' 'In sooth'
(answered Dametas with a graceless scorn) 'the lad may prove
well enough, if he over-soon think not too well of himself, and 15
will bear away that he heareth of his elders.' And therewith as
they walked to the other lodge, to make Zelmane find she
might have spent her time better with him, he began with a
wild method to run over all the art of husbandry, especially
employing his tongue about well dunging of a field; while poor 20
Zelmane yielded her ears to those tedious strokes, not warding
them so much as with any one answer, till they came to Basilius
and Gynecia, who attended for her in a coach to carry her
abroad to see some sports prepared for her. Basilius and
Gynecia, sitting in the one end, placed her at the other, with 25
her left side to Philoclea. Zelmane was moved in her mind to
have kissed their feet for the favour of so blessed a seat: for the
narrowness of the coach made them join from the foot to the
shoulders very close together; the truer touch whereof though
it were barred by their envious apparel, yet as a perfect magnes, 30
though put in an ivory box, will thorough the box send forth his
embracing virtue to a beloved needle; so this imparadised
neighbourhood made Zelmane's soul cleave unto her, both
thorough the ivory case of her body, and the apparel which did
overcloud it: all the blood of Zelmane's body stirring in her, 35
as wine will do when sugar is hastily put into it, seeking to suck
the sweetness of the beloved guest; her heart, like a lion new
imprisoned seeing him that restrains his liberty before the
grate, not panting, but striving violently (if it had been possible)
to have leapt into the lap of Philoclea. But Dametas, even then 40
proceeding from being master of a cart to be doctor of a coach,
not a little proud in himself that his whip at that time guided
the rule of Arcadia, drave the coach (the cover whereof was
made with such joints, that as they might to avoid the weather
pull it up close when they listed, so when they would they 45

16. *bear away:* keep in mind.
18–19. *with a wild method:* in disorderly order.
30. *magnes:* magnet.
45. *listed, would:* pleased.

NOTES: p. 231

might put each end down and remain as discovered and open-sighted as on horseback) till upon the side of the forest they had both greyhounds, spaniels, and hounds, whereof the first might seem the lords, the second the gentlemen, and the last the yeomen of dogs; a cast of merlins there was besides, which 50 flying of a gallant height over certain bushes would beat the birds that rose down unto the bushes, as falcons will do wild-fowl over a river. But the sport which for that day Basilius would principally show to Zelmane was the mountie at a hern, which getting up on his waggling wings with pain, till he was 55 come to some height (as though the air next to the earth were not fit for his great body to fly through), was now grown to diminish the sight of himself, and to give example to great persons that the higher they be, the less they should show: when a jerfalcon was cast off after him, who straight spying 60 where the prey was, fixing her eye with desire, and guiding her wing by her eye, used no more strength than industry. For as a good builder to a high tower will not make his stair upright, but winding almost the full compass about, that the steepness be the more unsensible; so she, seeing the towering of her 65 pursued chase, went circling and compassing about, rising so with the less sense of rising; and yet finding that way scantly serve the greediness of her haste, as an ambitious body will go far out of the direct way to win a point of height which he desires; so would she (as it were) turn tail to the heron, and fly 70 quite out another way, but all was to return in a higher pitch; which once gotten, she would either beat with cruel assaults the heron, who now was driven to the best defence of force, since flight would not serve; or else clasping with him, come down together, to be parted by the over-partial beholders. 75

Divers of which flights Basilius showing to Zelmane, thus

---

50. *cast:* number of hawks (usually a couple) flown together.
54. *mountie at a hern:* (French *montée*) rising to the chase of a heron.
60. *jerfalcon:* large falcon.
65. *unsensible:* imperceptible.
71. *pitch:* height from which a hawk stoops on its prey.
75. *over-partial:* taking sides (i.e., killing the heron).

was the richesse of the time spent, and the day decreased before
it was thought of, till night like a degenerating successor made
his departure the better remembered. And therefore (so constrained) they willed Dametas to drive homeward, who (half 80
sleeping, half musing about the mending of a wine-press)
guided the horses so ill, that the wheel coming over a great
stub of a tree, it overturned the coach. Which though it fell
violently upon the side where Zelmane and Gynecia sat, yet for
Zelmane's part she would have been glad of the fall which 85
made her bear the sweet burthen of Philoclea, but that she
feared she might receive some hurt. But indeed neither she did,
nor any of the rest, by reason they kept their arms and legs
within the coach, saving Gynecia, who with the only bruise of
the fall had her shoulder put out of joint; which though by one 90
of the falconers' cunning it was set well again, yet with much
pain was she brought to the lodge; and pain fetching his
ordinary companion a fever with him drave her to entertain
them both in her bed.

But neither was the fever of such impatient heat as the 95
inward plague-sore of her affection, nor the pain half so
noisome as the jealousy she conceived of her daughter Philoclea, lest this time of her sickness might give apt occasion to
Zelmane, whom she misdoubted. Therefore she called Philoclea to her, and though it were late in the night, commanded 100
her in her ear to go to the other lodge, and send Miso to her,
with whom she would speak, and she lie with her sister Pamela.
The meanwhile Gynecia kept Zelmane with her, because she
would be sure she should be out of the lodge before she
licensed Zelmane. Philoclea, not skilled in anything better 105
than obedience, went quietly down; and the moon then full
(not thinking scorn to be a torch-bearer to such beauty) guided
her steps, whose motions bare a mind which bare in itself far
more stirring motions. And alas (sweet Philoclea), how hath

77. *richesse:* wealth, i.e., greater part.
94. *them both:* pain and fever.
97. *noisome:* troublesome.
99. *misdoubted:* suspected.
105. *licensed:* gave leave (to go).

my pen till now forgot thy passions, since to thy memory 110
principally all this long matter is intended? Pardon the slack-
ness to come to those woes which having caused in others thou
didst feel in thyself.

The sweet-minded Philoclea was in their degree of well-
doing to whom the not knowing of evil serveth for a ground of 115
virtue, and hold their inward powers in better form with an
unspotted simplicity than many who rather cunningly seek to
know what goodness is than willingly take into themselves the
following of it. But as that sweet and simple breath of heavenly
goodness is the easier to be altered, because it hath not passed 120
through the worldly wickedness, nor feelingly found the evil
that evil carries with it; so now the Lady Philoclea (whose eyes
and senses had received nothing but according as the natural
course of each thing required; which from whose tender youth
had obediently lived under her parents' behests, without 125
framing out of her own will the fore-choosing of any thing),
when now she came to a point wherein her judgement was to
be practised in knowing faultiness by his first tokens, she was
like a young fawn, who coming in the wind of the hunters,
doth not know whether it be a thing or no to be eschewed; 130
whereof at this time she began to get a costly experience. For
after that Zelmane had a while lived in the lodge with her, and
that her only being a noble stranger had bred a kind of heedful
attention; her coming to that lonely place (where she had
nobody but her parents), a willingness of conversation; her wit 135
and behaviour, a liking and silent admiration; at length the
excellency of her natural gifts, joined with the extreme shows
she made of most devout honouring Philoclea (carrying thus in
one person the only two bands of goodwill, loveliness and
lovingness), brought forth in her heart a yielding to a most 140
friendly affection; which when it had gotten so full possession
of the keys of her mind that it would receive no message from

126. *fore-choosing:* preference.
130. *eschewed:* avoided.
133. *her only being:* the mere fact of her being.

NOTES: p. 231

her senses without that affection were the interpreter, then straight grew an exceeding delight still to be with her, with an unmeasurable liking of all that Zelmane did: matters being so 145 turned in her, that where at first liking her manners did breed goodwill, now goodwill became the chief cause of liking her manners; so that within a while Zelmane was not prized for her demeanour, but the demeanour was prized because it was Zelmane's. Then followed that most natural effect of conform- 150 ing oneself to that which she did like, and not only wishing to be herself such another in all things, but to ground an imitation upon so much an esteemed authority: so that the next degree was to mark all Zelmane's doings, speeches, and fashions, and to take them into herself, as a pattern of worthy proceeding. 155 Which when once it was enacted, not only by the commonalty of Passions, but agreed unto by her most noble Thoughts, and that Reason itself (not yet experienced in the issues of such matters) had granted his royal assent; then Friendship (a diligent officer) took care to see the statute thoroughly 160 observed. Then grew on that not only she did imitate the soberness of her countenance, the gracefulness of her speech, but even their particular gestures: so that as Zelmane did often eye her, she would often eye Zelmane; and as Zelmane's eyes would deliver a submissive but vehement desire in their look, 165 she, though as yet she had not the desire in her, yet should her eyes answer in like piercing kindness of a look. Zelmane, as much as Gynecia's jealousy would suffer, desired to be near Philoclea; Philoclea, as much as Gynecia's jealousy would suffer, desired to be near Zelmane. If Zelmane took her hand, 170 and softly strained it, she also (thinking the knots of friendship ought to be mutual) would with a sweet fastness show she was loth to part from it. And if Zelmane sighed, she would sigh also; when Zelmane was sad, she deemed it wisdom, and there- fore she would be sad too. Zelmane's languishing countenance 175 with crossed arms and sometimes cast-up eyes she thought to

143. *without that:* unless.
156. *commonalty:* common people.

NOTES: p. 231

have an excellent grace; and therefore she also willingly put on the same countenance: till at the last (poor soul), ere she were aware, she accepted not only the badge but the service; not only the sign but the passion signified. For whether it were, that her wit in continuance did find that Zelmane's friendship was full of impatient desire, having more than ordinary limits, and therefore she was content to second Zelmane, though herself knew not the limits; or that in truth true love (well considered) have an infective power, at last she fell in acquaintance with love's harbinger, wishing. First she would wish that they two might live all their lives together, like two of Diana's nymphs. But that wish she thought not sufficient, because she knew there would be more nymphs besides them, who also would have their part in Zelmane. Then would she wish that she were her sister, that such a natural band might make her more special to her. But against that, she considered that though being her sister, if she happened to be married she should be robbed of her. Then grown bolder, she would wish either herself or Zelmane a man, that there might succeed a blessed marriage betwixt them. But when that wish had once displayed his ensign in her mind, then followed whole squadrons of longings that so it might be, with a main battle of mislikings and repinings against their creation that so it was not. Then dreams by night began to bring more unto her than she durst wish by day, whereout waking did make her know herself the better by the image of those fancies. But as some diseases when they are easy to be cured they are hard to be known, but when they grow easy to be known they are almost impossible to be cured: so the sweet Philoclea, while she might prevent it, she did not feel it, now she felt it when it was past preventing; like a river, no rampiers being built against it, till already it have overflowed. For now indeed, Love pulled off his mask, and showed his face unto her, and told her plainly that she was his prisoner. Then needed she no more paint her face with pas-

181. *in continuance:* by and by.
198. *main battle:* principal armed force.
207. *rampiers:* walls, dikes.

sions; for passions shone thorough her face. Then her rosy colour was often increased with extraordinary blushing: and so another time perfect whiteness descended to a degree of paleness; now hot, then cold, desiring she knew not what, nor how, if she knew what. Then her mind (though too late) by the smart 215 was brought to think of the disease, and her own proof taught her to know her mother's mind; which (as no error gives so strong assault as that which comes armed in the authority of a parent) so greatly fortified her desires, to see that her mother had the like desires. And the more jealous her mother was, the 220 more she thought the jewel precious which was with so many locks guarded. But that prevailing so far as to keep the two lovers from private conference, then began she to feel the sweetness of a lover's solitariness, when freely with words and gestures, as if Zelmane were present, she might give passage to her 225 thoughts, and so as it were utter out some smoke of those flames wherewith else she was not only burned but smothered. As this night, that going from the one lodge to the other by her mother's commandment, with doleful gestures and uncertain paces, she did willingly accept the time's offer to be a while 230 alone: so that going a little aside into the wood, where many times before she had delighted to walk, her eyes were saluted with a tuft of trees, so close set together as (with the shade the moon gave thorough it) it might breed a fearful kind of devotion to look upon it. But true thoughts of love banished all vain 235 fancy of superstition. Full well she did both remember and like the place; for there had she often with their shade beguiled Phoebus of looking upon her. There had she enjoyed herself often, while she was mistress of herself, and had no other thoughts but such as might arise out of quiet senses. 240

But the principal cause that invited her remembrance was a goodly white marble stone, that should seem had been dedicated in ancient time to the sylvan gods: which she finding there a few days before Zelmane's coming, had written these

219. *so:* therefore.
234–5. *a fearful kind of devotion:* religious dread.
243. *sylvan:* woodland.

words upon it, as a testimony of her mind against the suspicion 245
her captivity made her think she lived in. The writing was this.

> You living powers enclos'd in stately shrine
> Of growing trees; you rural Gods that wield
> Your sceptres here, if to your ears divine
> A voice may come which troubled soul doth yield,   250
>   This vow receive, this vow O Gods maintain:
>   My virgin life no spotted thought shall stain.
>
> Thou purest stone, whose pureness doth present
> My purest mind; whose temper hard doth show
> My temper'd heart; by thee my promise sent   255
> Unto myself let after-livers know.
>   No fancy mine, nor others' wrong suspect,
>   Make me, O virtuous shame, thy laws neglect.
>
> O chastity, the chief of heavenly lights,
> Which mak'st us most immortal shape to wear,   260
> Hold thou my heart, establish thou my sprites:
> To only thee my constant course I bear.
>   Till spotless soul unto thy bosom fly,
>   Such life to lead, such death I vow to die.

But now that her memory served as an accuser of her change, 265
and that her own handwriting was there to bear testimony
against her fall, she went in among those few trees, so closed
in the tops together, as they might seem a little chapel: and
there might she by the help of the moonlight perceive the
goodly stone, which served as an altar in that woody devotion. 270
But neither the light was enough to read the words, and the
ink was already forworn and in many places blotted: which as
she perceived, 'Alas,' (said she) 'fair marble, which never

253. *present:* represent.
255. *temper'd:* firm, well-controlled.
257. *suspect:* suspicion.
261. *establish:* strengthen.
272. *forworn:* much worn away.

NOTES: p. 231

receivedst spot but by my writing, well do these blots become
a blotted writer. But pardon her which did not dissemble then, 275
although she have changed since. Enjoy, enjoy the glory of thy
nature, which can so constantly bear the marks of my incon-
stancy.' And herewith hiding her eyes with her soft hand, there
came into her head certain verses, which if she had had present
commodity she would have adjoined as a retractation to the 280
other. They were to this effect.

> My words, in hope to blaze my steadfast mind,
> This marble chose, as of like temper known:
> But lo, my words defac'd, my fancies blind,
> Blots to the stone, shame to myself I find,   285
>   And witness am, how ill agree in one
>   A woman's hand with constant marble stone.
>
> My words full weak, the marble full of might;
> My words in store, the marble all alone;
> My words black ink, the marble kindly white;   290
> My words unseen, the marble still in sight,
>   May witness bear, how ill agree in one
>   A woman's hand with constant marble stone.

But seeing she could not see means to join as then this
recantation to the former vow, laying all her fair length under 295
one of the trees, for a while she did nothing but turn up and
down, as if she had hoped to turn away the fancy that mastered
her, and hid her face, as if she could have hidden herself from
her own fancies. At length with a whispering note to herself,
'O me, unfortunate wretch,' (said she) 'what poisonous heats be 300
these which thus torment me? How hath the sight of this
strange guest invaded my soul? Alas, what entrance found
this desire, or what strength had it thus to conquer me?' Then,

280. *commodity:* opportunity (i.e., light and ink).
282. *blaze:* emblazon.
289. *in store:* in plenty.
290. *kindly:* by nature.
291. *still:* ever.

a cloud passing between her sight and the moon, 'O Diana,' (said she) 'I would either the cloud that now hides the light of 305 my virtue would as easily pass away, as you will quickly overcome this let; or else that you were for ever thus darkened, to serve for an excuse of my outrageous folly.' Then looking to the stars, which had perfectly as then beautified the clear sky, 'My parents' (said she) 'have told me, that in these fair heavenly 310 bodies, there are great hidden deities, which have their working in the ebbing and flowing of our estates. If it be so, then (O you stars) judge rightly of me, and if I have with wicked intent made myself a prey to fancy, or if by any idle lusts I framed my heart fit for such an impression, then let this plague daily 315 increase in me, till my name be made odious to womankind. But if extreme and unresistible violence have oppressed me, who will ever do any of you sacrifice (O you stars) if you do not succour me? No, no, you will not help me. No, no, you cannot help me. Sin must be the mother, and shame the daughter, of 320 my affection. And yet are these but childish objections, simple Philoclea: it is the impossibility that doth torment me: for unlawful desires are punished after the effect of enjoying; but unpossible desires are punished in the desire itself. O then, O ten times unhappy that I am, since where in all other hope 325 kindleth love, in me despair should be the bellows of my affection: and of all despairs the most miserable, which is drawn from impossibility. The most covetous man longs not to get riches out of a ground which never can bear anything. Why? because it is impossible. The most ambitious wight vexeth not 330 his wits to climb into heaven. Why? because it is impossible. Alas then, O love, why dost thou in thy beautiful sampler set such a work for my desire to take out, which is as much impossible? And yet, alas, why do I thus condemn my fortune, before I hear what she can say for herself? What do I, silly 335 wench, know what love hath prepared for me? Do I not see

307. *let:* hindrance, impediment.
312. *estates:* fortunes.
323. *effect:* accomplishment.
325. *all other:* all other beings.
333. *take out:* copy.

my mother as well, at least as furiously as myself, love Zelmane?
And should I be wiser than my mother? Either she sees a
possibility in that which I think impossible, or else impossible
loves need not misbecome me. And do I not see Zelmane (who 340
doth not think a thought which is not first weighed by wisdom
and virtue), doth not she vouchsafe to love me with like ardour?
I see it, her eyes depose it to be true; what then? and if she can
love poor me, shall I think scorn to love such a woman as
Zelmane? Away then, all vain exclamations of why and how! 345
Thou lovest me, excellent Zelmane, and I love thee.' And
with that, embracing the very ground whereon she lay, she
said to herself (for even to herself she was ashamed to speak it
out in words) 'O my Zelmane, govern and direct me: for I am
wholly given over unto thee.'   350

BOOK II, CHAPTER 5
*The bedfellow communication of Philoclea and Pamela. Pamela's
narration of her shepherd's making love; of his hot pursuit, and
her cold acceptance. His letter. Her relenting, and Philoclea's
sole complaint.*

In this depth of muses, and divers sorts of discourses, would   5
she ravingly have remained, but that Dametas and Miso (who
were round about to seek her, understanding she was to come
to their lodge that night) came hard by her; Dametas saying
that he would not deal in other bodies' matters, but for his
part he did not like that maids should once stir out of their   10
fathers' houses, but if it were to milk a cow, or save a chicken
from a kite's foot, or some such other matter of importance.
And Miso swearing that if it were her daughter Mopsa, she
would give her a lesson for walking so late, that should make
her keep within doors for one fortnight. But their jangling   15
made Philoclea rise, and pretending as though she had done it
but to sport with them, went with them (after she had willed

343. *depose:* witness.
     9. *deal in other bodies' matters:* meddle in other people's affairs.

Miso to wait upon her mother) to the lodge; where (being now accustomed by her parents' discipline, as well as her sister, to serve herself) she went up alone to Pamela's chamber: where 20 meaning to delight her eyes and joy her thoughts with the sweet conversation of her beloved sister, she found her (though it were in the time that the wings of night doth blow sleep most willingly into mortal creatures) sitting in a chair, lying backward, with her head almost over the back of it, and looking 25 upon a wax-candle which burnt before her; in one hand holding a letter, in the other her handkerchief, which had lately drunk up the tears of her eyes, leaving instead of them crimson circles, like red flakes in the element when the weather is hottest. Which Philoclea finding (for her eyes had learned to 30 know the badges of sorrow), she earnestly entreated to know the cause thereof, that either she might comfort or accompany her doleful humour. But Pamela rather seeming sorry that she had perceived so much than willing to open any further, 'O my Pamela,' (said Philoclea) 'who are to me a sister in nature, a 35 mother in counsel, a princess by the law of our country, and (which name methinks of all other is the dearest) a friend by my choice and your favour, what means this banishing me from your counsels? Do you love your sorrow so well as to grudge me part of it? Or do you think I shall not love a sad 40 Pamela so well as a joyful? Or be my ears unworthy, or my tongue suspected? What is it, my sister, that you should conceal from your sister, yea, and servant Philoclea?' These words won no further of Pamela but that telling her they might talk better as they lay together, they impoverished their clothes to enrich 45 their bed, which for that night might well scorn the shrine of Venus: and there cherishing one another with dear though chaste embracements, with sweet though cold kisses, it might seem that Love was come to play him there without dart, or that weary of his own fires he was there to refresh himself between 50 their sweet-breathing lips. But Philoclea earnestly again entreated Pamela to open her grief; who (drawing the curtain, that the candle might not complain of her blushing) was ready

49. *play him:* disport himself.

to speak; but the breath almost formed into words was again
stopped by her, and turned into sighs. But at last, 'I pray you,'   55
(said she) 'sweet Philoclea, let us talk of some other thing: and
tell me whether you did ever see anything so amended as our
pastoral sports be, since that Dorus came hither?' O Love,
how far thou seest with blind eyes! Philoclea had straight
found her, and therefore to draw out more, 'Indeed' (said she)   60
'I have often wondered to myself how such excellencies could
be in so mean a person; but belike Fortune was afraid to lay
her treasures where they should be stained with so many
perfections: only I marvel how he can frame himself to hide so
rare gifts under such a block as Dametas.' 'Ah,' (said Pamela)   65
'if you knew the cause – but no more do I neither; and to say
the truth – but Lord, how are we fallen to talk of this fellow?
and yet indeed if you were sometimes with me to mark him,
while Dametas reads his rustic lecture unto him (how to feed
his beasts before noon, where to shade them in the extreme   70
heat, how to make the manger handsome for his oxen, when to
use the goad and when the voice: giving him rules of a herd-
man, though he pretend to make him a shepherd), to see all
the while with what a grace (which seems to set a crown upon
his base estate) he can descend to those poor matters, certainly   75
you would – But to what serves this? No doubt we were better
sleep than talk of these idle matters.' 'Ah my Pamela,' (said
Philoclea) 'I have caught you, the constancy of your wit was not
wont to bring forth such disjointed speeches: you love, dissemble no further.' 'It is true' (said Pamela); 'now you have it;   80
and with less ado should, if my heart could have thought those
words suitable for my mouth. But indeed, my Philoclea, take
heed: for I think virtue itself is no armour of proof against
affection. Therefore learn by my example.' 'Alas,' (thought
Philoclea to herself) 'your shears come too late to clip the bird's   85
wings that already is flown away.'

But then Pamela, being once set in the stream of her love,

60. *found her:* detected her.
65. *block:* blockhead.
73. *pretend:* claims, undertakes.

NOTES: p. 232

went away amain withal, telling her how his noble qualities
had drawn her liking towards him; but yet ever weighing his
meanness, and so held continually in due limits; till seeking   90
many means to speak with her, and ever kept from it (as well
because she shunned it, seeing and disdaining his mind, as
because of her jealous jailors), he had at length used the finest
policy that might be, in counterfeiting love to Mopsa, and
saying to Mopsa whatsoever he would have her know: and in   95
how passionate manner he had told his own tale in a third person, making poor Mopsa believe that it was a matter fallen out
many ages before. 'And in the end, because you shall know my
tears come not neither of repentance nor misery, who think
you is my Dorus fallen out to be? Even the Prince Musidorus, 100
famous over all Asia for his heroical enterprises, of whom you
remember how much good the stranger Plangus told my
father; he not being drowned (as Plangus thought), though his
cousin Pyrocles indeed perished. Ah my sister, if you had
heard his words or seen his gestures, when he made me know 105
what and to whom his love was, you would have matched in
yourself those two rarely matched together, pity and delight.
Tell me, dear sister (for the gods are my witnesses I desire to do
virtuously), can I without the detestable stain of ungratefulness abstain from loving him, who (far exceeding the beautiful- 110
ness of his shape with the beautifulness of his mind, and the
greatness of his estate with the greatness of his acts) is content
so to abase himself as to become Dametas' servant for my sake?
You will say, But how know I him to be Musidorus, since the
handmaid of wisdom is slow belief? That consideration did 115
not want in me, for the nature of desire itself is no easier to
receive belief than it is hard to ground belief. For as desire is
glad to embrace the first show of comfort, so is desire desirous
of perfect assurance: and that have I had of him, not only by
necessary arguments to any of common sense, but by sufficient 120
demonstrations. Lastly he would have me send to Thessalia:
but truly, I am not as now in mind to do my honourable love

92. *mind:* intention.
93–94. *finest policy:* subtlest contrivance.

NOTES: p. 232

so much wrong as so far to suspect him; yet, poor soul, knows
he no other but that I do both suspect, neglect, yea and detest
him. For every day he finds one way or other to set forth him- 125
self unto me, but all are rewarded with like coldness of acceptation. . . . One time he danced the matachin dance in armour
(O with what a graceful dexterity!), I think to make me see
that he had been brought up in such exercises; another time
he persuaded his master (to make my time seem shorter) in 130
manner of a dialogue to play Priamus while he played Paris.
Think, sweet Philoclea, what a Priamus we had: but truly my
Paris was a Paris, and more than a Paris; who while in a savage
apparel, with naked neck, arms, and legs, he made love to
Oenone, you might well see by his changed countenance and 135
true tears that he felt the part he played. Tell me, sweet
Philoclea, did you ever see such a shepherd? Tell me, did you
ever hear of such a prince? And then tell me, if a small or unworthy assault have conquered me. Truly, I would hate my life,
if I thought vanity led me. But since my parents deal so 140
cruelly with me, it is time for me to trust something to my
own judgement. Yet hitherto have my looks been as I told you,
which continuing after many of these his fruitless trials, have
wrought such change in him, as I tell you true '(with that word
she laid her hand upon her quaking side)' I do not a little fear 145
him. See what a letter this is' (then drew she the curtain and
took the letter from under the pillow) 'which today, with an
afflicted humbleness, he delivered me, pretending before
Mopsa that I should read it unto her, to mollify (forsooth) her
iron stomach.' With that she read the letter containing thus 150
much.

Most blessed paper, which shalt kiss that hand whereto all
blessedness is in nature a servant, do not yet disdain to carry
with thee the woeful words of a miser now despairing: neither
be afraid to appear before her, bearing the base title of the 155

127. *matachin dance:* sword-dance.
145. *fear him:* fear for his welfare.
149–50. *mollify her iron stomach:* soften her inflexible disdain.
154. *miser:* wretch.

NOTES: p. 232

sender. For no sooner shall that divine hand touch thee, but that thy baseness shall be turned to most high preferment. Therefore mourn boldly, my ink; for while she looks upon you, your blackness will shine: cry out boldly, my lamentation; for while she reads you, your cries will be music. Say then (O happy messenger of a most unhappy message) that the too-soon-born, and too-late-dying creature, which dares not speak, no not look, no not scarcely think (as from his miserable self unto her heavenly highness), only presumes to desire thee (in the time that her eyes and voice do exalt thee) to say, and in this manner to say, not from him, O no, that were not fit, but of him, thus much unto her sacred judgement. O you, the only, the only honour to women, to men the only admiration, you that being armed by Love defy him that armed you; in this high estate wherein you have placed me, yet let me remember him to whom I am bound for bringing me to your presence; and let me remember him, who (since he is yours, how mean soever he be) it is reason you have an account of him. The wretch (yet your wretch), though with languishing steps, runs fast to his grave; and will you suffer a temple, how poorly-built soever, but yet a temple of your deity, to be rased? But he dieth; it is most true, he dieth; and he in whom you live, to obey you dieth. Whereof though he plain, he doth not complain: for it is a harm, but no wrong, which he hath received. He dies, because in woeful language all his senses tell him that such is your pleasure; for since you will not that he live, alas, alas, what followeth, what followeth of the most ruined Dorus, but his end? End then, evil-destinied Dorus, end; and end, thou woeful letter, end; for it sufficeth her wisdom to know that her heavenly will shall be accomplished.

'O my Philoclea, is he a person to write these words? And are these words lightly to be regarded? But if you had seen,

170. *me:* the letter (supposed to be addressing Pamela on his behalf).
176. *rased:* destroyed.
178. *plain:* grieve.
181. *will:* desire.

NOTES: p. 232

when with trembling hand he had delivered it, how he went
away, as if he had been but the coffin that carried himself to his
sepulchre! Two times, I must confess, I was about to take 190
courtesy into mine eyes; but both times the former resolution
stopped the entry of it: so that he departed without obtaining
any further kindness. But he was no sooner out of the door but
that I looked to the door kindly; and truly the fear of him ever
since hath put me into such perplexity as now you found me.' 195
'Ah, my Pamela,' (said Philoclea) 'leave sorrow. The river of
your tears will soon lose his fountain; it is in your hand as
well to stitch up his life again, as it was before to rent it.' And
so (though with self-grieved mind) she comforted her sister, till
sleep came to bathe himself in Pamela's fair weeping eyes.   200

Which when Philoclea found, wringing her hands, 'O me,'
(said she) 'indeed the only subject of the destinies' displeasure,
whose greatest fortunateness is more unfortunate than my
sister's greatest unfortunateness. Alas, she weeps because she
would be no sooner happy: I weep because I can never be 205
happy. Her tears flow from pity, mine from being too far
lower than the reach of pity. Yet do I not envy thee, dear
Pamela, I do not envy thee: only I could wish that, being thy
sister in nature, I were not so far off akin in fortune.'

BOOK II, CHAPTER 11

Dorus his suit to Pamela interrupted by Mopsa's waking. The
sisters' going with Zelmane to wash themselves. The pleasantness
of the river. The pleasure Zelmane had in seeing them, uttered
in speech and song. She led by a spaniel to know and hurt her noble
rival. The parting of that fray.   5

'I have heard' (said Pamela) 'that part of the story of Plangus
when he passed through this country: therefore you may (if you
list) pass over that war of Erona's quarrel, lest if you speak too

190–1. *take courtesy into mine eyes:* look kindly on him.
194. *the fear of him:* fear for him.
  6. *of Plangus:* from Plangus.

much of war matters, you should wake Mopsa, which might
happily breed a great broil.' He looked, and saw that Mopsa   10
indeed sat swallowing of sleep with open mouth, making such
a noise withal, as nobody could lay the stealing of a nap to her
charge. Whereupon, willing to use that occasion, he kneeled
down, and with humble-heartedness and hearty earnestness
printed in his graces, 'Alas,' (said he) 'divine Lady, who have   15
wrought such miracles in me, as to make a prince (none of the
basest) to think all principalities base in respect of the sheephook which may hold him up in your sight; vouchsafe now at
last to hear in direct words my humble suit, while this dragon
sleeps that keeps the golden fruit. If in my desire I wish, or in   20
my hopes aspire, or in my imagination feign to myself anything
which may be the least spot to that heavenly virtue which shines
in all your doings, I pray the eternal powers that the words I
speak may be deadly poisons while they are in my mouth, and
that all my hopes, all my desires, all my imaginations, may   25
only work their own confusion. But if love, love of you, love of
your virtues, seek only that favour of you which becometh that
gratefulness, which cannot misbecome your excellency, O do
not —' He would have said further, but Pamela calling aloud
'Mopsa!', she suddenly start up staggering, and rubbing her   30
eyes ran first out of the door and then back to them before she
knew how she went out or why she came in again: till at length,
being fully come to her little self, she asked Pamela why she had
called her. 'For nothing' (said Pamela) 'but that you might
hear some tales of your servant's telling; and therefore now'   35
(said she) 'Dorus, go on.'

But as he (who found no so good sacrifice as obedience) was
returning to the story of himself, Philoclea came in, and by
and by after her Miso; so as for that time they were fain to let
Dorus depart. But Pamela (delighted even to preserve in her   40
memory the words of so well-beloved a speaker) repeated the

10. *happily:* perhaps.
17. *principalities:* princely possessions.
17. *in respect of:* compared with.
30. *start:* sprang.
33. *little self:* small senses.

whole substance to her sister, till their sober dinner being
come and gone, to recreate themselves something (even tired
with the noisomeness of Miso's conversation), they determined to go, while the heat of the day lasted, to bathe them-   45
selves (such being the manner of the Arcadian nymphs often
to do) in the river of Ladon, and take with them a lute,
meaning to delight them under some shadow. But they could
not stir but that Miso with her daughter Mopsa was after
them: and as it lay in their way to pass by the other lodge,   50
Zelmane out of her window espied them, and so stale down
after them; which she might the better do because that Gynecia
was sick, and Basilius (that day being his birthday) according
to his manner was busy about his devotions; and therefore
she went after, hoping to find some time to speak with   55
Philoclea: but not a word could she begin, but that Miso would
be one of the audience; so that she was driven to recommend
thinking, speaking, and all, to her eyes, who diligently performed her trust, till they came to the river's side; which of all
the rivers of Greece had the price for excellent pureness and   60
sweetness, in so much as the very bathing in it was accounted
exceeding healthful. It ran upon so fine and delicate a ground,
as one could not easily judge whether the river did more wash
the gravel or the gravel did purify the river; the river not
running forth right, but almost continually winding, as if the   65
lower streams would return to their spring, or that the river
had a delight to play with itself. The banks of either side
seeming arms of the loving earth, that fain would embrace it;
and the river a wanton nymph which still would slip from it;
either side of the bank being fringed with most beautiful   70
trees, which resisted the sun's darts from overmuch piercing
the natural coldness of the river. There was among the rest a
goodly cypress, who bowing her fair head over the water, it
seemed she looked into it, and dressed her green locks by that
running river. There the Princesses determining to bathe them-   75
selves, (though it was so privileged a place, upon pain of death,

60. *had the price:* was judged best.

NOTES: p. 232

as nobody durst presume to come thither) yet for the more surety they looked round about, and could see nothing but a water-spaniel, who came down the river, showing that he hunted for a duck, and with a snuffling grace disdaining that his smelling force could not as well prevail thorough the water as thorough the air; and therefore waiting with his eye, to see whether he could espy the duck's getting up again; but then a little below them failing of his purpose, he got out of the river, and shaking off the water (as great men do their friends) now he had no further cause to use it, inweeded himself so as the Ladies lost the further marking his sportfulness: and inviting Zelmane also to wash herself with them, and she excusing herself with having taken a late cold, they began by piecemeal to take away the eclipsing of their apparel.

Zelmane would have put to her helping hand, but she was taken with such a quivering, that she thought it more wisdom to lean herself to a tree and look on, while Miso and Mopsa (like a couple of forswat melters) were getting the pure silver of their bodies out of the ore of their garments. But as the raiments went off to receive kisses of the ground, Zelmane envied the happiness of all, but of the smock was even jealous, and when that was taken away too, and that Philoclea remained (for her Zelmane only marked) like a diamond taken from out the rock, or rather like the sun getting from under a cloud, and showing his naked beams to the full view, then was the beauty too much for a patient sight, the delight too strong for a staid conceit: so that Zelmane could not choose but run to touch, embrace, and kiss her. But conscience made her come to herself, and leave Philoclea, who blushing and withal smiling, making shamefastness pleasant and pleasure shamefast, tenderly moved her feet, unwonted to feel the naked ground, till the touch of the cold water made a pretty kind of shrugging come over her body, like the twinkling of the fairest among

80

85

90

95

100

105

91. *put to:* lent.
94. *forswat melters:* sweaty furnace-men.
103. *a staid conceit:* a sober thought.
106. *shamefastness:* bashfulness.

NOTES: pp. 232–3

the fixed stars. But the river itself gave way unto her, so that 110
she was straight breast-high; which was the deepest that
thereabout she could be: and when cold Ladon had once fully
embraced them, himself was no more so cold to those Ladies,
but as if his cold complexion had been heated with love, so
seemed he to play about every part he could touch.   115

'Ah sweet, now sweetest Ladon,' (said Zelmane) 'why dost
thou not stay thy course to have more full taste of thy happiness? But the reason is manifest, the upper streams make
such haste to have their part of embracing, that the nether
(though lothly) must needs give place unto them. O happy 120
Ladon, within whom she is, upon whom her beauty falls,
thorough whom her eye pierceth. O happy Ladon, which art
now an unperfect mirror of all perfection, canst thou ever
forget the blessedness of this impression? If thou do, then let
thy bed be turned from fine gravel to weeds and mud; if thou 125
do, let some unjust niggards make weirs to spoil thy beauty; if
thou do, let some greater river fall into thee, to take away the
name of Ladon. O Ladon, happy Ladon, rather slide than run
by her, lest thou shouldst make her legs slip from her; and
then, O happy Ladon, who would then call thee but the most 130
cursed Ladon?' But as the ladies played them in the water,
sometimes striking it with their hands, the water (making lines
in his face) seemed to smile at such beating, and with twenty
bubbles, not to be content to have the picture of their face in
large upon him, but he would in each of those bubbles set 135
forth the miniature of them.

But Zelmane, whose sight was gainsaid by nothing but the
transparent veil of Ladon, (like a chamber where a great fire
is kept, though the fire be at one stay, yet with the continuance
continually hath his heat increased) had the coals of her 140
affection so kindled with wonder, and blown with delight, that
now all her parts grudged that her eyes should do more

111. *straight:* straightway.
114. *complexion:* constitution.
120. *lothly:* reluctantly.
126. *niggards:* covetous men.
139. *at one stay:* of a constant size.

homage than they to the princess of them. In so much that
taking up the lute, her wit began to be with a divine fury
inspired; her voice would in so beloved an occasion second 145
her wit; her hands accorded the lute's music to the voice; her
panting heart danced to the music; while I think her feet did
beat the time; while her body was the room where it should be
celebrated; her soul the queen which should be delighted. And
so together went the utterance and the invention, that one 150
might judge, it was Philoclea's beauty which did speedily
write it in her eyes; or the sense thereof, which did word by
word indite it in her mind, whereto she (but as an organ) did
only lend utterance. The song was to this purpose.

> What tongue can her perfections tell, 155
> In whose each part all pens may dwell?
> Her hair fine threads of finest gold
> In curled knots man's thought to hold:
> But that her forehead says, In me
> A whiter beauty you may see. 160
> Whiter indeed; more white than snow,
> Which on cold winter's face doth grow.
> That doth present those even brows,
> Whose equal line their angles bows,
> Like to the moon when after change 165
> Her horned head abroad doth range:
> And arches be to heavenly lids,
> Whose wink each bold attempt forbids.
> For the black stars those spheres contain,
> The matchless pair, even praise doth stain. 170
> No lamp, whose light by art is got,
> No sun, which shines and seeth not,

146. *accorded:* harmonized.
152. *thereof:* i.e., of Philoclea's beauty.
163. *that:* i.e., the forehead.
164. *their angles bows:* rounds their angles.
170. *even praise doth stain:* to which no praise can do justice.

NOTES: p. 233

Can liken them without all peer,
Save one as much as other clear:
Which only thus unhappy be,   175
Because themselves they cannot see.

Her cheeks with kindly claret spread,
Aurora-like new out of bed,
Or like the fresh queen-apple's side,
Blushing at sight of Phoebus' pride.   180

Her nose, her chin pure ivory wears:
No purer than the pretty ears.
So that therein appears some blood,
Like wine and milk that mingled stood;
In whose encirclets if ye gaze,   185
Your eyes may tread a lover's maze.
But with such turns the voice to stray,
No talk untaught can find the way.
The tip no jewel needs to wear:
The tip is jewel of the ear.   190

But who those ruddy lips can miss?
Which blessed still themselves do kiss.
Rubies, cherries, and roses new,
In worth, in taste, in perfect hue:
Which never part but that they show   195
Of precious pearl the double row,
The second sweetly-fenced ward,
Her heav'nly-dewed tongue to guard,
Whence never word in vain did flow.

Fair under these doth stately grow   200
The handle of this precious work,
The neck, in which strange graces lurk.
Such be I think the sumptuous towers
Which skill doth make in princes' bowers.

177. *kindly claret:* natural red.
178. *Aurora:* the dawn-goddess.
179. *queen-apple:* an early variety of apple.
185. *encirclets:* curves.
188. *untaught:* unguarded, loose.
197. *ward:* lock (the lips being the first).

So good a say invites the eye   205
A little downward to espy
The lively clusters of her breasts,
Of Venus' babe the wanton nests:
Like pommels round of marble clear,
Where azur'd veins well mixt appear,   210
With dearest tops of porphyry.
   Betwixt these two a way doth lie,
A way more worthy beauty's fame
Than that which bears the Milky name.
This leads into the joyous field   215
Which only still doth lilies yield:
But lilies such whose native smell
The Indian odours doth excel.
Waist it is call'd, for it doth waste
Men's lives, until it be embrac'd.   220
   There may one see, and yet not see,
Her ribs in white well armed be.
More white than Neptune's foamy face,
When struggling rocks he would embrace.
   In these delights the wand'ring thought   225
Might of each side astray be brought,
But that her navel doth unite,
In curious circle, busy sight:
A dainty seal of virgin wax,
Where nothing but impression lacks.   230
   Her belly there glad sight doth fill,
Justly entitled Cupid's hill.
A hill most fit for such a master,
A spotless mine of alabaster.
Like alabaster fair and sleek,   235
But soft and supple satin-like.

      205. *say:* sample.
      209. *pommels:* ornamental balls.
      216. *still:* continually.
      218. *The Indian odours:* spices from the East Indies.

NOTES: p. 233

In that sweet seat the Boy doth sport:
Loath, I must leave his chief resort,
For such a use the world hath gotten,
The best things still must be forgotten.   240
   Yet never shall my song omit
Those thighs, for Ovid's song more fit;
Which flanked with two sugar'd flanks
Lift up their stately swelling banks,
That Albion clives in whiteness pass,   245
With haunches smooth as looking glass.
   But bow all knees, now of her knees
My tongue doth tell what fancy sees.
The knots of joy, the gems of love,
Whose motion makes all graces move.   250
Whose bought incav'd doth yield such sight
Like cunning painter shadowing white.
The gart'ring place with child-like sign
Shows easy print in metal fine.
But then again the flesh doth rise   255
In her brave calves, like crystal skies,
Whose Atlas is a smallest small,
More white than whitest bone of whall.
   There oft steals out that round clean foot,
This noble cedar's precious root: 260
In show and scent pale violets,
Whose step on earth all beauty sets.
   But back unto her back, my Muse,
Where Leda's swan his feathers mews,
Along whose ridge such bones are met,   265
Like comfits round in marchpane set.

238. *loath:* reluctantly.
239. *use:* custom.
245. *Albion clives:* English cliffs.
248. *fancy:* the poetic imagination.
251. *bought incav'd:* inward-bending curve.
254. *metal fine:* i.e., her flesh.
258. *whall:* whale.
260. *cedar:* as being the king of trees.

NOTES: p. 233

Her shoulders be like two white doves,
Perching within square royal rooves,
Which leaded are with silver skin,
Passing the hate-spot ermelin.   270
And thence those arms derived are;
The Phoenix' wings are not so rare
For faultless length, and stainless hue.

Ah woe is me, my woes renew
Now course doth lead me to her hand,   275
Of my first love the fatal band,
Where whiteness doth for ever sit:
Nature herself enamell'd it.
For there with strange compact doth lie
Warm snow, moist pearl, soft ivory.   280
There fall those sapphire-colour'd brooks,
Which conduit-like, with curious crooks,
Sweet islands make in that sweet land.
As for the fingers of the hand,
The bloody shafts of Cupid's war,   285
With amethysts they headed are.

Thus hath each part his beauty's part,
But how the Graces do impart
To all her limbs a special grace,
Becoming every time and place,   290
Which doth even beauty beautify,
And most bewitch the wretched eye,
How all this is but a fair inn
Of fairer guest which dwells within,

264. *mews:* sheds.
266. *comfits:* sugared almonds.
266. *marchpane:* marzipan, sugar-and-almond paste.
268. *rooves:* roofs.
269. *leaded:* covered (as roofs with lead).
273. *stainless:* unfading.
279. *compact:* association.
281. *sapphire-colour'd brooks:* i.e., blue veins.
282. *conduit-like:* like watercourses.
294. *fairer guest:* i.e., her soul.

NOTES: p. 234

Of whose high praise and praiseful bliss 295
Goodness the pen, heav'n paper is,
The ink immortal fame doth lend –
As I began, so must I end:
No tongue can her perfections tell,
In whose each part all pens may dwell. 300

But as Zelmane was coming to the latter end of her song, she might see the same water-spaniel which before had hunted come and fetch away one of Philoclea's gloves; whose fine proportion showed well what a dainty guest was wont there to be lodged. It was a delight to Zelmane to see that the dog was 305 therewith delighted, and so let him go a little way withal, who quickly carried it out of sight among certain trees and bushes, which were very close together. But by and by he came again, and amongst the raiments (Miso and Mopsa being preparing sheets against their coming out) the dog lighted upon a 310 little book of four or five leaves of paper, and was bearing that away too. But then Zelmane (not knowing what importance it might be of) ran after the dog, who going straight to those bushes, she might see the dog deliver it to a gentleman who secretly lay there. But she hastily coming in, the gentleman rose 315 up, and with a courteous (though sad) countenance presented himself unto her. Zelmane's eyes straight willed her mind to mark him: for she thought in her life she had never seen a man of a more goodly presence, in whom strong making took not away delicacy, nor beauty fierceness: being indeed such a 320 right manlike man as Nature, often erring, yet shows she would fain make. But when she had a while (not without admiration) viewed him, she desired him to deliver back the glove and paper, because they were the Lady Philoclea's; telling him withal, that she would not willingly let them know of his close 325 lying in that prohibited place, while they were bathing themselves; because she knew they would be mortally offended withal. 'Fair Lady,' (answered he) 'the worst of the complaint

304. *dainty guest:* i.e., her hand.
310. *sheets:* towels, bath-sheets.

NOTES: p. 234

is already past, since I feel of my fault in myself the punishment. But for these things, I assure you it was my dog's wanton 330
boldness, not my presumption.' With that he gave her back the
paper: 'But for the glove,' (said he) 'since it is my Lady
Philoclea's, give me leave to keep it, since my heart cannot
persuade itself to part from it. And I pray you tell the lady
(lady indeed of all my desires) that owes it, that I will direct 335
my life to honour this glove with serving her.' 'O villain,' (cried
out Zelmane, madded with finding an unlooked-for rival, and
that he would make her a messenger) 'dispatch' (said she) 'and
deliver it, or by the life of her that owes it, I will make thy
soul (though too base a price) pay for it.' And with that drew 340
out her sword, which Amazon-like she ever ware about her.
The gentleman retired himself into an open place from among
the bushes; and then drawing out his too, he offered to deliver
it unto her, saying withal, 'God forbid I should use my sword
against you, since (if I be not deceived) you are the same 345
famous Amazon, that both defended my Lady's just title of
beauty against the valiant Phalantus, and saved her life in
killing the lion: therefore I am rather to kiss your hands, with
acknowledging myself bound to obey you.' But this courtesy
was worse than a bastinado to Zelmane: so that again with 350
rageful eyes she bade him defend himself, for no less than his
life should answer it. 'A hard case,' (said he) 'to teach my
sword that lesson, which hath ever used to turn itself to a
shield in a lady's presence.' But Zelmane, hearkening to no
more words, began with such witty fury to pursue him with 355
blows and thrusts, that nature and virtue commanded the
gentleman to look to his safety. Yet still courtesy, that seemed
incorporate in his heart, would not be persuaded by danger to
offer any offence, but only to stand upon the best defensive
guard he could; sometimes going back, being content in that 360

329–30. *the punishment:* i.e., the pangs of love.
330. *wanton:* playful.
335. *owes:* owns.
350. *bastinado:* cudgel.
355. *witty fury:* cunning (in swordsmanship) in the service
          of anger.

NOTES: p. 234

respect to take on the figure of cowardice; sometime with strong and well-met wards; sometime cunning avoidings of his body; and sometimes feigning some blows, which himself pulled back before they needed to be withstood. And so with play did he a good while fight against the fight of Zelmane, 365 who (more spited with that courtesy, that one that did nothing should be able to resist her) burned away with choler any motions which might grow out of her own sweet disposition, determining to kill him if he fought no better; and so re-doubling her blows, drave the stranger to no other shift, than 370 to ward and go back; at that time seeming the image of inno-cency against violence. But at length he found, that both in public and private respects, who stands only upon defence, stands upon no defence: for Zelmane seeming to strike at his head, and he going to ward it withal stepped back as he was 375 accustomed, she stopped her blow in the air, and suddenly turning the point, ran full at his breast; so as he was driven with the pommel of his sword (having no other weapon of defence) to beat it down: but the thrust was so strong, that he could not so wholly beat it away but that it met with his thigh, 380 thorough which it ran. But Zelmane retiring her sword, and seeing his blood, victorious anger was conquered by the before-conquered pity; and heartily sorry and even ashamed with herself she was, considering how little he had done, who well she found could have done more. In so much that she said, 385 'Truly I am sorry for your hurt, but yourself gave the cause, both in refusing to deliver the glove, and yet not fighting as I know you could have done. But' (said she) 'because I perceive you disdain to fight with a woman, it may be before a year come about, you shall meet with a near kinsman of mine, 390 Pyrocles Prince of Macedon, and I give you my word, he for me shall maintain this quarrel against you.' 'I would' (answered

361. *figure:* appearance.
368. *motions:* feelings (of kindness).
370. *shift:* resource.
373. *stands upon:* relies upon.
378. *pommel:* knob at end of sword-hilt.

NOTES: p. 234

Amphialus) 'I had many more such hurts, to meet and know
that worthy prince, whose virtues I love and admire, though
my good destiny hath not been to see his person.'   395

But as they were so speaking, the young Ladies came, to
whom Mopsa (curious in anything but her own good behaviour)
having followed and seen Zelmane fighting, had cried what she
had seen, while they were drying themselves, and the water
(with some drops) seemed to weep, that it should part from   400
such bodies. But they careful of Zelmane (assuring themselves
that any Arcadian would bear reverence to them), Pamela with
a noble mind, and Philoclea with a loving, (hastily hiding the
beauties whereof Nature was proud and they ashamed) they
made quick work to come to save Zelmane. But already they   405
found them in talk, and Zelmane careful of his wound. But
when they saw him they knew it was their cousin german, the
famous Amphialus; whom yet with a sweet-graced bitterness
they blamed for breaking their father's commandment,
especially while themselves were in such sort retired. But   410
he craved pardon, protesting unto them that he had only been
to seek solitary places, by an extreme melancholy that had a
good while possessed him, and guided to that place by his
spaniel, where while the dog hunted in the river, he had withdrawn himself to pacify with sleep his over-watched eyes: till   415
a dream waked him, and made him see that whereof he had
dreamed (and withal not obscurely signified that he felt the
smart of his own doings). But Philoclea (that was even jealous
of herself for Zelmane) would needs have her glove, and not
without so mighty a lour as that face could yield. As for   420
Zelmane, when she knew it was Amphialus, 'Lord Amphialus,'
(said she) 'I have long desired to know you, heretofore I must
confess with more goodwill, but still with honouring your
virtue, though I love not your person: and at this time I pray

397. *curious:* busy.
401. *careful of:* anxious for.
406. *careful of his wound:* attending to Amphialus's wound.
407. *cousin german:* first cousin.
411. *protesting:* swearing.
420. *lour:* angry look.

NOTES: p. 234

you let us take care of your wound, upon condition you shall 425
hereafter promise that a more knightly combat shall be performed between us.' Amphialus answered in honourable sort,
but with such excusing himself, that more and more accused
his love to Philoclea, and provoked more hate in Zelmane. But
Mopsa had already called certain shepherds not far off (who 430
knew and well observed their limits) to come and help to carry
away Amphialus, whose wound suffered him not without
danger to strain it: and so he leaving himself with them,
departed from them, faster bleeding in his heart than at his
wound: which bound up by the sheets wherewith Philoclea had 435
been wrapped, made him thank the wound, and bless the
sword for that favour.

BOOK II, CHAPTER 17
*Zelmane's tears, and tearful ditty. Philoclea enters conference
with her. She sues, and shows herself Pyrocles. Philoclea fears
much, but loves more. Their conclusion.*

So away departed Philoclea, with a new field of fancies for her
travailing mind. For well she saw, her father was grown her 5
adverse party, and yet her fortune such, as she must favour her
rival; and the fortune of that fortune such, as neither that did
hurt her, nor any contrary mean help her.

But she walked but a little on, before she saw Zelmane lying
upon a bank, with her face so bent over Ladon that (her tears 10
falling into the water) one might have thought that she began
meltingly to be metamorphosed to the under-running river. But
by and by, with speech she made known, as well that she lived,
as that she sorrowed. 'Fair streams,' (said she) 'that do
vouchsafe in your clearness to represent unto me my blubbered 15
face, let the tribute-offer of my tears unto you procure your
stay a while with me, that I may begin yet at last to find some

2. *she:* Zelmane.
6. *adverse party:* adversary, rival.
13–14. *as well . . . as:* both . . . and.
15. *blubbered:* tear-stained.

NOTES: pp. 234–5

F

thing that pities me: and that all things of comfort and pleasure do not fly away from me. But if the violence of your spring command you to haste away, to pay your duties to your great 20 prince, the Sea, yet carry with you these few words, and let the uttermost ends of the world know them. A love more clear than yourselves, dedicated to a love (I fear) more cold than yourselves, with the clearness lays a night of sorrow upon me; and with the coldness inflames a world of fire within me.' With 25 that she took a willow stick, and wrote in a sandy bank these few verses.

Over these brooks trusting to ease mine eyes
(Mine eyes even great in labour with their tears),
I laid my face, my face wherein there lies   30
Clusters of clouds, which no sun ever clears.
    In wat'ry glass my wat'ry eyes I see:
    Sorrows ill eas'd, where sorrows painted be.

My thoughts imprison'd in my secret woes,
With flamy breath do issue oft in sound: 35
The sound to this strange air no sooner goes,
But that it doth with Echo's force rebound,
    And make me hear the plaints I would refrain:
    Thus outward helps my inward griefs maintain.

Now in this sand I would discharge my mind,   40
And cast from me part of my burd'nous cares:
But in the sand my pains foretold I find,
And see therein how well the writer fares.
    Since stream, air, sand, mine eyes and ears conspire,
    What hope to quench, where each thing blows the fire?   45

And as soon as she had written them (a new swarm of thoughts stinging her mind) she was ready with her foot to give the new-born letters both death and burial. But Philoclea

29. *great in labour with:* ready to give birth to.
36. *strange:* foreign, unfriendly.

NOTES: p. 235

(to whom delight of hearing and seeing was before a stay from
interrupting her) gave herself to be seen unto her, with such a   50
lightning of beauty upon Zelmane, that neither she could look
on nor would look off. At last Philoclea (having a little mused
how to cut the thread even, between her own hopeless affection
and her father's unbridled hope), with eyes, cheeks, and lips
(whereof each sang their part, to make up the harmony of   55
bashfulness) began to say 'My father, to whom I owe myself,
and therefore —', when Zelmane (making a womanish habit to
be the armour of her boldness, giving up her life to the lips of
Philoclea, and taking it again by the sweetness of those kisses)
humbly besought her to keep her speech for a while within the   60
paradise of her mind. For well she knew her father's errand,
who should soon receive a sufficient answer. But now she
demanded leave not to lose this long-sought-for commodity of
time, to ease her heart thus far, that if in her agonies her
destiny was to be condemned by Philoclea's mouth, at least   65
Philoclea might know whom she had condemned. Philoclea
easily yielded to grant her own desire: and so making the green
bank the situation, and the river the prospect, of the two most
beautiful buildings of Nature, Zelmane doubting how to
begin, though her thoughts already had run to the end, with a   70
mind fearing the unworthiness of every word that should be
presented to her ears, at length brought it forth in this manner.

'Most beloved Lady, the incomparable excellencies of yourself (waited on by the greatness of your estate), and the importance of the thing (whereon my life consisteth), doth require   75
both many ceremonies before the beginning, and many circumstances in the uttering my speech, both bold and fearful. But
the small opportunity of envious occasion (by the malicious eye
hateful Love doth cast upon me) and the extreme bent of my

53. *cut the thread even:* express something midway (between the
    two extremes).
57. *a womanish habit:* i.e., of greeting with a kiss.
69. *buildings of Nature:* i.e., their bodies.
72. *her:* Philoclea's.
75. *the thing:* my subject.
79. *bent:* inclination.

affection (which will either break out in words, or break my 80
heart) compel me, not only to embrace the smallest time, but to
pass by the respects due unto you, in respect of your poor
caitiff's life, who is now or never to be preserved. I do therefore
vow unto you, hereafter nevermore to omit all dutiful form,
do you only now vouchsafe to hear the matter of a mind most 85
perplexed. If ever the sound of love have come to your ears, or
if ever you have understood what force it hath had to conquer
the strongest hearts, and change the most settled estates:
receive here an example of those strange tragedies; one, that
in himself containeth the particularities of all those mis- 90
fortunes: and from henceforth believe that such a thing may
be, since you shall see it is. You shall see (I say) a living image
and a present story of what Love can do, when he is bent to
ruin.

'But alas, whither goest thou, my tongue? or how doth my 95
heart consent to adventure the revealing his nearest-touching
secret? But peace, Fear, thou comest too late, when already the
harm is taken. Therefore I say again, O only Princess, attend
here a miserable miracle of affection. Behold here before your
eyes Pyrocles, Prince of Macedon, whom you only have 100
brought to this game of Fortune, and unused metamorphosis:
whom you only have made neglect his country, forget his
father, and lastly, forsake to be Pyrocles: the same Pyrocles
who (you heard) was betrayed by being put in a ship, which
being burned, Pyrocles was drowned. O most true presage: 105
for these traitors, my eyes, putting me into a ship of Desire,
which daily burneth, those eyes (I say) which betrayed me, will
never leave till they have drowned me. But be not, be not,
(most excellent Lady) you that Nature hath made to be the
lodestar of comfort, be not the rock of shipwreck: you whom 110
virtue hath made the princess of felicity, be not the minister of
ruin: you, whom my choice hath made the goddess of my

83. *caitiff*: wretch, prisoner.
85. *do you only*: if you will only.
101. *game*: toy, object of mockery.
111. *minister*: instrument.

safety, O let not, let not from you be poured upon me destruction. Your fair face hath many tokens in it of amazement at my
words: think then what his amazement is, from whence they 115
come: since no words can carry with them the life of the inward
feeling. I desire, that my desire may be weighed in the balances
of Honour, and let Virtue hold them. For if the highest love in
no base person may aspire to grace, then may I hope your
beauty will not be without pity. If otherwise you be (alas, but 120
let it never be so) resolved, yet shall not my death be comfortless, receiving it by your sentence.'

The joy which wrought into Pygmalion's mind, while he
found his beloved image was softer and warmer in his folded
arms, till at length it accomplished his gladness with a perfect 125
woman's shape (still beautified with the former perfections),
was even such, as by each degree of Zelmane's words creepingly
entered into Philoclea: till her pleasure was fully made up with
the manifesting of his being; which was such as in hope did
overcome Hope. Yet Doubt would fain have played his part in 130
her mind, and called in question how she should be assured
that Zelmane was Pyrocles. But Love straight stood up and
deposed, that a lie could not come from the mouth of Zelmane.
Besides, a certain spark of honour, which rose in her well-
disposed mind, made her fear to be alone with him, with whom 135
alone she desired to be (with all the other contradictions
growing in those minds which neither absolutely climb the rock
of Virtue nor freely sink into the sea of Vanity); but that spark
soon gave place, or at least gave no more light in her mind than
a candle doth in the sun's presence. But even sick with a surfeit 140
of joy, and fearful of she knew not what (as he that newly finds
huge treasures doubts whether he sleep or no; or like a fearful
deer, which then looks most about, when he comes to the best
feed), with a shrugging kind of tremor through all her principal
parts, she gave these affectionate words for answer. 'Alas, how 145
painful a thing it is to a divided mind to make a well-joined
answer! How hard it is to bring inward shame to outward

129. *manifesting of his being:* declaration of his identity.
133. *deposed:* testified.

NOTES: p. 235

confession! And what handsomeness, trow you, can be observed in that speech, which is made one knows not to whom? Shall I say O Zelmane? Alas, your words be against it. 150 Shall I say Prince Pyrocles? Wretch that I am, your show is manifest against it. But this, this I may well say: if I had continued as I ought Philoclea, you had either never been or ever been Zelmane; you had either never attempted this change, set on with hope, or never discovered it, stopped with 155 despair. But I fear me, my behaviour ill governed gave you the first comfort; I fear me, my affection ill hid hath given you this last assurance; I fear indeed, the weakness of my government before, made you think such a mask would be grateful unto me; and my weaker government since, makes you to pull 160 off the visor. What shall I do then? Shall I seek far-fetched inventions? Shall I labour to lay marble colours over my ruinous thoughts? or rather, though the pureness of my virgin mind be stained, let me keep the true simplicity of my word. True it is, alas, too true it is, O Zelmane (for so I love to call 165 thee, since in that name my love first began, and in the shade of that name my love shall best lie hidden), that even while so thou wert (what eye bewitched me I know not), my passions were fitter to desire, than to be desired. Shall I say then, I am sorry, or that my love must be turned to hate, since thou art 170 turned to Pyrocles? How may that well be, since when thou wert Zelmane, the despair thou mightest not be thus did most torment me? Thou hast then the victory: use it with virtue. Thy virtue won me: with virtue preserve me. Dost thou love me? Keep me then still worthy to be beloved.'   175

Then held she her tongue, and cast down a self-accusing look, finding that in herself she had (as it were) shot out of the bow of her affection a more quick opening of her mind than she minded to have done. But Pyrocles, so carried up with

151. *show:* appearance.
154–5. *this change:* this disguise.
158. *assurance:* cause of boldness.
158–9. *government:* behaviour, self-control.
172. *mightest not be thus:* couldst not be a man.

NOTES: p. 235

joy that he did not envy the gods' felicity, presented her with 180
some jewels of right princely value, as some little tokens of
his love and quality: and withal showed her letters from his
father King Euarchus unto him, which even in the sea had
amongst his jewels been preserved. But little needed those
proofs to one who would have fallen out with herself rather 185
than make any contrary conjectures to Zelmane's speeches; so
that with such embracements, as it seemed their souls desired
to meet, and their hearts to kiss, as their mouths did, they
passed the promise of marriage: which fain Pyrocles would
have sealed with the chief arms of his desire, but Philoclea 190
commanded the contrary.

BOOK III, CHAPTER 2
The young Ladies met, invited to the country-wenches' sports, go
thither, there are taken, and thence carried to Amphialus' castle.
Their entertainment there. Cecropia's auricular confession of her
proud carriage in prosperity, and ambitious practices in adversity.
Amphialus his affection in these actions.   5

What this would have wrought in her, she herself could not
tell: for, before her reason could moderate the disputation
between favour and faultiness, her sister and Miso called her
down to entertain Zelmane, who was come to visit the two
sisters; about whom, as about two poles, the sky of beauty was 10
turned: while Gynecia wearied her bed with her melancholy
sickness, and made Miso's shrewdness (who like a spirit set to
keep a treasure barred Zelmane from any further conference)
to be the lieutenant of her jealousy: both she and her husband
driving Zelmane to such a strait of resolution, either of 15
impossible granting or dangerous refusing, as the best escape
she had was (as much as she could) to avoid their company.
So as, this day, being the fourth day after the uproar, (Basilius

182. *quality:* rank.
   2. *taken:* captured.
   6. *this:* Musidorus's letter (see note).
  12. *shrewdness:* ill-nature.

NOTES: p. 236

being with his sick wife, conferring upon such examinations as Philanax and other of his noblemen had made of this late 20 sedition, all touching Cecropia with vehement suspicion of giving either flame or fuel unto it) Zelmane came with her body to find her mind, which was gone long before her, and had gotten his seat in Philoclea: who now with a bashful cheerfulness (as though she were ashamed that she could not choose 25 but be glad) joined with her sister in making much of Zelmane.

And so as they sat devising how to give more feathers to the wings of Time, there came to the lodge door six maids, all in one livery of scarlet petticoats, which were tucked up almost to their knees, the petticoats themselves being in many places 30 garnished with leaves, their legs naked, saving that above the ankles they had little black silk laces, upon which did hang a few silver bells; like which they had a little above their elbows, upon their bare arms. Upon their hair they ware garlands of roses and gilliflowers; and the hair was so dressed, as that 35 came again above the garlands, interchanging a mutual covering, so as it was doubtful whether the hair dressed the garlands, or the garlands dressed the hair. Their breasts liberal to the eye: the face of the foremost of them, in excellency fair; and of the rest lovely, if not beautiful; and beautiful might have been, 40 if they had not suffered greedy Phoebus over-often and hard to kiss them. Their countenances full of a graceful gravity; so as, the gesture matched with the apparel, it might seem a wanton modesty, and an enticing soberness. Each of them had an instrument of music in their hands, which consorting their 45 well-pleasing tunes, did charge each ear with unsensibleness that did not lend itself unto them. The music entering alone into the lodge, the Ladies were all desirous to see from whence so pleasant a guest was come: and therefore went out together; where, before they could take the pains to doubt, much less to 50 ask the question of their quality, the fairest of them (with a gay, but yet discreet demeanour) in this sort spake unto them.

35. *gilliflowers:* clove-scented pinks.
45. *consorting:* harmoniously accompanying.
50. *doubt:* suspect.

NOTES: p. 236

'Most excellent Ladies (whose excellencies have power to make
cities envy these woods, and solitariness to be accounted the
sweetest company), vouchsafe our message your gracious hear- 55
ing, which as it comes from Love, so comes it from lovely
persons. The maids of all this coast of Arcadia, understanding
the often access that certain shepherds of these quarters are
allowed to have in this forbidden place, and that their rural
sports are not disdained of you, have been stirred with emula- 60
tion to them, and affection to you, to bring forth something
which might as well breed your contentment: and therefore
hoping that the goodness of their intention, and the hurtlessness
of their sex shall excuse the breach of the commandment in
coming to this place unsent-for, they chose out us, to invite 65
both your princely parents and yourselves to a place in the
woods about half a mile hence: where they have provided
some such sports, as they trust your gracious acceptations will
interpret to be delightful. We have been at the other lodge,
but finding them there busied in weightier affairs, our trust is 70
that you yet will not deny the shining of your eyes upon us.'
The Ladies stood in some doubt whether they should go or
not, lest Basilius might be angry withal. But Miso (that had
been at none of the pastorals, and had a great desire to lead
her old senses abroad to some pleasure) told them plainly, they 75
should nor will nor choose but go thither, and make the honest
country people know that they were not so squeamish as folks
thought of them. The Ladies, glad to be warranted by her
authority, with a smiling humbleness obeyed her: Pamela only
casting a seeking look, whether she could see Dorus, who, poor 80
wretch, wandered half mad for sorrow in the woods, crying for
pardon of her who could not hear him but indeed was grieved
for his absence, having given the wound to him through her
own heart. But so the three Ladies and Miso went with those
six nymphs, conquering the length of the way with the force of 85
music, leaving only Mopsa behind, who disgraced weeping
with her countenance, because her mother would not suffer her

76. *will:* wish.
77. *squeamish:* dainty, stand-offish.

NOTES: p. 236

to show her new-scoured face among them. But the place
appointed (as they thought) met them half in their way, so well
were they pleased with the sweet tunes and pretty conversation   90
of their inviters. There found they in the midst of the thickest
part of the wood a little square place, not burdened with trees,
but with a board covered, and beautified with the pleasantest
fruits that sun-burned Autumn could deliver unto them. The
maids besought the Ladies to sit down, and taste of the swelling   95
grapes, which seemed great with child of Bacchus, and of the
divers coloured plums, which gave the eye a pleasant taste
before they came to the mouth. The Ladies would not show to
scorn their provision, but ate, and drank a little of their cool
wine, which seemed to laugh for joy to come to such lips.   100

But after the collation was ended, and that they looked for
the coming forth of such devices as were prepared for them,
there rushed out of the woods twenty armed men, who round
about environed them, and laying hold of Zelmane before she
could draw her sword, and taking it from her, put hoods over   105
the heads of all four, and so muffled by force set them on
horseback and carried them away; the sisters in vain crying for
succour, while Zelmane's heart was rent in pieces with rage of
the injury, and disdain of her fortune. But when they had
carried them a four or five mile further, they left Miso with   110
a gag in her mouth, and bound hand and foot, so as to take
her fortune; and brought the three Ladies (by that time that
the night seemed with her silence to conspire to their treason)
to a castle about ten mile off from the lodges; where they were
fain to take a boat which waited for them. For the castle stood   115
in the midst of a great lake, upon a high rock, where partly by
art, but principally by nature, it was by all men esteemed
impregnable.

> 93. *a board covered:* a table laid.
> 96. *great with child of Bacchus:* pregnant with wine.
> 98. *show:* seem.
> 99. *their provision:* what the girls had provided.
> 101. *collation:* refreshment.
> 102. *devices:* entertainments.

NOTES: p. 236

But at the castle gate their faces were discovered, and there were met with a great number of torches, after whom the sisters 120 knew their aunt-in-law Cecropia. But that sight increased the deadly terror of the Princesses, looking for nothing but death, since they were in the power of the wicked Cecropia: who yet came unto them, making courtesy the outside of mischief, and desiring them not to be discomforted, for they were in a place 125 dedicated to their service. Philoclea (with a look where love shined through the mist of fear) besought her to be good unto them, having never deserved evil of her. But Pamela's high heart disdaining humbleness to injury, 'Aunt,' (said she) 'what you have determined of us I pray you do it speedily: for my 130 part I look for no service, where I find violence.'

But Cecropia (using no more words with them) conveyed them all three to several lodgings (Zelmane's heart so swelling with spite, that she could not bring forth a word) and so left them: first taking from them their knives, because they should 135 do themselves no hurt, before she had determined of them; and then giving such order that they wanted nothing but liberty and comfort, she went to her son, who yet kept his bed, because of the wound he had received of Zelmane, and told him whom now he had in his power. Amphialus was but even 140 then returned from far countries, where he had won immortal fame, both of courage and courtesy, when he met with the Princesses and was hurt by Zelmane, so as he was utterly ignorant of all his mother's wicked devices; to which he would never have consented, being (like a rose out of a briar) an 145 excellent son of an evil mother: and now when he heard of this, was as much amazed as if he had seen the sun fall to the earth. And therefore desired his mother that she would tell him the whole discourse, how all these matters had happened.

'Son,' (said she) 'I will do it willingly, and since all is 150 done for you, I will hide nothing from you. And howsoever I might be ashamed to tell it strangers, who would think it

119. *discovered:* uncovered.
124. *outside:* cover, disguise.
129. *disdaining humbleness to injury:* scorning to behave humbly to her oppressor.

wickedness, yet what is done for your sake (how evil soever to others) to you is virtue. To begin then even with the beginning, this doting fool Basilius that now reigns, having lived 155 unmarried till he was nigh threescore years old (and in all his speeches affirming, and in all his doings assuring, that he never would marry), made all the eyes of this country to be bent upon your father, his only brother (but the younger by thirty years), as upon the undoubted successor: being indeed a man worthy 160 to reign, thinking nothing enough for himself; where this goose (you see) puts down his head before there be anything near to touch him. So that he holding place and estimation as heir of Arcadia, obtained me of my father the King of Argos, his brother helping to the conclusion with protesting his bachelorly 165 intention: for else you may be sure the King of Argos nor his daughter would have suffered their royal blood to be stained with the base name of subjection. So that I came into this country as apparent Princess thereof, and accordingly was courted and followed of all the Ladies of this country. My port 170 and pomp did well become a King of Argos' daughter: in my presence their tongues were turned into ears, and their ears were captives unto my tongue. Their eyes admired my majesty, and happy was he or she on whom I would suffer the beams thereof to fall. Did I go to church? it seemed the very Gods 175 waited for me, their devotions not being solemnized till I was ready. Did I walk abroad to see any delight? nay, my walking was the delight itself, for to it was the concourse; one thrusting upon another, who might show himself most diligent and serviceable towards me. My sleeps were inquired after, and 180 my wakings never unsaluted: the very gate of my house full of principal persons, who were glad if their presents had received a grateful acceptation. And in this felicity wert thou born, the very earth submitting itself unto thee to be trodden on as by his Prince; and to that pass had my husband's virtue (by my good 185

161. *where this goose:* whereas Basilius.
169. *apparent Princess:* Queen-apparent.
178. *concourse:* assembly, flocking.

NOTES: p. 236

help) within short time brought it, with a plot we laid, as we should not have needed to have waited the tedious work of a natural end of Basilius; when the heavens (I think envying my great felicity) then stopped thy father's breath, when he breathed nothing but power and sovereignty. Yet did not thy 190 orphancy, or my widowhood, deprive us of the delightful prospect which the hill of honour doth yield, while expectation of thy succession did bind dependencies unto us.

'But before (my son) thou wert come to the age to feel the sweetness of authority, this beast (whom I can never name 195 with patience) falsely and foolishly married this Gynecia, then a young girl, and brought her to sit above me in all feasts, to turn her shoulder to me-ward in all our solemnities. It is certain, it is not so great a spite to be surmounted by strangers as by one's own allies. Think then what my mind was, since 200 withal there is no question, the fall is greater from the first to the second, than from the second to the undermost. The rage did swell in my heart, so much the more as it was fain to be suppressed in silence, and disguised with humbleness. But above all the rest, the grief of griefs was when with these two 205 daughters (now thy prisoners) she cut off all hope of thy succession. It was a tedious thing to me, that my eyes should look lower than anybody's, that (myself being by) another's voice than mine should be more respected. But it was insupportable unto me, to think that not only I, but thou shouldst spend all 210 thy time in such misery, and that the sun should see my eldest son less than a Prince. And though I had been a saint I could not choose, finding the change this change of fortune bred unto me, for now from the multitude of followers, silence grew to be at my gate, and absence in my presence. The guess of 215 my mind could prevail more before, than now many of my earnest requests. And thou (my dear son) by the fickle multitude no more than an ordinary person, born of the mud of the

193. *bind dependencies unto us:* secure us a following.
203. *fain:* obliged.
207. *a tedious thing:* a trial, a burden.
215–16. *the guess of my mind:* people's guessing of my wishes.

people, regarded. But I (remembering that in all miseries weeping becomes fools, and practice wise folks) have tried divers 220 means to pull us out of the mire of subjection. And though many times fortune failed me, yet did I never fail myself. Wild beasts I kept in a cave hard by the lodges, which I caused by night to be fed in the place of their pastorals, I as then living in my house hard by the place; and against the hour they 225 were to meet, having kept the beasts without meat, then let them loose, knowing that they would seek their food there, and devour what they found. But blind Fortune, hating sharp-sighted inventions, made them unluckily to be killed. After, I used my servant Clinias to stir a notable tumult of country 230 people: but those louts were too gross instruments for delicate conceits. Now lastly, finding Philanax his examinations grow dangerous, I thought to play double or quit; and with a sleight I used of my fine-witted wench Artesia, with other maids of mine, would have sent these goodly inheritrixes of Arcadia to 235 have pleaded their cause before Pluto, but that over-fortunately for them, you made me know the last day how vehemently this childish passion of love doth torment you. Therefore I have brought them unto you, yet wishing rather hate than love in you. For Hate often begetteth victory: Love commonly is the 240 instrument of subjection. It is true, that I would also by the same practice have entrapped the parents, but my maids failed of it, not daring to tarry long about it. But this sufficeth, since (these being taken away) you are the undoubted inheritor, and Basilius will not long overlive this loss.' 245

'O Mother,' (said Amphialus) 'speak not of doing them hurt, no more than to mine eyes, or my heart, or if I have anything more dear than eyes or heart unto me. Let others find what sweetness they will in ever fearing, because they are ever feared: for my part, I will think myself highly entitled, if I 250 may be once by Philoclea accepted for a servant.' 'Well,' (said Cecropia) 'I would I had borne you of my mind, as well

220. *becomes:* suits.
226. *meat:* food.
231–2. *delicate conceits:* subtle intellects.

as of my body: then should you not have sunk under these base
weaknesses. But since you have tied your thoughts in so wilful
a knot, it is happy my policy hath brought matters to such a 255
pass, as you may both enjoy affection, and upon that build
your sovereignty.' 'Alas,' (said Amphialus) 'my heart would
fain yield you thanks for setting me in the way of felicity, but
that fear kills them in me, before they are fully born. For if
Philoclea be displeased, how can I be pleased? If she count it 260
unkindness, shall I give tokens of kindness? Perchance she
condemns me of this action, and shall I triumph? Perchance
she drowns now the beauties I love with sorrowful tears, and
where is then my rejoicing?' 'You have reason,' (said Cecropia,
with a feigned gravity); 'I will therefore send her away 265
presently, that her contentment may be recovered.' 'No, good
Mother' (said Amphialus); 'since she is here, I would not for
my life constrain presence, but rather would I die than consent
to absence.' 'Pretty intricate follies!' (said Cecropia); 'But get
you up, and see how you can prevail with her, while I go to the 270
other sister. For after we shall have our hands full to defend
ourselves, if Basilius hap to besiege us.' But remembering herself, she turned back, and asked him what he would have done
with Zelmane, since now he might be revenged of his hurt.
'Nothing but honourably,' (answered Amphialus) 'having 275
deserved no other of me, especially being (as I hear) greatly
cherished of Philoclea. And therefore I could wish they were
lodged together.' 'O no,' (said Cecropia). 'Company confirms
resolutions, and loneliness breeds a weariness of one's thoughts,
and so a sooner consenting to reasonable proffers.'   280

258–9. *but that:* were it not that.
264. *have reason:* are right.
271. *after:* afterwards.

BOOK III, CHAPTER 3

Amphialus' addressing him to Philoclea. Her melancholy habit.
His humble suit. Her pitiful answer: and his compassionate reply.
Their parting with cold comfort.

But Amphialus (taking of his mother Philoclea's knives, which
he kept as a relic, since she had worn them) gat up, and calling   5
for his richest apparel, nothing seemed sumptuous enough for
his mistress's eyes: and that which was costly, he feared were
not dainty; and though the invention were delicate, he misdoubted the making. As careful he was too of the colour; lest if
gay, he might seem to glory in his injury, and her wrong; if   10
mourning, it might strike some evil presage unto her of her
fortune. At length he took a garment more rich than glaring,
the ground being black velvet, richly embroidered with great
pearl and precious stones, but they set so among certain tuffs of
cypress, that the cypress was like black clouds, through which   15
the stars might yield a dark lustre. About his neck he ware a
broad and gorgeous collar; whereof the pieces interchangeably
answering, the one was of diamonds and pearl, set with a white
enamel, so as by the cunning of the workman it seemed like a
shining ice, and the other piece being of rubies and opals had a   20
fiery glistering, which he thought pictured the two passions of
fear and desire, wherein he was enchained. His hurt (not yet
fully well) made him a little halt, but he strave to give the best
grace he could unto his halting.

And in that sort he went to Philoclea's chamber: whom he   25
found (because her chamber was over-lightsome) sitting of that
side of her bed which was from the window; which did cast
such a shadow upon her, as a good painter would bestow upon
Venus, when under the trees she bewailed the murther of
Adonis: her hands and fingers (as it were) indented one within   30

1. *habit:* condition.
4. *of:* from.
14. *tuffs:* tufts.
17–18. *interchangeably answering:* arranged in alternating pattern.
23. *halt:* limp.
30. *indented:* interlaced.

NOTES: pp. 236–7

the other: her shoulder leaning to her bed's head, and over her head a scarf, which did eclipse almost half her eyes, which under it fixed their beams upon the wall by, with so steady a manner, as if in that place they might well change, but not mend their object: and so remained they a good while after his coming in, he not daring to trouble her, nor she perceiving him, till that (a little varying her thoughts something quickening her senses) she heard him as he happed to stir his upper garment: and perceiving him, rose up, with a demeanour where in the book of beauty there was nothing to be read but sorrow; for kindness was blotted out, and anger was never there.

But Amphialus that had entrusted his memory with long and forcible speeches, found it so locked up in amazement, that he could pick nothing out of it, but the beseeching her to take what was done in good part, and to assure herself there was nothing but honour meant unto her person. But she making no other answer, but letting her hands fall one from the other, which before were joined, (with eyes something cast aside, and a silent sigh) gave him to understand, that considering his doings, she thought his speech as full of incongruity as her answer would be void of purpose. Whereupon he kneeling down, and kissing her hand (which she suffered with a countenance witnessing captivity, but not kindness), he besought her to have pity of him, whose love went beyond the bounds of conceit, much more of uttering: that in her hands the balance of his life or death did stand; whereto the least motion of hers would serve to determine, she being indeed the mistress of his life, and he her eternal slave; and with true vehemency besought her that he might hear her speak, whereupon she suffered her sweet breath to turn itself into these kind of words.

'Alas, cousin,' (said she) 'what shall my tongue be able to do, which is informed by the ears one way, and by the eyes another? You call for pity, and use cruelty; you say you love me, and yet do the effects of enmity. You affirm your death is in my hands, but you have brought me to so near a degree to death as, when you will, you may lay death upon me: so that

33. *by:* beside.
55. *conceit:* thought.

while you say I am mistress of your life, I am not mistress of
mine own. You entitle yourself my slave, but I am sure I am
yours. If then violence, injury, terror, and depriving of that
which is more dear than life itself, liberty, be fit orators for　70
affection, you may expect that I will be easily persuaded. But if
the nearness of our kindred breed any remorse in you, or there
be any such thing in you, which you call love toward me, then
let not my fortune be disgraced with the name of imprisonment: let not my heart waste itself by being vexed with feeling　75
evil, and fearing worse. Let not me be a cause of my parents'
woeful destruction; but restore me to myself; and so doing I
shall account I have received myself of you. And what I say for
myself, I say for my dear sister, and my friend Zelmane: for I
desire no well-being, without they may be partakers.' With that　80
her tears rained down from her heavenly eyes, and seemed to
water the sweet and beautiful flowers of her face.

But Amphialus was like the poor woman, who loving a tame
doe she had above all earthly things, having long played withal,
and made it feed at her hand and lap, is constrained at last by　85
famine (all her flock being spent, and she fallen into extreme
poverty) to kill the deer to sustain her life. Many a pitiful look
doth she cast upon it, and many a time doth she draw back her
hand before she can give the stroke. For even so Amphialus by
a hunger-starved affection was compelled to offer this injury,　90
and yet the same affection made him with a tormenting grief
think unkindness in himself, that he could find in his heart any
way to restrain her freedom. But at length, neither able to
grant nor deny, he thus answered her. 'Dear Lady,' (said he)
'I will not say unto you (how justly soever I may do it) that I am　95
neither author nor accessory unto this your withholding. For
since I do not redress it, I am as faulty as if I had begun it. But
this I protest unto you (and this protestation of mine, let the
heavens hear, and if I lie, let them answer me with a deadly
thunderbolt), that in my soul I wish I had never seen the light,　100
or rather, that I had never had a father to beget such a child,
than that by my means those eyes should overflow their own

96. *withholding:* confinement.

beauties, than by my means the sky of your virtue should be overclouded with sorrow. But woe is me, most excellent Lady, I find myself most willing to obey you: neither truly do mine 105 ears receive the least word you speak with any less reverence than as absolute and unresistible commandments. But alas, that tyrant Love (which now possesseth the hold of all my life and reason) will no way suffer it. It is Love, it is Love, not I, which disobey you. What then shall I say, but that I, who am 110 ready to lie under your feet; to venture, nay to lose my life at your least commandment, I am not the stay of your freedom, but Love, Love, which ties you in your own knots. It is you yourself, that imprison yourself: it is your beauty which makes these castle walls embrace you: it is your own eyes which 115 reflect upon themselves this injury. Then is there no other remedy, but that you some way vouchsafe to satisfy this Love's vehemency; which (since it grew in yourself) without question you shall find it (far more than I) tractable.'

But with these words Philoclea fell to so extreme a quaking, 120 and her lively whiteness did degenerate to so dead a paleness, that Amphialus feared some dangerous trance: so that taking her hand, and feeling that it (which was wont to be one of the chief firebrands of Cupid) had all the sense of it wrapped up in coldness, he began humbly to beseech her to put away all 125 fear, and to assure herself upon the vow he made thereof unto God, and herself, that the uttermost forces he would ever employ to conquer her affection, should be Desire and Desert. That promise brought Philoclea again to herself, so that slowly lifting up her eyes upon him, with a countenance ever 130 courteous, but then languishing, she told him, that he should do well to do so, if indeed he had ever tasted what true love was; for that where now she did bear him goodwill, she should (if he took any other way) hate, and abhor the very thought of him: assuring him withal, that though his mother had taken 135 away her knives, yet the house of Death had so many doors, as she would easily fly into it, if ever she found her honour endangered.

121. *lively*: belonging to life.

Amphialus having the cold ashes of Care cast upon the coals of Desire, leaving some of his mother's gentlewomen to wait 140 upon Philoclea, himself indeed a prisoner to his prisoner, and making all his authority to be but a footstool to humbleness, went from her to his mother. To whom with words which affection endited, but amazement uttered, he delivered what had passed between him and Philoclea: beseeching her to try 145 what her persuasions could do with her, while he gave order for all such things as were necessary against such forces as he looked daily Basilius would bring before his castle. His mother bade him quiet himself, for she doubted not to take fit times. But that the best way was, first to let her own passion a little 150 tire itself.

BOOK III, CHAPTER 6
Fresh motives to Philoclea. Cecropia's new fetch to attempt Pamela. Pamela's prayer, and saint-like graces in it. Her aunt's fruitless arguments.

But neither her witty words in an enemy, nor those words made more than eloquent with passing through such lips, could 5 prevail in Cecropia, no more than her persuasions could win Philoclea to disavow her former vow, or to leave the prisoner Zelmane for the commanding Amphialus. So that both sides being desirous, and neither granters, they brake off conference, Cecropia sucking up more and more spite out of her denial, 10 which yet for her son's sake she disguised with a visard of kindness, leaving no office unperformed which might either witness or endear her son's affection. Whatsoever could be imagined likely to please her was with liberal diligence performed: musics at her window, and especially such musics as 15 might (with doleful embassage) call the mind to think of sorrow,

144. *endited:* composed.
4. *witty:* wise.
11. *visard:* mask.

NOTES: p. 237

and think of it with sweetness; with ditties so sensibly expressing Amphialus' case, that every word seemed to be but a
diversifying of the name of Amphialus. Daily presents, as it
were oblations to pacify an angry deity, sent unto her: wherein,   20
if the workmanship of the form had striven with the sumptuous-
ness of the matter, as much did the invention in the application
contend to have the chief excellency: for they were as so
many stories of his disgraces, and her perfections; where the
richness did invite the eyes, the fashion did entertain the eyes,   25
and the device did teach the eyes the present misery of the
presenter himself, awefully serviceable: which was the more
notable, as his authority was manifest. And for the bondage
wherein she lived, all means used to make known, that if it
were a bondage, it was a bondage only knit in love-knots. But   30
in heart already understanding no language but one, the music
wrought indeed a dolefulness, but it was a dolefulness to be in
his power: the ditty intended for Amphialus, she translated to
Zelmane: the presents seemed so many tedious clogs of a
thralled obligation: and his service, the more diligent it was,   35
the more it did exprobate (as she thought) unto her, her unworthy estate: that even he that did her service, had authority
of commanding her, only construing her servitude in his own
nature, esteeming it a right, and a right bitter servitude: so
that all their shots (how well soever levelled) being carried   40
awry from the mark by the storm of her mislike, the Prince
Amphialus affectionately languished, and Cecropia spitefully
cunning, disdained at the barrenness of their success.

Which willingly Cecropia would have revenged, but that she
saw her hurt could not be divided from her son's mischief: 45

16. *embassage:* embassy.
17. *sensibly:* feelingly.
22. *invention:* ingenuity.
24. *disgraces:* wretchednesses.
27. *awefully serviceable:* proffering his service with awe.
36. *exprobate:* show to her shame.
41–42. *affectionately languished:* languishing with love.
43. *disdained at:* disliked.
45. *mischief:* harm.

NOTES: p. 237

wherefore, she bethought herself to attempt Pamela, whose
beauty being equal, she hoped, if she might be won, that her
son's thoughts would rather rest on a beautiful gratefulness,
than still be tormented with a disdaining beauty. Wherefore,
giving new courage to her wicked inventions, and using the   50
more industry, because she had missed in this, and taking even
precepts of prevailing in Pamela, by her failing in Philoclea,
she went to her chamber, and (according to her own ungracious
method of subtle proceeding) stood listening at the door,
because that out of the circumstance of her present behaviour   55
there might kindly arise a fit beginning of her intended
discourse.

And so she might perceive that Pamela did walk up and
down, full of deep (though patient) thoughts. For her look and
countenance was settled, her pace soft, and almost still of one   60
measure, without any passionate gesture or violent motion: till
at length (as it were) awakening, and strengthening herself,
'Well,' (said she) 'yet this is the best, and of this I am sure,
that howsoever they wrong me, they cannot overmaster God.
No darkness blinds his eyes, no jail bars him out. To whom   65
then else should I fly but to him for succour?' And therewith
kneeling down, even in the same place where she stood, she
thus said. 'O all-seeing Light, and eternal Life of all things, to
whom nothing is either so great, that it may resist; or so small,
that it is contemned: look upon my misery with thine eye of   70
mercy, and let thine infinite power vouchsafe to limit out some
proportion of deliverance unto me, as to thee shall seem most
convenient. Let not injury, O Lord, triumph over me, and let
my faults by thy hand be corrected, and make not mine unjust
enemy the minister of thy justice. But yet, my God, if in thy   75
wisdom, this be the aptest chastisement for my inexcusable
folly; if this low bondage be fittest for my over-high desires;

47. *equal:* i.e., to Philoclea's.
52. *precepts:* lessons (from experience).
55. *her:* Pamela's.
56. *kindly:* naturally.
56. *her:* Cecropia's.

if the pride of my not-enough-humble heart be thus to be broken, O Lord, I yield unto thy will, and joyfully embrace what sorrow thou wilt have me suffer. Only thus much let me 80 crave of thee (let my craving, O Lord, be accepted of thee, since even that proceeds from thee), let me crave, even by the noblest title which in my greatest affliction I may give myself, that I am thy creature, and by thy goodness (which is thyself), that thou wilt suffer some beam of thy majesty so to shine into 85 my mind, that it may still depend confidently upon thee. Let calamity be the exercise, but not the overthrow of my virtue: let their power prevail, but prevail not to destruction; let my greatness be their prey: let my pain be the sweetness of their revenge: let them (if so it seem good unto thee) vex me with 90 more and more punishment. But, O Lord, let never their wickedness have such a hand, but that I may carry a pure mind in a pure body.' (And pausing a while) 'And O most gracious Lord,' (said she) 'what ever become of me, preserve the virtuous Musidorus.' 95

The other part Cecropia might well hear, but this latter prayer for Musidorus her heart held it, as so jewel-like a treasure that it would scarce trust her own lips withal. But this prayer, sent to heaven from so heavenly a creature, with such a fervent grace as if Devotion had borrowed her body to make of 100 itself a most beautiful representation; with her eyes so lifted to the sky-ward, that one would have thought they had begun to fly thitherward, to take their place among their fellow stars; her naked hands raising up their whole length, and as it were kissing one another, as if the right had been the picture of Zeal 105 and the left of Humbleness, which both united themselves to make their suits more acceptable. Lastly, all her senses being rather tokens than instruments of her inward motions, altogether had so strange a working power, that even the hard-hearted wickedness of Cecropia, if it found not a love of that 110

87. *exercise:* trial, test.
92. *such a hand:* such power.
98. *it:* her heart.

NOTES: p. 237

goodness, yet it felt an abashment at that goodness; and if she had not a kindly remorse, yet had she an irksome accusation of her own naughtiness, so that she was put from the bias of her fore-intended lesson. For well she found there was no way at that time to take that mind, but with some at least image of 115 Virtue, and what the figure thereof was her heart knew not.

Yet did she prodigally spend her uttermost eloquence, leaving no argument unproved, which might with any force invade her excellent judgement: the justness of the request, being but for marriage; the worthiness of the suitor; then her 120 own present fortune, if she would not only have amendment but felicity; besides falsely making her believe, that her sister would think herself happy if now she might have his love which before she had contemned; and obliquely touching what danger it should be for her, if her son should accept Philoclea 125 in marriage, and so match the next heir apparent, she being in his power; yet plentifully perjuring, how extremely her son loved her, and excusing the little shows he made of it with the dutiful respect he bare unto her, and taking upon herself that she restrained him, since she found he could set no limits 130 to his passions. And as she did to Philoclea, so did she to her, with the tribute of gifts, seek to bring her mind into servitude: and all other means, that might either establish a beholding-ness, or at the least awake a kindness; doing it so, as by reason of their imprisonment, one sister knew not how the other was 135 wooed; but each might think that only she was sought. But if Philoclea with sweet and humble dealing did avoid their assaults, she with the majesty of virtue did beat them off.

112. *kindly:* natural.
113. *put from the bias of:* distracted from.
119. *her:* Pamela's.
125. *her:* Pamela.
129. *taking upon herself:* alleging.
133–4. *beholdingness:* indebtedness.
134. *so, as:* in such manner, that.

BOOK III, CHAPTER 16
*The unknown Knights will not be known. The Knight of the
Tomb's show, and challenge accepted by Amphialus. Their fight,
with the death of the Tomb-knight. Who that Knight was. The
dying speeches, and the lamentable funerals.*

The fight being ceased, and each side withdrawn within their   5
strengths, Basilius sent Philanax to entertain the strange
Knights, and to bring them unto him, that he might acknowledge
what honour was due to their virtue. But they excused
themselves, desiring to be known first by their deeds, before
their names should accuse their unworthiness: and though the   10
other replied according as they deserved, yet (finding that
unwelcome courtesy is a degree of injury) he suffered them to
retire themselves to a tent of their own without the camp,
where they kept themselves secret: Philanax himself being
called away to another strange Knight, strange not only by the   15
unlookedforness of his coming, but by the strange manner of
his coming.

For he had before him four damosels, and so many behind
him, all upon palfreys, and all apparelled in mourning weeds;
each of them a servant of each side, with like liveries of sorrow. 20
Himself in an armour all painted over with such a cunning of
shadow, that it represented a gaping sepulchre, the furniture
of his horse was all of cypress branches, wherewith in old time
they were wont to dress graves. His bases (which he ware so
long, as they came almost to his ankle) were embroidered only   25
with black worms, which seemed to crawl up and down, as
ready already to devour him. In his shield, for *impresa*, he had
a beautiful child, but having two heads; whereof the one
showed that it was already dead; the other alive, but in that
case, necessarily looking for death. The word was, *No way to be* 30
rid from death, but by death.

This Knight of the Tomb (for so the soldiers termed him)

10–11. *the other:* Philanax.
24. *bases:* skirts.
27. *impresa:* (Italian) heraldic device.
NOTES: pp. 237–8

sent to Basilius, to demand leave to send in a damosel into the town, to call out Amphialus, according as beforetime some others had done. Which being granted (as glad any would 35 undertake the charge which nobody else in that camp was known willing to do), the damosel went in, and having with tears sobbed out a brave challenge to Amphialus from the Knight of the Tomb, Amphialus, honourably entertaining the gentlewoman, and desiring to know the Knight's name (which 40 the doleful gentlewoman would not discover), accepted the challenge, only desiring the gentlewoman to say thus much to the strange Knight from him: that if his mind were like to his title, there were more cause of affinity than enmity between them. And therefore presently (according as he was wont) as 45 soon as he perceived the Knight of the Tomb, with his damosels and judge, was come into the island, he also went over in accustomed manner; and yet for the courtesy of his nature desired to speak with him.

But the Knight of the Tomb, with silence, and drawing his 50 horse back, showed no will to hear, nor speak: but with lance on high, made him know it was fit for him to go to the other end of the career, whence waiting the start of the unknown Knight, he likewise made his spurs claim haste of his horse. But when his staff was in his rest, coming down to meet with 55 the Knight, now very near him, he perceived the Knight had missed his rest: wherefore the courteous Amphialus would not let his lance descend, but with a gallant grace ran over the head of his therein-friended enemy: and having stopped his horse, and with the turning of him blessed his sight with the 60 window where he thought Philoclea might stand, he perceived the Knight had lighted from his horse, and thrown away his staff, angry with his misfortune, as having missed his rest, and drawn his sword to make that supply his fellow's fault. He also lighted, and drew his sword, esteeming victory by advantage 65 rather robbed than purchased: and so the other coming eagerly

53. *career:* ground over which they would run together.
59. *therein-friended:* befriended because spared.
64. *his fellow:* its fellow, i.e., the lance.

toward him, he with his shield out and sword aloft with more
bravery than anger drew unto him; and straight made their
swords speak for them a pretty while with equal fierceness.
But Amphialus (to whom the earth brought forth few matches)   70
having both much more skill to choose the places, and more
force to work upon the chosen, had already made many
windows in his armour for death to come in at, when (the
nobleness of his nature abhorring to make the punishment
overgo the offence) he stepped back, and withal, 'Sir Knight,'   75
(said he) 'you may easily see, that it pleaseth God to favour my
cause; employ your valour against them that wish you hurt:
for my part, I have not deserved hate of you.' 'Thou liest,
false traitor', said the other, with an angry but weak voice. But
Amphialus, in whom abused kindness became spiteful rage,   80
'Ah, barbarous wretch,' (said he) 'only courageous in dis-
courtesy; thou shalt soon see whether thy tongue hath betrayed
thy heart or no': and with that, redoubling his blows, gave him
a great wound upon his neck, and closing with him overthrew
him, and with the fall thrust him mortally into the body: and   85
with that went to pull off his helmet, with intention to make him
give himself the lie for having so said, or to cut off his head.

But the headpiece was no sooner off, but that there fell about
the shoulders of the overcome Knight the treasure of fair
golden hair, which with the face (soon known by the badge of   90
excellency) witnessed that it was Parthenia, the unfortunately
virtuous wife of Argalus: her beauty then even in despite of the
passed sorrow or coming death assuring all beholders that it
was nothing short of perfection. For her exceeding fair eyes
having with continual weeping gotten a little redness about   95
them; her roundy sweetly-swelling lips a little trembling, as
though they kissed their neighbour death; in her cheeks the
whiteness striving by little and little to get upon the rosiness of
them; her neck, a neck indeed of alabaster, displaying the
wound which with most dainty blood laboured to drown his   100
own beauties, so as here was a river of purest red, there an

80. *abused:* ill-used, rejected.
96. *roundy:* rounded.

island of perfittest white, each giving lustre to the other; with
the sweet countenance (God knows) full of an unaffected
languishing: though these things to a grossly-conceiving sense
might seem disgraces, yet indeed were they but apparelling 105
beauty in a new fashion, which all looked upon thorough the
spectacles of pity did even increase the lines of her natural fairness, so as Amphialus was astonished with grief, compassion,
and shame, detesting his fortune, that made him unfortunate
in victory. 110

Therefore, putting off his headpiece and gauntlet, kneeling
down unto her, and with tears testifying his sorrow, he offered
his (by himself accursed) hands to help her: protesting his
life and power to be ready to do her honour. But Parthenia
(who had inward messengers of the desired death's approach) 115
looking upon him, and straight turning away her feeble sight
as from a delightless object, drawing out her words, which
her breath (loth to part from so sweet a body) did faintly
deliver, 'Sir,' (said she) 'I pray you (if prayers have place
in enemies) to let my maids take my body untouched by you: 120
the only honour I now desire by your means is, that I have
no honour of you. Argalus made no such bargain with you,
that the hands which killed him should help me. I have of
them (and I do not only pardon you, but thank you for it) the
service which I desired. There rests nothing now, but that 125
I go live with him, since whose death I have done nothing
but die.' Then pausing, and a little fainting, and again coming
to herself, 'O sweet life, welcome' (said she). 'Now feel I the
bands untied of the cruel death which so long hath held me.
And O life, O death, answer for me, that my thoughts have not 130
so much as in a dream tasted any comfort, since they were
deprived of Argalus. I come, my Argalus, I come: and O God,
hide my faults in thy mercies, and grant (as I feel thou dost
grant) that in thy eternal love, we may love each other eternally.

102. *perfittest:* most perfect.
103. *unaffected:* unfeigned.
104. *grossly-conceiving:* superficially-judging.
119-20. *if prayers have place in enemies:* if enemies' prayers are
heeded.

And this, O Lord —' But there Atropos cut off her sentence: 135
for with that, casting up both eyes and hands to the skies, the
noble soul departed (one might well assure himself) to heaven,
which left the body in so heavenly a demeanour.

But Amphialus (with a heart oppressed with grief, because
of her request) withdrew himself; but the judges, as full of 140
pity, had been all this while disarming her, and her gentlewomen with lamentable cries labouring to stanch the remediless
wounds; and a while she was dead before they perceived it;
death being able to divide the soul, but not the beauty, from
that body. But when the infallible tokens of death assured 145
them of their loss, one of the women would have killed herself,
but that the squire of Amphialus, perceiving it, by force held
her. Others that had as strong passions, though weaker resolution, fell to cast dust upon their heads, to tear their garments:
all falling upon the earth, and crying upon their sweet mistress; 150
as if their cries could persuade the soul to leave the celestial
happiness, to come again into the elements of sorrow: one time
calling to remembrance her virtue, chasteness, sweetness,
goodness to them; another time accursing themselves, that
they had obeyed her, they having been deceived by her words, 155
who assured them that it was revealed unto her that she should
have her heart's desire in the battle against Amphialus, which
they wrongly understood. Then kissing her cold hands and feet,
weary of the world, since she was gone who was their world.
The very heavens seemed, with a cloudy countenance, to lour 160
at the loss, and fame itself (though by nature glad to tell such
rare accidents) yet could not choose but deliver it in lamentable
accents, and in such sort went it quickly all over the camp:
and, as if the air had been infected with sorrow, no heart was
so hard but was subject to that contagion; the rareness of the 165
accident, matching together (the rarely matched together) pity
with admiration, Basilius himself came forth, and brought the
fair Gynecia with him, who was come into the camp under

152. *elements:* of which the body is formed.
160. *lour:* frown.
162. *accidents:* happenings.

NOTES: p. 238

colour of visiting her husband and hearing of her daughters: but indeed Zelmane was the saint to which her pilgrimage was 170 intended; cursing, envying, blessing, and in her heart kissing the walls which imprisoned her. But both they with Philanax, and the rest of the principal nobility, went out, to make honour triumph over death, conveying that excellent body (whereto Basilius himself would needs lend his shoulder) to a church a 175 mile from the camp, where the valiant Argalus lay entombed; recommending to that sepulchre the blessed relics of faithful and virtuous love: giving order for the making of marble images, to represent them, and each way enriching the tomb. Upon which, Basilius himself caused this epitaph to be written. 180

> His being was in her alone:
> And, he not being, she was none.
> They joy'd one joy, one grief they griev'd,
> One love they lov'd, one life they liv'd.
> The hand was one, one was the sword,   185
> That did his death, her death, afford.
> As all the rest, so now the stone
> That tombs the two is justly one.

BOOK III, CHAPTER 20
The sweet resistance of the true sisters to the sour assaults of their false aunt. The whipping of Philoclea and Pamela. The patience of both, and passions for their lovers.

Cecropia by this means rid of the present danger of the siege (desiring Zoilus and Lycurgus to take the care, till their 5 brother recovered, of revictualling and furnishing the city both with men and what else wanted, against any new occasion should urge them, she herself disdaining to hearken to Basilius

182. *she was none:* she had no being.
186. *his death, her death:* his death and hers.
187. *all the rest:* all else they shared.

3. *passions:* feelings.
7. *against:* in case.

NOTES: p. 238

without he would grant his daughter in marriage to her son,
which by no means he would be brought unto), bent all the   10
sharpness of her malicious wit how to bring a comfortable
grant to her son: whereupon she well found no less than his
life depended. Therefore for a while she attempted all means
of eloquent praying and flattering persuasion, mingling sometimes gifts, sometimes threatenings, as she had cause to hope   15
that either open force or undermining would best win the castle
of their resolution. And ever as much as she did to Philoclea, so
much did she to Pamela, though in manner sometimes differing, as she found fit to level at the one's noble height and the
other's sweet lowliness. For though she knew her son's heart   20
had wholly given itself to Philoclea, yet seeing the equal gifts in
Pamela, she hoped a fair grant would recover the sorrow of a
fair refusal: cruelly intending the present empoisoning the one,
as soon as the other's affection were purchased.

But in vain was all her vain oratory employed. Pamela's   25
determination was built upon so brave a rock, that no shot of
hers could reach unto it: and Philoclea (though humbly
seated) was so environed with sweet rivers of clear virtue as
could neither be battered nor undermined: her witty persuasions had wise answers; her eloquence recompensed with   30
sweetness; her threatenings repelled with disdain in the one,
and patience in the other; her gifts either not accepted, or
accepted to obey, but not to bind. So as Cecropia, in nature
violent; cruel, because ambitious; hateful, for old rooted
grudge to their mother, and now spiteful because she could   35
not prevail with girls, as she counted them; lastly, drawn on by
her love to her son, and held up by a tyrannical authority,
forthwith followed the bias of her own crooked disposition,
and doubling and redoubling her threatenings, fell to confirm
some of her threatened effects: first withdrawing all comfort,   40
both of servants and service from them. But that these excellent
Ladies had been used unto, even at home, and then found in

9. *without:* unless.
23. *the present empoisoning:* immediately to poison.
29. *her:* Cecropia's.

themselves how much good the hardness of education doth to
the resistance of misery. Then dishonourably using them both
in diet and lodging, by a contempt to pull down their thoughts   45
to yielding. But as before the consideration of a prison had
disgraced all ornaments, so now the same consideration made
them attend all diseasefulness. Then still, as she found these
not prevail, would she go forward with giving them terrors,
sometimes with noises of horror, sometimes with sudden   50
frightings in the night, when the solitary darkness thereof might
easier astonish the disarmed senses. But to all virtue and love
resisted, strengthened one by the other, when each found
itself over-vehemently assaulted. Cecropia still sweetening
her fiercenesses with fair promises, if they would promise   55
fair; that feeling evil, and seeing a way far better, their minds
might the sooner be mollified. But they that could not taste her
behaviour when it was pleasing, indeed could worse now,
when they had lost all taste by her injuries.

She resolving all extremities rather than fail of conquest,   60
pursued on her rugged way: letting no day pass without new
and new perplexing the poor Ladies' minds, and troubling
their bodies: and still swelling the more she was stopped, and
growing hot with her own doings, at length abominable rage
carried her to absolute tyrannies, so that taking with her certain 65
old women (of wicked dispositions, and apt for envy's sake to
be cruel to youth and beauty), with a countenance empoisoned
with malice, flew to the sweet Philoclea, as if so many kites
should come about a white dove, and matching violent
gestures with mischievous threatenings, she having a rod in   70
her hand (like a Fury that should carry wood to the burning of
Diana's temple) fell to scourge that most beautiful body: Love
in vain holding the shield of Beauty against her blind cruelty.
The sun drew clouds up to hide his face from so pitiful a sight;
and the very stone walls did yield drops of sweat for agony of   75

48. *attend all diseasefulness:* put up with any discomfort.
57. *taste:* appreciate, like.
61. *rugged:* harsh, cruel.
70. *mischievous threatenings:* threats of harm.

NOTES: p. 238

such a mischief: each senseless thing had sense of pity; only
they that had sense were senseless. Virtue rarely found her
worldly weakness more than by the oppression of that day: and
weeping Cupid told his weeping mother, that he was sorry he
was not deaf, as well as blind, that he might never know so   80
lamentable a work. Philoclea, with tearful eyes and sobbing
breast (as soon as her weariness rather than compassion gave
her respite) kneeled down to Cecropia, and making pity in her
face honourable, and torment delightful, besought her, since
she hated her (for what cause she took God to witness she   85
knew not), that she would at once take away her life, and not
please herself with the tormenting of a poor gentlewoman. 'If'
(said she) 'the common course of humanity cannot move you,
nor the having me in your own walls cannot claim pity; nor
womanly mercy, nor near alliance, nor remembrance (how   90
miserable soever now) that I am a Prince's daughter; yet let the
love you have often told me your son bears me, so much
procure, that for his sake, one death may be thought enough
for me; I have not lived so many years but that one death may
be able to conclude them: neither have my faults, I hope,   95
been so many, but that one death may satisfy them. It is no
great suit to an enemy, when but death is desired. I crave but
that; and as for the granting your request, know for certain
you lose your labours, being every day further-off-minded
from becoming his wife, who useth me like a slave.' But that   100
instead of getting grace renewed again Cecropia's fury: so that
(excellent creature) she was newly again tormented by those
hellish monsters, Cecropia using no other words but that she
was a proud and ungrateful wench, and that she would teach
her to know her own good, since of herself she would not con-   105
ceive it.

So that with silence and patience (like a fair gorgeous armour
hammered upon by an illfavoured smith) she abode their

77. *they:* Cecropia and the old women.
82. *her:* Cecropia's.
105–6. *conceive:* understand.
108. *illfavoured:* ugly-looking.

NOTES: p. 239

G

pitiless dealing with her: till, rather reserving her for more, than meaning to end, they left her to an uncomfortable leisure, 110 to consider with herself her fortune; both helpless herself, being a prisoner, and hopeless, since Zelmane was a prisoner: who therein only was short of the bottom of misery, that she knew not how unworthily her angel by these devils was abused; but wanted (God wot) no stings of grief, when those words did but 115 strike upon her heart, that Philoclea was a captive, and she not able to succour her. For well she knew the confidence Philoclea had in her, and well she knew Philoclea had cause to have confidence: and all trodden underfoot by the wheel of senseless Fortune. Yet if there be that imperious power in the soul, as it 120 can deliver knowledge to another, without bodily organs; so vehement were the workings of their spirits, as one met with other, though themselves perceived it not, but only thought it to be the doubling of their own loving fancies. And that was the only worldly thing whereon Philoclea rested her mind, that 125 she knew she should die beloved of Zelmane, and should die rather than be false to Zelmane. And so this most dainty nymph, easing the pain of her mind with thinking of another's pain; and almost forgetting the pain of her body through the pain of her mind, she wasted, even longing for the conclusion 130 of her tedious tragedy.

But for a while she was unvisited, Cecropia employing her time in using the like cruelty upon Pamela, her heart growing not only to desire the fruit of punishing them, but even to delight in the punishing them. But if ever the beams of per- 135 fection shined through the clouds of affliction, if ever Virtue took a body to show his (else unconceivable) beauty, it was in Pamela. For when reason taught her there was no resistance (for to just resistance first her heart was inclined), then with so heavenly a quietness, and so graceful a calmness, did she suffer 140 the divers kinds of torments they used to her, that while they vexed her fair body, it seemed that she rather directed than obeyed the vexation. And when Cecropia ended, and asked whether her heart would yield, she a little smiled, but such a

125. *rested her mind:* relied.

NOTES: p. 239

smiling as showed no love, and yet could not but be lovely. 145
And then, 'Beastly woman,' (said she) 'follow on, do what thou
wilt and canst upon me: for I know thy power is not unlimited.
Thou mayst well wrack this silly body, but me thou canst never
overthrow. For my part, I will not do thee the pleasure to
desire death of thee: but assure thyself, both my life and death 150
shall triumph with honour, laying shame upon thy detestable
tyranny.'

And so, in effect, conquering their doing with her suffering,
while Cecropia tried as many sorts of pains as might rather
vex them than spoil them (for that she would not do while 155
she were in any hope to win either of them for her son), Pamela
remained almost as much content with trial in herself what
virtue could do, as grieved with the misery wherein she found
herself plunged: only sometimes her thoughts softened in her,
when with open wings they flew to Musidorus. For then she 160
would think with herself, how grievously Musidorus would
take this her misery; and she, that wept not for herself, wept
yet Musidorus's tears, which he would weep for her. For gentle
Love did easlier yield to lamentation than the constancy of
virtue would else admit. Then would she remember the case 165
wherein she had left her poor shepherd, and she that wished
death for herself feared death for him; and she that condemned
in herself the feebleness of sorrow, yet thought it great reason
to be sorry for his sorrow: and she that long had prayed for the
virtuous joining themselves together, now thinking to die 170
herself, heartily prayed that long time their fortunes might be
separated. 'Live long, my Musidorus,' (would she say) 'and let
my name live in thy mouth, in thy heart my memory. Live
long, that thou mayst love long the chaste love of thy dead
Pamela.' Then would she wish to herself that no other woman 175
might ever possess his heart: and yet scarcely the wish was

146. *beastly:* inhuman.
148. *wrack:* destroy, ruin.
148. *silly:* poor, weak.
155. *spoil:* destroy, kill.
164. *easlier:* more easily.
168. *great reason:* fully allowable.

NOTES: p. 239

made a wish, when herself would find fault with it, as being too unjust, that so excellent a man should be banished from the comfort of life. Then would she fortify her resolution with bethinking the worst, taking the counsel of virtue and comfort 180 of love.

BOOK III, CHAPTER 23
A Lady's kind comforts to Pyrocles' comfortless unkindness. His hardly knowing her. Her unmasking of Cecropia's fruitless sophistry. Their medley of solace and sorrow.

Then stopping his words with sighs, drowning his sighs in tears, and drying again his tears in rage, he would sit a while 5 in a wandering muse, which represented nothing but vexations unto him: then throwing himself sometimes upon the bed: then up again, till walking was wearisome, and rest loathsome: and so neither suffering food nor sleep to help his afflicted nature, all that day and night he did nothing but weep 10 Philoclea, sigh Philoclea, and cry out Philoclea: till as it happened (at that time upon his bed) toward the dawning of the day, he heard one stir in his chamber, by the motion of garments; and with an angry voice asked who was there. 'A poor gentlewoman' (answered the party) 'that wish long life 15 unto you.' 'And I soon death to you' (said he) 'for the horrible curse you have given me.' 'Certainly' (said she) 'an unkind answer, and far unworthy the excellency of your mind; but not unsuitable to the rest of your behaviour. For most part of this night I have heard you (being let into your chamber, you 20 never perceiving it, so was your mind estranged from your senses), and have heard nothing of Zelmane in Zelmane, nothing but weak wailings, fitter for some nurse of a village, than so famous a creature as you are.' 'O God!' (cried out Pyrocles) 'that thou wert a man that usest these words unto 25 me! I tell thee I am sorry: I tell thee I will be sorry in despite of thee, and all them that would have me joyful.' 'And yet' (replied she) 'perchance Philoclea is not dead, whom you so

2. *hardly:* with difficulty.

NOTES: p. 239

much bemoan.' 'I would we were both dead, on that con- dition,' said Pyrocles. 'See the folly of your passion,' (said she) 30 'as though you should be nearer to her, you being dead, and she alive, than she being dead, and you alive: and if she be dead, was she not born to die? What then do you cry out for? Not for her, who must have died one time or other; but for some few years: so as it is time, and this world, that seem so 35 lovely things, and not Philoclea unto you.' 'O noble Sisters,' (cried Pyrocles) 'now you be gone (who were the only exalters of all womankind), what is left in that sex, but babbling and business?' 'And truly' (said she) 'I will yet a little longer trouble you.' 'Nay, I pray you do,' (said Pyrocles) 'for I wish 40 for nothing in my short life, but mischiefs and cumbers: and I am content you shall be one of them.' 'In truth' (said she) 'you would think yourself a greatly privileged person, if since the strongest buildings and lastingest monarchies are subject to end, only your Philoclea (because she is yours) should be 45 exempted. But indeed you bemoan yourself, who have lost a friend: you cannot her, who hath in one act both preserved her honour, and left the miseries of this world.' 'O woman's philosophy, childish folly!' (said Pyrocles) 'as though if I do bemoan myself, I have not reason to do so, having lost more 50 than any monarchy, nay than my life can be worth unto me.' 'Alas,' (said she) 'comfort yourself, Nature did not forget her skill, when she had made them: you shall find many their superiors, and perchance such as (when your eyes shall look abroad) yourself will like better.' 55

But that speech put all good manners out of the conceit of Pyrocles: in so much that, leaping out of his bed, he ran to have stricken her: but coming near her (the morning then winning the field of darkness) he saw, or he thought he saw, indeed, the very face of Philoclea; the same sweetness, the same 60

29. *we:* i.e., himself and the lady to whom he is speaking.
39. *business:* meddling.
41. *mischiefs and cumbers:* harms and troubles.
53. *them:* the 'noble Sisters'.
56. *conceit:* mind.
59. *winning the field of:* defeating.

grace, the same beauty: with which carried into a divine
astonishment, he fell down at her feet. 'Most blessed angel,'
(said he) 'well hast thou done to take that shape, since thou
wouldest submit thyself to mortal sense; for a more angelical
form could not have been created for thee. Alas, even by that   65
excellent beauty, so beloved of me, let it be lawful for me to ask
of thee what is the cause, that she, that heavenly creature whose
form you have taken, should by the heavens be destined to so
unripe an end? Why should unjustice so prevail? Why was she
seen to the world, so soon to be ravished from us? Why was she   70
not suffered to live, to teach the world perfection?' 'Do not
deceive thyself;' (answered she) 'I am no angel; I am Philoclea,
the same Philoclea, so truly loving you, so truly beloved of
you.' 'If it be so' (said he) 'that you are indeed the soul of
Philoclea, you have done well to keep your own figure: for no   75
heaven could have given you a better. Then alas, why have
you taken the pains to leave your blissful seat to come to this
place most wretched, to me who am wretchedness itself, and
not rather obtain for me that I might come where you are,
there eternally to behold, and eternally to love your beauties?   80
You know (I know) that I desire nothing but death, which I
only stay, to be justly revenged of your unjust murtherers.'
'Dear Pyrocles,' (said she) 'I am thy Philoclea, and as yet
living: not murdered, as you supposed, and therefore be
comforted.' And with that gave him her hand. But the sweet   85
touch of that hand seemed to his astrayed powers so heavenly a
thing, that it rather for a while confirmed him in his former
belief: till she with vehement protestations (and desire that it
might be so, helping to persuade that it was so) brought him
to yield; yet doubtfully to yield to this height of all comfort,   90
that Philoclea lived: which witnessing with tears of joy, 'Alas,'
(said he) 'how shall I believe mine eyes any more? Or do you
yet but appear thus unto me, to stay me from some desperate
end? For alas, I saw the excellent Pamela beheaded: I saw
your head (the head indeed and chief part of all Nature's works)   95

75. *figure:* appearance.
88. *desire:* his desire.

standing in a dish of gold, too mean a shrine (God wot) for such
a relic. How can this be, my only dear, and you live? Or if this
be not so, how can I believe mine own senses? And if I cannot
believe them, why should I now believe these blessed tidings
they bring me?'   100

'The truth is,' (said she) 'my Pyrocles, that neither I (as
you find) nor yet my dear sister is dead: although the mis-
chievously subtle Cecropia used sleights to make either of
us think so of other. For, having in vain attempted the farthest
of her wicked eloquence to make either of us yield to her son, 105
and seeing that neither it, accompanied with great flatteries
and rich presents, could get any ground of us, nor yet the
violent way she fell into of cruelly tormenting our bodies could
prevail with us; at last, she made either of us think the other
dead, and so hoped to have wrested our minds to the forgetting 110
of virtue: and first she gave to mine eyes the miserable spectacle
of my sister's (as I thought) death: but indeed not my sister: it
was only Artesia, she who so cunningly brought us to this
misery. Truly I am sorry for the poor gentlewoman, though
justly she be punished for her double falsehood: but Artesia 115
muffled so as you could not easily discern her, and in my
sister's apparel (which they had taken from her under colour
of giving her other), did they execute. And when I (for thy
sake especially, dear Pyrocles) could by no force nor fear be
won, they assayed the like with my sister, by bringing me down 120
under the scaffold, and (making me thrust my head up through
a hole they had made therein) they did put about my poor
neck a dish of gold, whereout they had beaten the bottom, so
as having set blood in it, you saw how I played the part of
death (God knows even willing to have done it in earnest), 125
and so had they set me that I reached but on tiptoes to the
ground, so as scarcely I could breathe, much less speak. And
truly, if they had kept me there any whit longer, they had
strangled me, instead of beheading me: but then they took
me away, and seeking to see their issue of this practice, they 130

109. *either:* each.
NOTES: pp. 239–40

found my noble sister (for the dear love she vouchsafeth to bear me) so grieved withal, that she willed them to do their uttermost cruelty unto her; for she vowed never to receive sustenance of them that had been the causers of my murther: and finding both of us, even given over, not like to live many 135 hours longer, and my sister Pamela rather worse than myself (the strength of her heart worse bearing those indignities), the good woman Cecropia (with the same pity as folks keep fowl when they are not fat enough for their eating) made us know her deceit, and let us come one to another; with what 140 joy you can well imagine, who I know feel the like; saving that we only thought ourselves reserved to miseries, and therefore fitter for condoling than congratulating. For my part, I am fully persuaded, it is but with a little respite, to have a more feeling sense of the torments she prepares for us. 145 True it is, that one of my guardians would have me to believe that this proceeds of my gentle cousin Amphialus: who having heard some inkling that we were evil entreated, had called his mother to his bedside, from whence he never rose since his last combat, and besought and charged her upon all the love she 150 bare him, to use us with all kindness: vowing, with all the imprecations he could imagine, that if ever he understood for his sake that I received further hurt than the want of my liberty, he would not live an hour longer. And the good woman sware to me that he would kill his mother, if he knew 155 how I had been dealt with; but that Cecropia keeps him from understanding things how they pass, only having heard a whispering, and myself named, he had (of abundance, forsooth, of honourable love) given this charge for us. Whereupon this enlargement of mine was grown: for my part I know too well 160 their cunning (who leave no money unoffered that may buy mine honour) to believe any word they say, but (my dear Pyrocles) even look for the worst, and prepare myself for the same. Yet I must confess, I was content to rob from death, and

135. *given over:* about to die.
146. *guardians:* jailors.
148. *evil entreated:* ill-treated.
154-5. *the good woman:* the jailor.

borrow of my misery, the sweet comfort of seeing my sweet 165
sister, and most sweet comfort of thee, my Pyrocles. And so
having leave, I came stealing into your chamber: where (O
Lord) what a joy it was unto me, to hear you solemnize the
funerals of the poor Philoclea! That I myself might live to hear
my death bewailed: and by whom? by my dear Pyrocles. 170
That I saw death was not strong enough to divide thy love from
me. O my Pyrocles, I am too well paid for my pains I have
suffered: joyful is my woe for so noble a cause; and welcome be
all miseries, since to thee I am so welcome. Alas, how I
pitied to hear thy pity of me; and yet a great while I could 175
not find in my heart to interrupt thee, but often had even
pleasure to weep with thee: and so kindly came forth thy
lamentations, that they enforced me to lament too, as if indeed
I had been a looker-on to see poor Philoclea die. Till at last I
spake with you, to try whether I could remove thee from 180
sorrow, till I had almost procured myself a beating.'

And with that she prettily smiled, which, mingled with her
tears, one could not tell whether it were a mourning pleasure or
a delightful sorrow: but like when a few April drops are scat-
tered by a gentle Zephyrus among fine-coloured flowers. But 185
Pyrocles, who had felt (with so small distance of time) in himself the overthrow both of hope and despair, knew not to what
key he should tune his mind, either of joy or sorrow. But
finding perfit reason in neither, suffered himself to be carried
by the tide of his imagination, and his imaginations to be raised 190
even by the sway which hearing or seeing might give unto
them: he saw her alive, he was glad to see her alive: he saw
her weep, he was sorry to see her weep: he heard her comfortable speeches, nothing more gladsome: he heard her
prognosticating her own destruction, nothing more doleful. 195
But when he had a little taken breath from the panting motion
of such contrariety in passions, he fell to consider with her of
her present estate, both comforting her, that certainly the

189. *perfit reason:* perfect fitness.
193–4. *comfortable:* expressing comfort.
195. *prognosticating:* foretelling.

worst of this storm was past, since already they had done the
worst which man's wit could imagine: and that if they had 200
determined to have killed her, they would have now done it:
and also earnestly counselling her, and enabling his counsels
with vehement prayers that she would so far second the hopes
of Amphialus as that she might but procure him liberty;
promising then as much to her, as the liberality of loving 205
courage durst promise to himself.

BOOK III, CHAPTER 24
*Amphialus excuseth. The Princesses accuse. Cecropia seeking their
death findeth her own. Amphialus his death-pangs and self-
killing. The woeful knowledge of it.*

But who would lively describe the manner of these speeches,
should paint out the lightsome colours of affection, shaded 5
with the deepest shadows of sorrow, finding then between hope
and fear, a kind of sweetness in tears: till Philoclea, content
to receive a kiss, and but a kiss, of Pyrocles, sealed up his
moving lips, and closed them up in comfort: and herself
(for the passage was left between them open) went to her 10
sister: with whom she had stayed but a while, fortifying one
another (while Philoclea tempered Pamela's just disdain, and
Pamela ennobled Philoclea's sweet humbleness), when
Amphialus came unto them: who never since he had heard
Philoclea named, could be quiet in himself, although none of 15
them about him (fearing more his mother's violence than his
power) would discover what had passed: and many messages
he sent to know her estate, which brought answers back
according as it pleased Cecropia to endite them, till his heart
full of unfortunate affection more and more misgiving him, 20
having impatiently borne the delay of the night's unfitness,

199. *they:* Cecropia and her servants.
202. *enabling:* reinforcing.

4. *lively:* faithfully, to the life.
5. *paint out:* paint, use.
21. *unfitness:* i.e., for a visit.

NOTES: p. 240

this morning he gat up, and though full of wounds (which not without danger could suffer such exercise), he apparelled himself, and with a countenance that showed strength in nothing but in grief, he came where the sisters were; and weakly kneeling down, he besought them to pardon him, if they had not been used in that castle according to their worthiness and his duty; beginning to excuse small matters, poor gentleman, not knowing in what sort they had been handled.

But Pamela's high heart (having conceived mortal hate for the injury offered to her and her sister) could scarcely abide his sight, much less hear out his excuses; but interrupted him with these words. 'Traitor' (said she) 'to thine own blood, and false to the profession of so much love as thou hast vowed, do not defile our ears with thy excuses; but pursue on thy cruelty, that thou and thy godly mother have used towards us: for my part, assure thyself, and so do I answer for my sister (whose mind I know), I do not more desire mine own safety than thy destruction.' Amazed with this speech, he turned his eye, full of humble sorrowfulness, to Philoclea. 'And is this (most excellent Lady) your doom of me also?' She, sweet lady, sat weeping: for as her most noble kinsman she had ever favoured him, and loved his love, though she could not be in love with his person; and now partly unkindness of his wrong, partly pity of his case, made her sweet mind yield some tears before she could answer; and her answer was no other, but that she had the same cause as her sister had. He replied no further, but delivering from his heart two or three untaught sighs, rose, and with most low reverence went out of their chamber: and straight, by threatening torture, learned of one of the women in what terrible manner those Princesses had been used. But when he heard it, crying out 'O God!', and then not able to say any more (for his speech went back to rebound woe upon his heart), he needed no judge to go upon him: for no man could ever think any other worthy of greater punishment than he thought himself.

Full therefore of the horriblest despair which a most guilty

54. *go upon him:* pronounce his verdict and sentence.

NOTES: p. 240

conscience could breed, with wild looks promising some
terrible issue, understanding his mother was upon the top
of the leads, he caught one of his servants' swords from him,　60
and none of them daring to stay him, he went up, carried by
fury instead of strength, where she was at that time musing
how to go thorough with this matter, and resolving to make
much of her nieces in show, and secretly to empoison them;
thinking, since they were not to be won, her son's love would　65
no otherwise be mitigated.

But when she saw him come in with a sword drawn, and a
look more terrible than the sword, she straight was stricken
with the guiltiness of her own conscience: yet the well-known
humbleness of her son somewhat animated her, till he coming　70
nearer her, and crying to her, 'Thou damnable creature, only
fit to bring forth such a monster of unhappiness as I am —',
she fearing he would have stricken her (though indeed he
meant it not, but only intended to kill himself in her presence),
went back so far till, ere she were aware, she overthrew herself　75
from over the leads, to receive her death's kiss at the ground:
and yet was she not so happy as presently to die, but that she
had time with hellish agony to see her son's mischief (whom
she loved so well) before her end; when she confessed (with
most desperate, but not repenting, mind) the purpose she had　80
to empoison the Princesses, and would then have had them
murthered. But everybody seeing and glad to see her end, had
left obedience to her tyranny.

And (if it could be) her ruin increased woe in the noble heart
of Amphialus, who when he saw her fall, had his own rage　85
stayed a little with the suddenness of her destruction. 'And
was I not enough miserable before,' (said he) 'but that before
my end I must be the death of my mother? who how wicked
soever, yet I would she had received her punishment by some
other. O Amphialus, wretched Amphialus; thou hast lived to　90

60. *the leads:* the leaden roof-top walk.
77. *presently:* instantly.
78. *mischief:* destruction.
81. *then:* i.e., even as her last wish.
83. *left obedience to:* ceased obeying.

be the death of thy most dear companion and friend Philoxenus, and of his father, thy most careful foster-father. Thou hast lived to kill a lady with thine own hands, and so excellent and virtuous a lady as the fair Parthenia was. Thou hast lived to see thy faithful Ismenus slain in succouring thee, and thou not 95 able to defend him. Thou hast lived to show thyself such a coward as that one unknown knight could overcome thee in thy lady's presence. Thou hast lived to bear arms against thy rightful Prince, thine own uncle. Thou hast lived to be accounted, and justly accounted, a traitor, by the most excellent 100 persons that this world holdeth. Thou hast lived to be the death of her that gave thee life. But ah, wretched Amphialus, thou hast lived for thy sake and by thy authority to have Philoclea tormented: O heavens, in Amphialus' castle, where Amphialus commanded. Tormented, tormented! Torment of 105 my soul, Philoclea tormented! And thou hast had such comfort in thy life, as to live all this while. Perchance this hand (used only to mischievous acts) thinks it were too good a deed to kill me; or else, filthy hand, only worthy to kill women, thou art afraid to strike a man. Fear not, cowardly hand, for thou shalt 110 kill but a cowardly traitor: and do it gladly, for thou shalt kill him whom Philoclea hateth.' With that, furiously he tare open his doublet, and setting the pommel of the sword to the ground, and the point to his breast, he fell upon it. But the sword more merciful than he to himself, with the slipping of 115 the pommel the point swerved and rased him but upon the side: yet with the fall, his other wounds opened so, as he bled in such extremity, that Charon's boat might very well be carried in that flood: which yet he sought to hasten by this means. As he opened his doublet and fell, there fell out 120 Philoclea's knives, which Cecropia at the first had taken from her, and delivered to her son; and he had ever worn them next his heart, as the only relic he had of his saint: now seeing them by him, (his sword being so, as weakness could not well draw

108. *mischievous:* hurtful.
116. *rased:* glancingly wounded.
NOTES: pp. 240–1

it out from his doublet) he took the knives, and pulling one 125
of them out, and many times kissing it, and then first with the
passions of kindness and unkindness melting in tears, 'O dear
knives, you are come in a good time, to revenge the wrong I
have done you all this while, in keeping you from her blessed
side, and wearing you without your mistress' leave. Alas, be 130
witness with me, yet before I die, (and well you may, for you
have lain next my heart) that by my consent, your excellent
mistress should have had as much honour as this poor place
could have brought forth, for so high an excellency: and now I
am condemned to die by her mouth. Alas, other, far other 135
hope would my desire often have given me: but other event it
hath pleased her to lay upon me. Ah Philoclea,' (with that his
tears gushed out, as though they would strive to overflow his
blood) 'I would yet thou knewest how I love thee. Unworthy I
am, unhappy I am, false I am; but to thee, alas, I am not false. 140
But what a traitor am I, any way to excuse him whom she con-
demneth? Since there is nothing left me wherein I may do her
service, but in punishing him who hath so offended her. Dear
knife, then do your noble mistress's commandment.' With
that, he stabbed himself into divers places of his breast and 145
throat, until those wounds (with the old, freshly bleeding)
brought him to the senseless gate of death.

By which time, his servants having (with fear of his fury)
abstained a while from coming unto him, one of them (preferring dutiful affection before fearful duty) came in, and 150
there found him swimming in his own blood, giving a pitiful
spectacle, where the conquest was the conqueror's overthrow,
and self-ruin the only triumph of a battle fought between him
and himself. The time full of danger, the person full of
worthiness, the manner full of horror, did greatly astonish all 155
the beholders; so as by and by, all the town was full of it, and
then of all ages came running up to see the beloved body;
everybody thinking their safety bled in his wounds, and their
honour died in his destruction.

149–50. *preferring . . . before:* putting before.
156. *by and by:* straightway.

NOTES: p. 241

MISCELLANEOUS POEMS

I

My true love hath my heart and I have his,
By just exchange one for the other giv'n.
I hold his dear, and mine he cannot miss:
There never was a better bargain driv'n.
    His heart in me keeps me and him in one,   5
My heart in him his thoughts and senses guides:
He loves my heart for once it was his own;
I cherish his because in me it bides.

His heart his wound received from my sight;
My heart was wounded with his wounded heart,   10
For as from me on him his hurt did light,
So still methought in me his hurt did smart.
    Both equal hurt, in this change sought our bliss:
    My true love hath my heart and I have his.

II

Lock up, fair lids, the treasures of my heart;
Preserve those beams, this age's only light;
To her sweet sense, sweet Sleep, some ease impart,
Her sense too weak to bear her spirit's might.
    And while, O Sleep, thou closest up her sight   5
(Her sight where Love did forge his fairest dart),
O harbour all her parts in easeful plight;
Let no strange dream make her fair body start.

I. 3. *miss:* do without.
    9. *his wound:* its wound.
    9. *my sight:* the sight of me.
  13. *change:* exchange.

NOTES: pp. 241–2

But yet, O Dream, if thou wilt not depart
   In this rare subject from thy common right,   10
   But wilt thyself in such a seat delight,
Then take my shape, and play a lover's part:
   Kiss her from me, and say unto her sprite
   Till her eyes shine I live in darkest night.

III

Poor painters oft with silly poets join
To fill the world with strange but vain conceits:
One brings the stuff, the other stamps the coin,
Which breeds naught else but gloses of deceits.
   Thus painters Cupid paint, thus poets do,   5
   A naked god, young, blind, with arrows two.

Is he a god, that ever flies the light?
Or naked he, disguis'd in all untruth?
If he be blind, how hitteth he so right?
How is he young, that tam'd old Phoebus' youth?   10
   But arrows two, and tipt with gold or lead?
   Some, hurt, accuse a third with horny head.

No, nothing so: an old false knave he is,
By Argus got on Io, then a cow,
What time for her Juno her Jove did miss,   15
And charge of her to Argus did allow.
   Mercury kill'd his false sire for this act;
   His dam, a beast, was pardon'd beastly fact.

II. 9–10 *depart . . . from:* yield, waive.
III. 4. *gloses of deceits:* deceitful appearances.
    14. *got:* begot.
    15. *for her:* because of her.
    18. *fact:* deed, crime.

NOTES: p. 242

With father's death and mother's guilty shame,
With Jove's disdain at such a rival's seed,   20
The wretch compell'd a runagate became,
And learn'd what ill a miser state doth breed:
 To lie, feign, gloze, to steal, pry, and accuse;
 Naught in himself, each other to abuse.

Yet bears he still his parents' stately gifts,   25
A horned head, clov'n foot, and thousand eyes,
Some gazing still, some winking wily shifts,
With long large ears where never rumour dies.
 His horned head doth seem the heaven to spite,
 His cloven foot doth never tread aright.   30

Thus, half a man, with man he eas'ly haunts,
Cloth'd in the shape which soonest may deceive:
Thus, half a beast, each beastly vice he plants
In those weak hearts that his advice receive.
 He prowls each place, still in new colours deckt,   35
 Sucking one's ill, another to infect.

To narrow breasts he comes all wrapt in gain;
To swelling hearts he shines in honour's fire;
To open eyes all beauties he doth rain,
Creeping to each with flattering of desire.   40
 But for that love's desire most rules the eyes,
 Therein his name, there his chief triumph lies.

20. *seed:* offspring.
21. *runagate:* vagabond.
22. *ill:* wickedness.
22. *miser state:* wretched lot.
24. *naught:* wicked.
24. *each other:* everyone else.
27. *winking wily shifts:* shut, to countenance the crafty tricks of
  lovers.
41. *for that:* because.
42. *name:* 'Cupiditas', desire (of the eyes: cf. line 48); also, reputation.

Millions of years this old drivel Cupid lives,
While still more wretch, more wicked he doth prove;
Till now at length that Jove him office gives   45
(At Juno's suit who much did Argus love)
    In this our world a hangman for to be
    Of all those fools that will have all they see.

IV

Let mother Earth now deck herself in flowers,
To see her offspring seek a good increase,
Where justest love doth vanquish Cupid's powers,
And war of thoughts is swallow'd up in peace,
    Which never may decrease,   5
    But, like the turtles fair,
Live one in two, a well-united pair;
    Which that no chance may stain,
O Hymen, long their coupled joys maintain!

O heav'n, awake, show forth thy stately face;   10
Let not these slumbering clouds thy beauties hide,
But with thy cheerful presence help to grace
The honest Bridegroom and the bashful Bride,
    Whose loves may ever bide,
    Like to the elm and vine,   15
With mutual embracements them to twine:
    In which delightful pain,
O Hymen, long their coupled joys maintain!

Ye Muses all, which chaste affects allow,
And have to Lalus show'd your secret skill,   20
To this chaste love your sacred favours bow,
And so to him and her your gifts distil
    That they all vice may kill,

43. *drivel:* dirty rascal.
IV. 6. *turtles:* turtle doves.
    19. *affects:* affections, emotions.
    21. *bow:* send down.

NOTES: p. 242

And, like to lilies pure,
Do please all eyes, and spotless do endure,   25
   Where that all bliss may reign:
O Hymen, long their coupled joys maintain!

Ye Nymphs which in the waters empire have,
Since Lalus' music oft doth yield you praise,
Grant to the thing which we for Lalus crave: 30
Let one time (but long first) close up their days,
   One grave their bodies seize;
   And like two rivers sweet,
When they though divers do together meet,
   One stream both streams contain,   35
O Hymen, long their coupled joys maintain!

Pan, father Pan, the god of silly sheep,
Whose care is cause that they in number grow,
Have much more care of them that them do keep,
Since from these good the others' good doth flow,   40
   And make their issue show
   In number like the herd
Of younglings which thyself with love hast rear'd,
   Or like the drops of rain.
O Hymen, long their coupled joys maintain!   45

Virtue, if not a god, yet God's chief part,
Be thou the knot of this their open vow,
That still he be her head, she be his heart,
He lean to her, she unto him do bow,
   Each other still allow;   50
   Like oak and mistletoe,
Her strength from him, his praise from her do grow:
   In which most lovely train,
O Hymen, long their coupled joys maintain!

40. *these good:* the good of these.
47. *open:* public.
50. *each other still allow:* let each always bear with the other.
53. *train:* course.

NOTES: p. 242

But thou, foul Cupid, sire to lawless lust,   55
Be thou far hence with thy empoison'd dart,
Which, though of glittering gold, shall here take rust,
Where simple love, which chasteness doth impart,
    Avoids thy hurtful art,
    Not needing charming skill   60
Such minds with sweet affections for to fill:
    Which being pure and plain,
O Hymen, long their coupled joys maintain!

All churlish words, shrewd answers, crabbed looks,
All privateness, self-seeking, inward spite,   65
All waywardness which nothing kindly brooks,
All strife for toys and claiming master's right,
    Be hence aye put to flight!
    All stirring husband's hate
'Gainst neighbours good, for womanish debate,   70
    Be fled, as things most vain!
O Hymen, long their coupled joys maintain!

All peacock pride, and fruits of peacock's pride,
Longing to be with loss of substance gay,
With recklessness what may thy house betide,   75
So that you may on higher slippers stay,
    For ever hence away!
    Yet let not sluttery,
The sink of filth, be counted huswifery,
    But keeping wholesome mean.   80
O Hymen, long their coupled joys maintain!

60. *charming:* enchanting.
66. *which nothing kindly brooks:* which takes nothing well.
67. *toys:* trifles.
69–70. *stirring . . . womanish debate:* women's quarrels which make
     enmity between the husband and his good neighbours.
79. *sink:* cess-pit.
79. *huswifery:* domestic economy.
80. *wholesome mean:* the healthy middle way.

But above all, away vile jealousy,
The evil of evils, just cause to be unjust!
How can he love, suspecting treachery?
How can she love, where love cannot win trust?   85
   Go, snake, hide thee in dust,
   Ne dare once show thy face
Where open hearts do hold so constant place
   That they thy sting restrain.
O Hymen, long their coupled joys maintain!   90

The earth is deckt with flowers, the heav'ns display'd,
Muses grant gifts, nymphs long and joined life,
Pan store of babes, virtue their thoughts well staid;
Cupid's lust gone, and gone is bitter strife.
   Happy man, happy wife!   95
   No pride shall them oppress,
Nor yet shall yield to loathsome sluttishness,
   And jealousy is slain;
For Hymen will their coupled joys maintain.

V

   The lad Philisides
   Lay by a river side,
In flowery field a gladder eye to please:
   His pipe was at his foot,
   His lambs were him beside,   5
A widow turtle near on bared root
   Sat wailing without boot.
   Each thing both sweet and sad
   Did draw his boiling brain
   To think and think with pain   10
Of Mira's beams, eclipst by absence bad.
   And thus, with eyes made dim
With tears, he said, or sorrow said for him:

V. 3. *to please:* able to please.
   6. *turtle:* turtle dove.
   7. *boot:* remedy.
    NOTES: p. 242

'O earth, once answer give,
    So may thy stately grace   15
By north or south still rich adorned live;
    So Mira long may be
    On thy then blessed face,
Whose foot doth set a heav'n on cursed thee;
    I ask, now answer me,   20
    If th'author of thy bliss,
    Phoebus, that shepherd high,
    Do turn from thee his eye,
Doth not thyself, when he long absent is,
    Like rogue all ragged go,   25
And pine away with daily wasting woe?

'Tell me, you wanton brook,
    So may your sliding race
Shun loathed-loving banks with cunning crook;
    So in you ever new   30
    Mira may look her face,
And make you fair with shadow of her hue;
    So when to pay your due
    To mother Sea you come,
    She chide you not for stay,   35
    Nor beat you for your play;
Tell me, if your diverted springs become
    Absented quite from you,
Are you not dried? Can you yourself renew?

'Tell me, you flowers fair,   40
    Cowslip and columbine,
So may your make, this wholesome springtime air,
    With you embraced lie,
    And lately thence untwine,
But with dew drops engender children high;   45
    So may you never die,

29. *crook:* turning aside.
42. *make:* mate.

But, pull'd by Mira's hand,
Dress bosom hers or head,
Or scatter on her bed;
Tell me, if husband Springtime leave your land   50
   When he from you is sent,
Wither not you, languisht with discontent?

'Tell me, my silly pipe,
   So may thee still betide
A cleanly cloth thy moistness for to wipe;   55
   So may the cherries red
   Of Mira's lips divide
Their sugar'd selves to kiss thy happy head;
   So may her ears be led
   (Her ears where music lives)   60
   To hear and not despise
   Thy liribliring cries;
Tell if that breath, which thee thy sounding gives,
   Be absent far from thee,
Absent, alone, canst thou then piping be?   65

'Tell me, my lamb of gold,
   So mayst thou long abide
The day well fed, the night in faithful fold;
   So grow thy wool of note
   In time, that richly dyed   70
It may be part of Mira's petticoat;
   Tell me, if wolves the throat
   Have caught of thy dear dam,
   Or she from thee be stay'd,
   Or thou from her be stray'd,   75
Canst thou, poor lamb, become another's lamb,
   Or rather, till thou die,
Still for thy dam with bae-waymenting cry?

62. *liribliring:* word imitating a pipe's sound.
69. *of note:* famous.
78. *bae-waymenting:* lamenting by crying bae.

NOTES: p. 242

'Tell me, O turtle true,
　　So may no fortune breed　　　　　　　80
To make thee nor thy better-loved rue;
　　So may thy blessings swarm,
　　That Mira may thee feed
With hand and mouth, with lap and breast keep warm;
　　Tell me, if greedy arm　　　　　　　85
　　Do fondly take away,
　　With traitor lime, the one,
　　The other left alone,
Tell me, poor wretch, parted from wretched prey,
　　Disdain you not the green,　　　　　　90
Wailing till death, shun you not to be seen?

　　'Earth, brook, flowers, pipe, lamb, dove,
　　Say all, and I with them,
Absence is death, or worse, to them that love.
　　So I, unlucky lad,　　　　　　　95
　　Whom hills from her do hem,
What fits me now but tears and sighings sad?
　　O Fortune too too bad,
　　I rather would my sheep
　　Th'adst killed with a stroke,　　　　　100
　　Burnt cabin, lost my cloak,
Than want one hour those eyes which my joys keep.
　　O, what doth wailing win?
Speech without end were better not begin.

　　'My song, climb thou the wind　　　　　105
Which Holland sweet now gently sendeth in,
That on his wings the level thou mayst find
　　To hit, but kissing hit
　　Her ears, the weights of wit.

86. *fondly:* madly.
87. *lime:* bird-lime.
89. *prey:* your captured mate.
96. *hem:* shut out.
107. *level:* aim.
109. *the weights of wit:* the scales in which wit is weighed.
NOTES: p. 243

If thou know not for whom thy master dies,   110
   These marks shall make thee wise:
She is the herdess fair that shines in dark,
And gives her kids no food but willow's bark.'

   This said, at length he ended
   His oft sigh-broken ditty,   115
Then rase, but rase on legs with faintness bended,
   With skin in sorrow dyed,
   With face the plot of pity,
With thoughts which thoughts their own tormenters tried,
   He rase, and straight espied   120
   His ram, who, to recover
   The ewe another loved,
   With him proud battle proved.
He envied such a death in sight of lover,
   And always westward eyeing,   125
More envied Phoebus for his western flying.

VI

STREPHON.   KLAIUS.

STREPH. Ye goat-herd gods, that love the grassy mountains,
   Ye nymphs which haunt the springs in pleasant valleys,
   Ye satyrs joy'd with free and quiet forests,
   Vouchsafe your silent ears to plaining music,
   Which to my woes gives still an early morning,   5
   And draws the dolour on till weary evening.
KLAI. O Mercury, foregoer to the evening,
   O heavenly huntress of the savage mountains,
   O lovely star, entitl'd of the morning,
   While that my voice doth fill these woeful valleys,   10

116. *rase:* rose.
118. *plot:* map, plan.
  119. *which thoughts . . . tried:* which suffered the torment of themselves.
VI. 4. *plaining:* lamenting.

NOTES: p. 243

Vouchsafe your silent ears to plaining music,
Which oft hath Echo tir'd in secret forests.

STREPH. I that was once free-burgess of the forests,
Where shade from sun, and sports I sought at evening,
I that was once esteem'd for pleasant music,   15
Am banisht now among the monstrous mountains
Of huge despair, and foul affliction's valleys;
Am grown a screech-owl to myself each morning.

KLAI. I that was once delighted every morning,
Hunting the wild inhabiters of forests,   20
I that was once the music of these valleys,
So darken'd am, that all my day is evening;
Heart-broken so, that mole-hills seem high mountains;
And fill the vales with cries instead of music.

STREPH. Long since, alas, my deadly swannish music   25
Hath made itself a crier of the morning,
And hath with wailing strength climb'd highest mountains;
Long since my thoughts more desert be than forests;
Long since I see my joys come to their evening,
And state thrown down to over-trodden valleys.   30

KLAI. Long since the happy dwellers of these valleys
Have pray'd me leave my strange exclaiming music,
Which troubles their day's work, and joys of evening;
Long since I hate the night, more hate the morning;
Long since my thoughts chase me like beasts in forests,   35
And make me wish myself laid under mountains.

STREPH. Meseems I see the high and stately mountains
Transform themselves to low dejected valleys;
Meseems I hear in these ill-changed forests
The nightingales do learn of owls their music;   40
Meseems I feel the comfort of the morning
Turn'd to the mortal serene of an evening.

KLAI. Meseems I see a filthy cloudy evening
As soon as sun begins to climb the mountains;

25. *deadly swannish music:* music like the song of the dying swan.
42. *serene:* unhealthy dew or mist.

NOTES: p. 243

Meseems I feel a noisome scent, the morning,   45
When I do smell the flowers of these valleys;
Meseems I hear, when I do hear sweet music,
The dreadful cries of murder'd men in forests.
STREPH. I wish to fire the trees of all these forests;
    I give the sun a last farewell each evening;   50
    I curse the fiddling finders-out of music;
    With envy do I hate the lofty mountains,
    And with despite despise the humble valleys;
    I do detest night, evening, day, and morning.
KLAI. Curse to myself my prayer is, the morning;   55
    My fire is more than can be made with forests;
    My state more base than are the basest valleys;
    I wish no evenings more to see, each evening;
    Shamed, I hate myself in sight of mountains,
    And stop mine ears, lest I go mad with music.   60
STREPH. For she whose parts maintain'd a perfect music,
    Whose beauty shin'd more than the blushing morning,
    Who much did pass in state the stately mountains,
    In straightness pass'd the cedars of the forests,
    Hath cast me, wretch, into eternal evening,   65
    By taking her two suns from these dark valleys.
KLAI. For she to whom compar'd the Alps are valleys,
    She whose least word brings from the spheres their music,
    At whose approach the sun rose in the evening,
    Who, where she went, bare in her forehead morning,   70
    Is gone, is gone from these our spoiled forests,
    Turning to deserts our best pastur'd mountains.
STREPH. KLAI. These mountains witness shall, so shall these valleys,
    These forests eke, made wretched by our music,
    Our morning hymn is this, and song at evening.   75

> 45. *feel:* smell.
> 45. *the morning:* in the morning.
> 55. *curse . . . my prayer is:* I pray for death.
> 56. *fire:* passion.
> 66. *her two suns:* her eyes.
> 70. *bare:* bore.

NOTES: p. 243

VII

The nightingale, as soon as April bringeth
Unto her rested sense a perfect waking,
While late bare earth, proud of new clothing, springeth,
Sings out her woes, a thorn her song-book making;
　　And mournfully bewailing,　　　　　　　　　　　5
　　Her throat in tunes expresseth
　　What grief her breast oppresseth
For Tereus' force on her chaste will prevailing.
O Philomela fair, O take some gladness
That here is juster cause of plaintful sadness:　　　10
　　Thine earth now springs, mine fadeth;
Thy thorn without, my thorn my heart invadeth.

Alas, she hath no other cause of anguish
But Tereus' love, on her by strong hand wroken,
Wherein she suffering all her spirits' languish　　　15
Full womanlike complains her will was broken.
　　But I who, daily craving,
　　Cannot have to content me,
　　Have more cause to lament me,
Since wanting is more woe than too much having.　　20
O Philomela fair, O take some gladness
That here is juster cause of plaintful sadness:
　　Thine earth now springs, mine fadeth;
Thy thorn without, my thorn my heart invadeth.

VIII

Ring out your bells, let mourning shows be spread,
　　For love is dead:
All love is dead, infected
With plague of deep disdain;
Worth, as nought worth, rejected,　　　　　　　　　5

VII. 10. *plaintful:* full of lamentation.
　　14. *wroken:* inflicted.
　　18. *cannot have to content me:* cannot have what would satisfy me.
VIII. 1. *mourning shows:* signs of mourning, black hangings.

And faith fair scorn doth gain.
  From so ungrateful fancy,
  From such a female franzy,
  From them that use men thus,
  Good Lord, deliver us.   10

Weep, neighbours, weep, do you not hear it said
  That Love is dead?
His death-bed, peacock's folly;
His winding-sheet is shame;
His will, false-seeming holy;   15
His sole executor, blame.
  From so ungrateful fancy,
  From such a female franzy,
  From them that use men thus,
  Good Lord, deliver us.   20

Let dirge be sung, and trentals rightly read,
  For Love is dead.
Sir Wrong his tomb ordaineth,
My mistress' marble heart,
Which epitaph containeth,   25
'Her eyes were once his dart.'
  From so ungrateful fancy,
  From such a female franzy,
  From them that use men thus,
  Good Lord, deliver us.   30

Alas, I lie: rage hath this error bred.
  Love is not dead.
Love is not dead, but sleepeth
In her unmatched mind,
Where she his counsel keepeth   35
Till due desert she find.

    8. *franzy:* frenzy, madness.
    13. *peacock's folly:* (feminine) pride.
    21. *trentals:* thirty masses for the soul.
    34. *unmatched:* matchless.

NOTES: p. 244

Therefore from so vile fancy,
To call such wit a franzy,
Who love can temper thus,
Good Lord, deliver us.   40

IX

Thou blind man's mark, thou fool's self-chosen snare,
Fond fancy's scum, and dregs of scatter'd thought,
Band of all evils, cradle of causeless care,
Thou web of will, whose end is never wrought;
    Desire, Desire, I have too dearly bought,   5
With price of mangled mind, thy worthless ware;
Too long, too long asleep thou hast me brought,
Who should my mind to higher things prepare.
But yet in vain thou hast my ruin sought,
    In vain thou mad'st me to vain things aspire,   10
    In vain thou kindlest all thy smoky fire;
For Virtue hath this better lesson taught,
    Within myself to seek my only hire,
    Desiring nought but how to kill Desire.

X

Leave me, O Love, which reachest but to dust,
And thou, my mind, aspire to higher things:
Grow rich in that which never taketh rust:
Whatever fades, but fading pleasure brings.
    Draw in thy beams, and humble all thy might   5
To that sweet yoke where lasting freedoms be;
Which breaks the clouds and opens forth the light
That doth both shine and give us sight to see.

39. *temper:* control.
IX. 1. *mark:* target.
    2. *scatter'd:* confused.
    3. *band:* leash.
    4. *web:* piece of weaving.
    8. *who:* I myself.
    13. *hire:* reward.

NOTES: p. 244

O take fast hold, let that light be thy guide
In this small course which birth draws out to death,   10
And think how evil becometh him to slide
Who seeketh heav'n and comes of heav'nly breath.
    Then farewell world, thy uttermost I see:
    Eternal Love, maintain thy life in me.

Splendidis longum valedico nugis.

    11. *how evil becometh:* how badly it befits.

Notes

THE DEFENCE OF POESY

1–2 *at the Emperor's Court together:* From autumn 1574 to spring 1575, Sidney (then aged 20) and Wotton (aged 26) were at the Court of the Emperor Maximilian II in Vienna.

18 *pedanteria:* pedantry. Sidney makes us hear Pugliano's derogatory tone by quoting his Italian word.

40 *philosophers:* especially Plato, who urged the banishment of poetry from his ideal Republic (*Republic*, Book X).

49 *his host:* a snake which invited him to hibernate in its crevice.

50 *kill their parents:* by eating them, according to Pliny's *Natural History*, the fancies of which were repeated as facts by medieval books.

51–52 *Musaeus, Homer and Hesiod* are historical, and their works survive (though the Musaeus to whom Sidney refers, who wrote of Hero and Leander, was not the early Musaeus but a much later writer); *Orpheus, Linus,* and *Amphion* are mythical.

90 *Gyges' Ring:* Gyges, a shepherd, found a magic ring and thereby made himself invisible at will; by this means he killed the king of Lydia and gained the kingdom (Plato, *Republic*, Book II).

91 *walk into Apollo's garden:* recognize and enjoy poetry (of which Apollo was the patron). Sidney's own style continually employs metaphor and simile, as here.

112 *Areytos:* (plural of Spanish *aréito*) song-dances for individual and chorus, used among the American Indians (who are always meant by Sidney's 'Indians').

136 *Sortes Virgilianae:* the use of Virgil's works to tell one's fortune (*sortes*, the oracle's replies). Virgil had a traditional reputation as a magician.

139 *Albinus:* governor of Britain, A.D. 192. *Arma amens capio . . . armis:* 'Madly I seize my arms, nor is there much purpose in arms' (*Aeneid*, II, 314: Aeneas describing his reaction to the

213

Greeks' midnight entry into Troy). Albinus fulfilled the prophecy when he led his army against the Emperor Septimius
Severus and lost his life.

179 *a maker:* used in this sense since Chaucer's time.

198-9 *which still are compassed . . . proposed matter:* which are
always confined by their application to the subject discussed;
cf. p. 36, l. 580, 'learn a conceit out of a matter'.

201-2 *though it be in the second and abstract notions:* though it re-
gards things not as independent objects, but as parts of a
system.

212 *so rich tapestry:* With the renaissance admiration for art and
ornament, Sidney portrays Nature as a decorator and furnisher;
cf. Astrophel and Stella, IX.

215 *the too much loved earth:* a phrase suggesting the tension in
Sidney's mind, as in Spenser's, between the claims of earth and
heaven.

219 *Theagenes:* the lover of Chariclea in Heliodorus's Greek
romance *Aethiopica,* one of the books which inspired *Arcadia.*

220 *Pylades:* the faithful friend of Orestes in the Greek tragedies.

220 *Orlando:* the chivalrous hero of Ariosto's romantic epic
Orlando Furioso.

221 *Cyrus:* King of Persia. W. Barker's translation, *The Books of
Xenophon containing the Discipline and Education of Cyrus,* was
published in 1560.

225 *Idea or foreconceit:* mental image. That is, it is imagination,
not technique, that makes a great artist.

243 *erected wit; infected will:* a strong antithesis between reason and
passion, the higher and the lower parts of human nature; *cf.
Astrophel and Stella,* V ; and p. 29, 'our degenerate souls, made
worse by their clayey lodgings'.

253 *Aristotle:* in his *Poetics.* This book, and Horace's *Art of Poetry,*
are the corner-stones of renaissance criticism and literary theory.

264 *Emanuel Tremellius and Franciscus Junius:* Protestant theolo-
gians of Heidelberg. They translated the Old Testament into
Latin.

269 *St James's counsel:* in his general epistle, V, 13: 'Is any among
you afflicted? Let him pray. Is any merry? Let him sing psalms.'

288 *Lucretia:* the type of Roman heroic chastity. Raped by Tar-quin, she killed herself: see Shakespeare's poem *The Rape of Lucrece.*

334 *by his works, and then by his parts:* The 'works' of poetry are its effects (namely teaching and delighting); the 'parts' are its kinds or species (heroic, lyric, tragic, etc.).

345 *high and heavenly:* Sidney obtains a touch of irony by combin-ing the literal and figurative senses of the words.

361 ἀρχιτεκτονικη (*architektonike*): from the opening of Aristotle's *Ethics:* the highest knowledge is that which leads to virtue and right action. Sidney refers to the same passage on p. 35.

376–7 *whereto they set their names:* and thus betray their own desire for the earthly fame which their books disparage.

396–8 *better acquainted . . . wit runneth:* ignorant of the present time, and still more ignorant of himself.

402–3 *Testis temporum . . . nuntiavet ustatis:* the witness of times, the light of truth, the life of memory, the teacher of life, the messenger of antiquity (Cicero, *De Oratore*, II).

416–17 *Brutus; Alphonsus of Aragon:* Roman and medieval exam-ples of great men who were copious readers of histories.

420–1 *since the question . . . school of learning:* since the question is, which of these should take precedence in the academy where virtue is studied and taught? Sidney again develops a metaphor, this time from academic disputation: a *moderator* is the arbitra-tor between the challenger and the defender of a thesis.

432 *rather formidine poenae than virtutis amore:* rather by fear of punishment than by love of virtue (Horace, *Epistles*, I, xvi).

493 *the tragedy writer:* Euripides (as Plutarch reports him), answering objections to the impious character of his Ixion, who, taken by Jupiter to heaven, attempted to seduce Juno.

498 *Miltiades:* the victor of Marathon.

503–4 *virtuous Cato: rebel Caesar:* Caesar used force to overthrow the Republic and make himself dictator; Cato killed himself rather than submit to him.

543–4 *Hoc opus, hic labor est:* This is the task, this is the toil (Virgil, *Aeneid*, VI, 128, referring to the difficulty of returning from the Underworld).

589 *our Saviour Christ:* Sidney has shown the poetical nature of parables, citing those of Dives and Lazarus and the Prodigal Son.

ASTROPHEL AND STELLA

I. 'This introductory sonnet performs the double function of praising Stella as the ground of all poetical invention and of providing a brief essay on the proper method of writing love poetry' (Ringler). Like five other sonnets in *Astrophel and Stella*, it is written in alexandrines.

2 *the dear She:* the beloved, my dear Lady; cf. *Twelfth Night*, I, v, 225, 'the cruellest she alive'. A variant reading is 'she (dear she)'; this parenthesis is characteristic of Sidney (cf. p. 97) 'her body (O sweet body) . . .'), yet the noun phrase seems preferable to a pronoun.

7 *others' leaves:* Sidney's use of images is free. From the leaves of others' books of poetry, there flow showers to refresh the brain, which is a field parched with drought, the hot sun being rays of Stella's beauty. Likewise, in ll. 9–10, Invention is first a crutch and immediately afterwards a child.

14 *look in thy heart and write:* 'What the poet will see when he looks in his heart is the image of Stella' (Ringler).

II. 10 *slave-born Muscovite:* Russian serf.

14 *a feeling skill:* cf. Pope, *Eloisa to Abelard*, l. 366: 'He best can paint 'em [a lover's woes] who shall feel 'em most.'

III. A profession of sincerity in love and of consequent simplicity in art. The poet's 'one Muse' is Stella, and he treats the other love-poets' extravagances with amused irony.

3 *Pindar's apes:* the French sonneteers, especially Ronsard, and their English imitators. Pindar was a master of the grand style in Greek poetry.

7 *strange similes:* a fashion brought in by Lyly in his prose romance *Euphues:* thus Euphues, trying to convince Lucilla that not all lovers are inconstant, tells her 'though Polypus change his hue, yet the Salamander keepeth his colour'.

IV. The theme of a conflict between virtue and love (sometimes between reason and love) appears often in the sonnets. It has nothing to do with the poet's scruples in loving a married woman, but is about his scruples in giving to love time and talents that could be better employed; cf. pp. 81–87, where Musidorus reproves Pyrocles on these general grounds. 'Fundamentally, the debate between virtue and love is utilized in the cycle to give it drama' (Hallett Smith).

5 *Cato:* a Roman moralist.

V. A series of concessions, countered by a final assertion. Sidney allows that the soul is above the body, reason above the senses, virtue above love; and yet love is irresistible. The flippant tone of ll. 5–8 prepares for the final surprise, which, however, remains a surprise.

10–11 *this beauty . . . breed:* this mortal beauty, compounded of mortal physical elements, is but a shadow of that real beauty which is virtue. Platonic doctrine.

IX. A sustained and elaborate metaphor: Stella's face as Virtue's palace.

5 *her Grace:* Virtue's title. She 'comes forth' whenever Stella speaks, because all Stella's words are virtuous.

10–11 *nothing such . . . name of best:* nothing which can challenge the excellence of those windows.

IX. 12 *touch:* 'a form of lignite that has the property of attracting light bodies when static electricity is induced by rubbing. The windows (Stella's black eyes) are made of "touch" (glossy black stone) that without "touch" (contact) doth "touch" (affect with emotion)' (Ringler).

X. 2 *Sense and Love:* Sidney often half-personifies abstract nouns. This sonnet starts with a brawl ('brabbling') which prepares for the sword-play in the sestet; but in the middle the personification is dropped, and love is classified as a province of emotion ('will'). When this happens it seems best not to use capital initials throughout, since this would artificially sustain the personification.

10 *giving wounds of dispraise:* disparaging earthly beauty, as in V, 10–11.

11 *downright blows; cunning fence:* a good antithesis. The subtle arguments of reason are powerless against the strong impact of the passions and the senses.

XII. 2 *day-nets:* 'In Wiltshire [where Sidney's married sister the Countess of Pembroke lived] larks were caught with "day-nets" by attracting them with a brightly-shining lure made of small mirrors (Stella's eyes) and then capturing them with a net (her locks)' (Ringler).

8 *her clear voice:* when she sings (as opposed to 'speaks' in l. 7).

XIV. A justification of love against the traditional objections that it is sinful. See note to IV. 'It is another Musidorus to whom this sonnet is addressed' (Pollard).

3 *him who first stale down the fire:* Prometheus, whom Jove punished by chaining him to a mountain where a vulture fed on his liver.

XV. Further mockery of literary affectations.

2 *old Parnassus:* seat of the Muses. Sidney alludes to the imitation of Greek poetry; cf. III, 3.

5 *dictionary's method:* alliteration (of which the next line gives an example).

8 *denizen'd wit:* 'native English intelligence', in a derogatory sense ('How unlike the great Italian!'); cf. the mocking antithesis of 'long-deceased' and 'new-born', and of 'far-fet helps' and 'inward touch'.

12–13 *But if . . . breasts of Fame:* but if you wish to become famous both for your love and for your poetry.

XVI. 9 *this young lion:* growing love: a traditional metaphor, lion cubs being playful and harmless, old lions fierce and dangerous.

XVII. A fanciful elaboration of a conceit (that his mistress's eyebrow is Cupid's bow) into a story.

9 *his grandam Nature:* Nature is called Cupid's grandmother, partly to make her presence (and her spoiling the child) plausible, and partly to show that Nature begets Beauty (Venus) and Beauty begets Desire (Cupid).

XIX. 5 *my best wits . . . disgrace invent:* I use my brains to write love-poetry, a discreditable pursuit and a fruitless one.

12 *prop my mind:* The metaphor is from husbandry: the 'growing' mind is a 'fruit'-tree, to be 'propped' in one way (according to reason), or 'bent' in another (according to Love).

XX. Cupid lurks in ambush in Stella's eye-lashes; like an Elizabethan highway-robber, he is armed with a gun, though in l. 13 it has become his traditional dart.

XXI. 1 *caustics:* used medically, to burn away diseased living tissue.

5–6 *that Plato . . . coltish gyres:* 'Sidney has in mind the passage in the *Phaedrus* [of Plato] in which Socrates describes the struggles of the soul to control the horses by which its chariot is drawn' (Wilson).

XXII. Stella is compared with the sun: she shines in beauty as he does in light and heat (l. 10), and the sun's harmless kiss is a tribute to her beauty.

1 *In highest way of heav'n:* in the noonday height of his heavenly course. There is also word-play on 'highway'; for the sun is 'progressing' from the Twins' 'place', like a king on a state journey from one noble's house to another; cf. *Hamlet*, IV, iii, 30: 'how a king may go a progress through the guts of a beggar'.

2 *Twins:* Castor and Pollux, the zodiacal sign of Gemini, where the sun is in the last third of May and the first two-thirds of June.

9 *marcht:* a vigorous verb continuing the metaphor of 'foe's wounds' and 'unarmed'.

XXIV. 1 *Rich:* a play on the name of Penelope Devereux's husband, Lord Rich (see Introduction, p. 8); also *cf.* the parable of the Rich Fool, Luke XII, 16–20.

3 *Tantal:* Tantalus, punished in Hades by being starved in the midst of plenty.

5–14: 'Heaven makes these fools wise enough to know what they have got (i.e., money), knowledge makes them love it, love makes them treasure it as too sacred to touch. But there is one rich fool (i.e., Lord Rich) who uses no such abstinence, and for his punishment is exiled from all knowledge of the treasures of Stella's mind' (Pollard).

XXVII. The turn of the thought is a good surprise: the ambition of which he accuses himself (or boasts) is a wholly private one, and is contrasted with the self-advancement which is the accepted ambition of a courtier.

XXXI. The pathos of this sonnet comes from the indirect nature of the lover's complaint, expressed in his sympathy for the moon.

14 *Do they call virtue there ungratefulness?:* Muir interprets this question as 'aimed at himself for stigmatizing Stella's virtue, or chastity, as ingratitude', and says that Lamb's explanation (see footnote) 'would make the line intolerably clumsy, more difficult to read, and less subtle'. But it is clumsier to change the sense of the pronoun 'they'; Sidney's inversion throws the whole weight of the sestet upon 'ungratefulness'; and it is possible to be too subtle an interpreter. Ringler refers to Italian poetic examples of disdain and cruelty being miscalled honour.

XXXIII. The 'heav'nly day' which he might have had is Stella's hand in marriage; deprived of this, he is plunged in 'infernal [hellish] night'. The 'rising morn' was the dawn of Stella's love.

14 *That I had been more foolish or more wise!:* O that I had offered my love without calculating the consequences (i.e., lack of money upon which to marry?)! This, though apparent folly, would have been true wisdom.

XXXIV. An internal dialogue, reaching its crisis with ll. 9–10, where the antithesis sharpens the conflict. In ll. 12–14, it seems necessary to supply another 'while': i.e., Thus, while I hesitate between writing and not writing, any observer might see how Stella's excellence has power to disturb my mind.

5–6 *Art not asham'd ... so rare:* His disease is rare because it is completely sincere love.

XXXV. 4 *Where nature doth with infinite agree:* where infinite beauty can exist within a limited natural form; cf. p. 106: 'the goddess, who in a definite compass can set forth infinite beauty'.
11 *rich:* another play on Stella's married name.

XXXVIII. 8 *sings:* an arresting end to the octave, throwing the interest forward to the sestet ('I start, look, *heark*').

XXXIX. This sonnet anticipates some of Shakespeare's passages about Sleep, e.g., *2 Henry IV*, III, i, 1–31; *Macbeth*, II, ii, 35–40.
1 *knot:* 'the place where peace frayed by day is knitted up again' (Wilson).
13 *Move not thy heavy grace:* obtain thy weighty favour; 'heavy' is used paradoxically, as it usually refers metaphorically to retribution, not to favour, but it is here appropriate to the boon of deep sleep which the poet desires.

XL. 3–4 *That hast my mind . . . to moan:* That hast brought my mind to lament my unchanging course of love. *None of the basest:* Sidney's lovers show a proper sense of their worth; cf. pp. 136 and 153.

14 *O do not let thy temple be destroy'd:* The temple is the lover's heart in which he worships Stella. In *Arcadia*, Musidorus makes the same appeal to Pamela, p. 134.

XLI. 9–10 *because of both sides . . . excel in this:* 'Sidney's father and grandfather, and his maternal uncles the earls of Leicester and Warwick, had been frequent participants in tournaments in their younger days' (Ringler).

XLII. 12–14 *And if from majesty . . . doth breed:* And if my death should proceed from the overwhelming of my mortal powers by the power of these stars, I shall think such destruction (caused by aspiring too high in love) a triumph.

XLV. 10 *free scope:* in contrast with the restriction which |honour (i.e., care for one's reputation, cf. Eighth Song, l. 95) imposes upon her sympathy.

XLVII. 2 *black beams:* Stella's black eyes, which engrave burning marks as of a brand identifying a slave.

3 *born a slave:* as opposed to becoming one, ll. 1–3.

LII. 'The sonnet must, of course, be taken as Sidney's playful raillery of his own Platonic meditations' (Pollard).

12 *demur:* an admission of the facts, but a denial that they constitute a legal claim to possession.

LIII. In this sonnet, contrary to Sidney's usual practice, the break comes not at the end of the octave but after l. 9.

7 *I would no less:* I wanted (deserved) no other title. Sometimes printed as part of Love's speech, and interpreted as 'I insist'.

9 *made a window send forth light:* thus reversing its function.

LIV. 2 *set colours:* colours appointed to a lover, either by convention (the green and yellow of sorrow, the blue of constancy) or by his lady (like Malvolio's yellow stockings in *Twelfth Night*).

6 *in their lips:* contrast 'in the heart', l. 12.

H

LXI. 7 *selfness:* selfish passions. 'Apparently a coinage by Sidney' (Wilson).

12 *Doctor Cupid:* Cupid is given an academic title, with some humour, because he is being engaged as a logician.

14 *That I love not without I leave to love:* a paradox, like the last line of the next sonnet.

LXIV. A rhetorical and eloquent protestation that he has no ambition besides Stella's favour.

LXVI. 10 *last fair night, nay day:* 'night' is used literally to mean evening, 'day' metaphorically to mean the dawn of happiness.

LXIX. 12–13 *And though ... virtuous course I take:* Stella has granted her love on condition that Astrophel does not demand her body. Compare the last line of the next sonnet, and p. 155: 'they passed the promise of marriage: which fain Pyrocles would have sealed with the chief arms of his desire, but Philoclea commanded the contrary'.

LXXIII. 1 *Love ... a wanton is:* Love (Cupid) is always a boy (i.e., he never grows up, but is always pictured so), and is often a naughty one.

5 *my Star:* Stella; *cf.* Second Song, l. 1, 'my heav'nly jewel'. This song immediately precedes this sonnet in the sequence of the best texts.

LXXIV. Sidney laughs at sonneteers who insist on their originality. At the same time he seriously insists – though with humour and a light touch – that Stella is his inspiration.

1 *Aganippe well:* a fountain situated at the foot of Mount Helicon and sacred to the Muses.

2 *Tempe:* a valley where Daphne, pursued by Apollo, was changed to a laurel tree; the laurel is the poet's crown.

5 *poets' fury;* poetical inspiration, a divine madness according to Plato.

7 *by blackest brook of hell:* to swear by the Styx was the Olympian gods' most solemn and binding oath. Sidney's style here, with its omission of the definite article and its alliteration, mocks a

passing fashion (cf. XV. 6); contrast the flowing smoothness of
ll. 9–11. There is further rhythmical contrast when the smooth
and complete l. 14 follows the abrupt questionings and denials
of ll. 12–13.

LXXVIII. A 'character' of Jealousy, identified in the ambiguity
of the last line as Stella's husband.

14 *wants horns:* literally, lacks horns to complete his devilish
   ugliness: figuratively, is not made a cuckold (of whom horns are,
   for reasons unknown, the traditional crest).

LXXXIII. To a sparrow. Skelton (died 1529) had written a famous
poem, *Philip Sparrow*, in which a girl lamented her pet sparrow's
death (he was killed by a cat) and praised his virtues. Sidney calls
the sparrow brother (l. 1) because they share the same Christian
name, and humorously affects jealousy at the favours the sparrow
receives from Stella. Some readers insist that Astrophel is not Sidney; but Astrophel's name is not Philip.

LXXXIV. 1 *since you my chief Parnassus be:* since Sidney com-
poses many of his poems on horseback, as he states in ll. 2–4, he
calls the road Parnassus, i.e., the seat of the Muses, where poetry
originates.

   6 *where I my heart safeliest shall meet:* Since he left it with her, he
   will most surely find it with her; cf. p. 156: 'Zelmane came
   with her body to find her mind, which was gone long before her,
   and had gotten his seat in Philoclea.'

LXXXVI. 5 *spotless ermine:* the white fur of the ermine (stoat in
winter colouring) was much prized; here its colour is taken as a
symbol of purity.

LXXXVIII. 3–4 *she that . . . oft shows a present pay:* another
woman who freely offers her love. The metaphor is that of a re-
cruiting officer.

LXXXIX. This sonnet is built upon the paradoxical conceit of the
last two lines; and to sharpen the antithesis, the two words 'night'
and 'day' provide its only rhymes. There is no break between octave
and sestet. Instead, a long cumulative sentence runs from l. 7 to
the end. Its sense is sufficiently clear, but its syntax is confused.

XC. 11 *Without my plumes . . . I take:* alluding to Aesop's fable of the upstart crow beautified with the other birds' feathers. Its use perhaps suggested to Sidney the 'nest' metaphor in l. 6 (where the laurel tree is used, as always, to symbolize poetic fame).

XCII. 6 *Phoenix Stella:* Stella, like the Phoenix, is unique.

Second Song. 24 *Who will read must first learn spelling:* spelling is to reading as a first kiss is to further favours.

Fourth Song. The lovers are imagined in Stella's bedroom after the rest of the household has gone to bed. She gently refuses Astrophel's demands, in the refrain of each stanza. The last stanza draws the dialogue to a good conclusion: she still does not yield to his passion, but she assuages his despair.

14 *Cupid's yoke to loose or bind:* i.e., to confirm love by releasing passion.

43 *why strive you thus?:* Astrophel's embrace brings the situation to its crisis.

Eighth Song. The course of this poem resembles that of the Fourth Song, except that the grounds of Stella's refusal are here given in detail. The setting this time is an outdoor one in spring, and the joyous mood of nature contrasts with the pathetic mood of the lovers, whose pathos is increased by their joy in each other's rare company.

19 *with arms crost:* crossed or folded arms were a sign of grief; cf. pp. 88, 123.

69–100: 'Nowhere in literature is there a refusal which is more like yielding; nowhere a more generous bestowal of the heart such as makes the refusal of the body seem of no account' (Legouis).

Eleventh Song. A nocturnal dialogue at Stella's window. She attempts to dissuade Astrophel from his hopeless love, but he counters all her arguments.

24 *Image-like of saints' perfection:* Such poetic imagery had survived the Reformation: compare the sonnet-dialogue shared by Romeo and Juliet at their first meeting.

42 *Argus' eyes:* for Argus, see note to p. 196. From this stanza and the preceding one, it seems that Stella is either in her husband's house or within sight of his spies.

ARCADIA

For a general account of the story, see Introduction. The contexts of the extracts are given in these notes as the extracts are reached.

The division of the Books into Chapters, and the summary headings, are not by Sidney but by 'the overseer of the print' of 1590, probably Sidney's lifelong friend Fulke Greville. They are not only useful but skilful, pithily summing up situations in order to bring out their narrative and moral interest, and preserving the suspense where necessary.

BOOK I, CHAPTER 12

Musidorus (calling himself Palladius) and Pyrocles (calling himself Daiphantus) were wrecked off the coast of Laconia. Musidorus, flung on shore, was revived by two Arcadian shepherds; Pyrocles, clinging to the wreckage, was captured by slave-trading pirates. The shepherds took Musidorus to their country and left him in the care of Kalander, a nobleman. Learning that Kalander's son had been taken prisoner in a civil war between the gentlemen and helots (slaves) of Laconia, Musidorus volunteered to go to his rescue, where he encountered Pyrocles, whose merits had raised him to be captain of the helots. Peace was made, and the two princes returned to Kalander's house. There Pyrocles saw Philoclea's picture, fell in love with her, and soon afterwards vanished during a hunting party, leaving a note for his friend explaining that love was the reason for his going.

22–23 *resembling her he had once loved:* Zelmane, daughter to King Plexirtus. Her story is told to Philoclea by Pyrocles in Book II, Chapters 20–23. She loved Pyrocles and followed him disguised as a page, revealing her identity only as she was dying: ' "Think of me after my death with kindness, though ye cannot with love. And whensoever ye shall make any other lady happy with your well-placed affection, if you tell her my folly, I pray you speak of it not with scorn but with pity." . . . And then kissing me, and often desiring me not to condemn her of lightness [immodesty], in mine arms she delivered her pure soul to the purest place [heaven]: leaving me as full of agony, as kindness, pity and sorrow could make an honest heart. For I must confess for true, that if my stars had not wholly reserved me for you, there else perhaps I might have loved, and (which had been most

strange) begun my love after death: whereof let it be the less
marvel, because somewhat she did resemble you: though as far
short of your perfection as herself dying was of herself flourishing' (Book II, Chapter 23).

27 *discreet stays make speedy journeys:* the converse of the proverb,
More haste, less speed. Sidney frequently, as in this passage,
lightens romance with humour.

31 *a sorrowful memory:* of his friend's loss.

61 *Omphale:* Queen of Lydia, to whom Hercules was in bondage
for three years. Pyrocles uses Hercules spinning as a symbol of
his own condition, grown superficially like a woman because of
his love, but *Never more valiant.*

72–73 *beautiful; full of harmony:* strikingly transposed epithets.

123–4 *the reasonable part . . . absolute commandment:* cf. *Astrophel
and Stella*, V, and Pyrocles's own song, p. 80.

129–30 *we must do it . . . we will do it:* cf. *Astrophel and Stella*,
XLVII.

191–3 *I am not yet come . . . have my life:* Contrast Sidney's attitude
to woman (expressed in this speech, and shown in Pamela's
and Philoclea's behaviour in Cecropia's castle later) with Milton's. Notice also the argumentative skill of the speech, with its
systematic reasoning and telling illustrations. There is much
argument and debate, both in dialogue and in soliloquy, in
Arcadia.

257–8 *And in that heavenly love since there are two parts:* Renaissance neo-platonism, based upon Plato's 'ladder' image in the
Symposium: from natural love (for a human being) one proceeds
to mystical love (for the ideal perfection).

265–7 *since I assure you . . . this enterprise:* A touch of bold wit.

272–3 *'O Lord,' (said Musidorus) . . . answered Pyrocles:* The debate
quickens in this use of repartee, which corresponds to the
stichomythia or line-by-line exchange of classical drama, imported into Elizabethan drama about this time.

285 *end:* used in the two senses of 'object' and 'conclusion'.

340 *gushing out abundance of tears:* Passionate feelings receive
passionate expression in Sidney's works: compare the similar
behaviour of Chaucer's Troilus and Shakespeare's Romeo.

351-2 *But even this kindness . . . former unkindness:* But this very sympathy made Pyrocles think with more emotion of Musidorus's former unsympathetic behaviour.

365-6 *said he, smiling:* Sidney's control of mood is exquisite in this scene. He is now lightening the tone and working towards Pyrocles's exposition, in the next chapter, of the growth of his love and his fortunes therein.

BOOK I, CHAPTER 13

9 *the Lady Zelmane:* see note on pp. 225-6.

13 *his declaration:* his account of how Basilius had withdrawn into the country with his wife and daughters to avoid the fulfilment of the prophecy. (See Introduction, pp. 13-14.)

34 *Parthenia:* whose marriage to Argalus the two princes had attended as Kalander's guests. Her beauty drew from Pyrocles the significant exclamation, 'O Jupiter, how happens it that beauty is only confined to Arcadia?' (Book I, Chapter 8). For the end of Parthenia's story, see below, pp. 173-8.

58-59 *the last day of my parting and speaking with you:* Kalander's invitation to go hunting had interrupted Pyrocles's confession to Musidorus that he was in love.

71 *Philanax:* the regent of Arcadia in Basilius's retirement. He had written a letter vainly dissuading Basilius from his course.

98 *but never had his fancy in his head:* but could form no mental picture of Hercules. Compare *Defence of Poesy*, p. 26, where the artist needs a 'foreconceit'; this applies to the actor also. Dametas makes himself ridiculous by speaking big and looking aggressive. To Dametas, 'the Prince's pleasure' is a less fitting climax than 'Dametas' pleasure'.

112-13 *look so like an ape . . . purgation:* thus making his ugly face uglier. The image seems to be drawn from experience, apes being shown at fairs, and sometimes kept as pets.

113-14 *spake these words to myself:* In the Old *Arcadia* Sidney related this incident in the third person. By giving the narration to Pyrocles, he unavoidably makes it a little unnatural, and thereby reduces the comedy of this dialogue at cross-purposes.

130-1 *clowns . . . turned into frogs:* when they drove away Latona, then pregnant with Apollo and Diana.

181 *Penthesilea:* the Queen of the Amazons who helped the Trojans after the death of Hector.

199–200 *being in the strength of her age:* The princes and princesses of this story are very young. Musidorus, 'whose age could not be above one-and-twenty years' (Book I, Chapter 2), is 'elder by three or four years' than Pyrocles (Book II, Chapter 7): this makes their ardent heroism and their mature wisdom and tact the more impressive, and also makes plausible Pyrocles's disguise as an Amazon. Pamela and Philoclea may be assumed to be seventeen and sixteen, Gynecia under thirty-five, and Cecropia her sister-in-law a few years older, to make Amphialus about the same age as Musidorus. Only Basilius, who was nearly sixty years old when he married (p. 160), is old, now approaching the 'fourscore years' which Pyrocles attributes to him (p. 100).

214–15 *a very rich diamond set but in a black horn:* symbolizing, with its motto, her present condition, in bondage to Dametas.

225 *a net:* the Old *Arcadia* adds 'made only of itself', thus explaining why this net could have caught Jupiter: compare *Astrophel and Stella*, XII, 'her locks, [Cupid's] day-nets'.

230 *black eyes:* compare *Astrophel and Stella*, VII, where the same conceits are developed. Sidney says later (p. 122) that 'to [Philoclea's] memory principally all this long matter is intended', and it is tempting to suppose that in Philoclea he is idealizing Stella. But against this we must set the fact that the phrase also appears in his Old *Arcadia*, probably written before he saw Penelope Devereux. Thus, though we know from external evidence (cited by Ringler, *Poems*, p. 436) that Penelope Devereux had black eyes and gold hair, it seems that Sidney had always admired this unusual combination of beauties.

250 *taking by force her hand, and kissing it:* Sidney's delicacy. Pyrocles is so far from taking any unfair advantage that by kissing her hand (after kissing the faces of her mother and sister) he shows his adoration.

287 *built in the form of a star:* a not improbable Elizabethan architectural conceit. Compare Triangular Lodge, Rushton, Northamptonshire, allegorizing the Trinity, and incorporating the trefoil which was the emblem of its owner Sir Thomas Tresham, who built it in 1593–5. (A full description is in N. Pevsner, *Northamptonshire:* 'The Buildings of England' series, 1961.) The Elizabethans delighted in geometry.

BOOK I, CHAPTER 14

6–7 *artificial inventions:* more Elizabethan ingenuity. Note, however, that the revolving table is not an irrelevance, but amusingly symbolizes Pyrocles's situation, getting no closer to Philoclea.

13 *the heavenly Iris:* messenger of the gods, and personification of the rainbow.

21 *as a mill:* like the rotating mill-stones which are indirectly worked by a water-wheel.

77 *these avoidings of company:* such as Basilius's withdrawal of his family out of temptation's way.

84–85 *carried with the bier of violent love:* The metaphor symbolizes her dangerous and deadly passion.

87 *the unevitable Philoclea:* Philoclea, from whose presence Pyrocles cannot keep himself.

93 *to have lodged us together:* dramatic irony, such as the story frequently allows; cf. Amphialus' expression of the same thought, p. 163. But even while he brings out the irony, Sidney carefully and plausibly avoids an actual embarrassing situation.

119–20 *the praise and yet the stain:* cf. *Astrophel and Stella*, First Song, l. 10.

135–6 *Zelmane dismissed Musidorus:* Hereafter Sidney calls Pyrocles Zelmane and uses the feminine pronoun.

BOOK I, CHAPTER 18

Meanwhile a grand tournament was proclaimed, the general challenger being Phalantus, who affirmed that his lady Artesia was more beautiful than any other. He defeated many knights who produced their ladies' pictures, but at length was worsted by a knight who appeared in poor apparel to champion Philoclea. This knight proved afterwards to be the supposed Amazon Zelmane, really Pyrocles. In encountering Phalantus, Pyrocles had forestalled and disappointed another challenger, an unknown knight in black armour, who championed Pamela.

28 *Menalcas:* a shepherd with whom Musidorus has been lodging; see p. 105.

51 *smiling at him:* By again treating love with some humour (and foreshadowing Shakespeare's treatment of it in his comedies), Sidney makes a virtue out of the symmetry of his

plot. Pyrocles first pretends to turn Musidorus's own words against him, and then pretends to think that he is only feigning love. But then the thought that Musidorus may be his rival alarms him, so that the dramatic irony of the situation is partly at his expense also. Musidorus is, of course, in love with Pamela.

121–2 *I shaked the stake:* cf. *Astrophel and Stella*, Eleventh Song, ll. 33–35.

136–8 *that very evening . . . horse and armour:* when he answered Phalantus's challenge.

167–9 *the highest point . . . miserable:* one of the many moral maxims which Sidney introduces; cf. ll. 176–8, 'the most servile flattery is lodged most easily in the grossest capacity'.

BOOK I, CHAPTER 19

8 *forest-bill:* for hacking off tree-branches, a significant increase on his 'hedging bill', p. 92.

82 *so changeable in men's estates:* Pyrocles is thinking of Musidorus's disguise (the dramatic irony of which has been underlined by the ladies' patronizing attitude to his shyness), and of his own.

99 *swiftness of desire: force of affection:* imagery drawing attention to his love for Philoclea which inspires his courage.

109 *Arethusa:* a fountain-nymph pursued by the passionate river-god Alpheus: see Shelley's poem *Arethusa*. The simile is very apt, drawing attention to Philoclea's streaming draperies, and introducing Pyrocles's amorous pursuit of her.

113 *twice-wounded:* first by the lion's paw, and now by Philoclea's beauty.

124 *a new sight:* again a deliberate, and delicate, touch of the absurd; cf. 'a notable dumb show of Cupid's kingdom', p. 101.

224 *scorn borrowing the countenance of mirth:* In the Old *Arcadia*, Dametas's inglorious conduct is narrated in the third person. By giving the narration to Pamela, Sidney here further creates her character. The wit is, however, Sidney's own.

245 *plainness and honesty:* Basilius shows his poor judgement by his besotted over-estimation of Dametas, which is described brilliantly in Book I, Chapter 3 (Kalander is relating the story to Musidorus): 'The beginning of his credit was by the Prince's straying out of the way, one time he hunted, where meeting this

fellow and asking the way, and so falling into other questions, he found some of his answers (as a dog, sure, if he could speak, had wit enough to describe his kennel) not unsensible, and all uttered with such rudeness, which he interpreted plainness (though there be great difference between them), that Basilius conceiving a sudden delight, took him to his Court, with apparent show of his good opinion: where the flattering courtier had no sooner taken the Prince's mind but that there were straight reasons to confirm the Prince's doing, and shadows of virtues found for Dametas. His silence grew wit, his bluntness integrity, his beastly ignorance virtuous simplicity . . .'

299 *Cecropia:* see her own account of the incident, with the full explanation of her motives, in Book III, Chapter 2 (pp. 159–62).

BOOK II, CHAPTER 4
Having obtained admission to Dametas's lodge, Musidorus pretended courtship to Dametas's daughter: he addressed his words to Mopsa, but his eyes to Pamela, who soon understood his meaning. Therefore he told her a story of a prince called Musidorus who loved an Arcadian king's elder daughter and disguised himself as a shepherd. All this he recounts at his next meeting with Pyrocles.

26–40 *Zelmane was moved . . . lap of Philoclea:* Sidney uses a series of elaborate conceits to define Pyrocles's sensuous delight and strong emotion.

41 *proceeding . . . doctor of a coach:* comic academic metaphor; a scholar first 'proceeds bachelor (of arts)', next 'proceeds master (of arts – of which 'master of a cart' is a verbal echo)', and finally 'proceeds doctor (of divinity)'.

42–43 *that his whip guided the rule:* that he had the king as his passenger; a witty mixture of literal and metaphorical.

114–16 *The sweet-minded Philoclea . . . ground of virtue:* her virtue was her innocence; she had felt no temptation to do ill. Sidney's analysis of her growing love is pretty.

156–61 *Which when once it was enacted . . . statute thoroughly observed:* metaphor from parliamentary procedure, the Passions representing the Commons, the Thoughts the Lords, and Reason the Sovereign.

245–6 *the suspicion her captivity made her think she lived in:* The oracle (see Introduction, p. 13) had foretold that she should enjoy an unnatural love.

BOOK II, CHAPTER 5

28 *the tears of her eyes:* In this passage Sidney further enlarges
Pamela's character, showing that in spite of her firmness of
purpose she has tender feelings.

62-64 *but belike Fortune . . . so many perfections:* Fortune's gifts are
rank and wealth: Philoclea implies that these are most evident
when there is no other merit in their possessor.

84 *Therefore learn by my example:* dramatic irony, as Philoclea's
aside makes clear.

102 *the stranger Plangus:* Plangus, Prince of Iberia, had visited
Arcadia, and told Basilius and his family how Musidorus and
Pyrocles were drowned in a shipwreck. Pamela had therefore
been at first incredulous of Musidorus's confession, but he
cleverly turned her incredulity to his advantage, replying, 'I
perceive indeed you have neither heard nor read the story of
that unhappy Prince; for this was the very objection which that
peerless Princess did make unto him, when he sought to appear
such as he was before her wisdom' (Book II, Chapter 3).

131 *while he played Paris:* Paris, the son of Priam of Troy, was
brought up by a shepherd (being abandoned by his parents because of his foretold destiny to destroy the kingdom), and
courted Oenone. The little drama exposes the incongruous self-
esteem of Dametas and the secret love of Musidorus.

175-6 *suffer a temple . . . to be rased:* cf. *Astrophel and Stella*, XL.

204-5 *because she would be no sooner happy:* because she refuses
immediately to embrace the happiness which is offered to her.

BOOK II, CHAPTER 11

The next day, when the sisters rose, Pamela (who was ready before
Philoclea) asked Dorus to continue his story of Pyrocles and his
friend. He recounted their education, and several of their adventures, and proceeded to their going to the defence of 'the fair and
virtuous Queen Erona of Lycia, besieged by the puissant King of
Armenia'.

72 *There was among the rest:* Sidney left a gap here (doubtless intending to insert a catalogue of trees picturesquely described),
thus: 'There was the [space] But among the rest . . .'

97 *but of the smock was even jealous:* the smock, being the inmost
undergarment, touched Philoclea's body. Sidney skilfully
implies her beauty in this passage, to avoid anticipating Pyro-

cles's enthusiastic recital of it later. Thus he never so much as states that Philoclea is naked, instead using imagery (the sun 'showing his naked beams to the full view') and tactile sensation ('her feet, unwonted to feel the naked ground'; 'the touch of the cold water'; 'so that she was straight breast-high'; 'so seemed he to play about every part he could touch').

155 *What tongue can her perfections tell:* This poem appeared in the Old *Arcadia* in a different context, and is much better suited to its present position. It is a 'blason', a form of poem originating in the thirteenth century, in which a systematic catalogue of bodily beauties is followed by a brief tribute to the soul. 'A few of Sidney's images derive from stock comparisons such as "hair like golden wire" or "white as whale's bone"; but most of his details are original rather than conventional. His poem is highly ingenious, for it uses a shock technique which at first surprises by the exaggeration and apparent incongruity of the images, and then delights when further consideration reveals their essential appropriateness and unexpected relationships' (Ringler).

168 *Whose wink each bold attempt forbids:* To 'wink' was to close the eye, not to wink in the modern sense. The lids are lowered when the eyes are cast down in avoiding the bold glance of a lover.

214 *that which bears the Milky name:* the Milky Way among the stars.

219 *Waist; waste:* a typically Elizabethan play upon words.

242 *Ovid's song:* Sidney is probably thinking of Ovid's fifth Elegy of the first Book, in which an unexpected sight of Corinna's naked body is thus celebrated:

> What arms and shoulders did I touch and see!
> How apt her breasts were to be press'd by me!
> How smooth a belly under her waist saw I,
> How large a leg, and what a lusty thigh!
> (Marlowe's translation.)

257 *Whose Atlas is a smallest small:* Atlas, the mythical giant who held up the heavens, is (with intentional contrast) likened to the slender small of Philoclea's legs beneath her calves ('like crystal skies').

264 *Leda's swan:* Jupiter courted Leda in the shape of a swan.

270 *Passing the hate-spot ermelin:* surpassing the ermine, which keeps its white fur spotless: cf. *Astrophel and Stella*, LXXXVI.

271 *And thence those arms derived are:* 'arms' is another play upon words, meaning heraldic devices (which are 'derived', inherited) as well as the bodily arms which spring from the shoulders.

287 *Thus hath each part his beauty's part:* Thus each part of her body has its own share of beauty.

295-7 *Of whose high praise . . . doth lend –:* The praise of her soul is written in heaven's records by her virtue, immortal fame supplying the means. The long sentence (begun at l. 287) is broken off, for the reason explained in the last couplet.

316 *with a courteous (though sad) countenance:* Amphialus's character is well sketched, and his future rôle suggested, in the description which follows. He is indeed a worthy rival to Pyrocles, showing courtesy as well as passion and valour.

332-3 *'But for the glove, . . . give me leave to keep it':* Pyrocles had been anxious to recover the book and had been content to let the glove go. Amphialus wants the glove because it has enclosed Philoclea's hand. By the consequent reversal of Pyrocles's feelings, Sidney neatly stresses the drama of the situation.

390 *a near kinsman of mine:* dramatic irony on Pyrocles's part, unconsciously continued in Amphialus's reply. The phrase *answered Amphialus* is a slip: his identity should not have been revealed to the reader until his cousins recognized him.

409 *breaking their father's commandment:* in approaching their bathing place.

417-18 *and withal . . . his own doings:* He showed clearly that he had been dreaming of Philoclea, had waked to see her beauty, and had thereby further wounded himself with love.

418-19 *that was even jealous of herself for Zelmane:* who (sharing as she did all Zelmane's feelings) felt Zelmane's resentment of Amphialus's presumption.

435-6 *bound up by the sheets . . . wrapped:* Sidney loses no opportunity of showing his lovers' romantic sensibility.

BOOK II, CHAPTER 17

Meanwhile, both Gynecia and Basilius continued their advances to the disguised Pyrocles. While discouraging Basilius's courtship, Pyrocles thought of a way of profiting by his folly: 'and therefore, with a relented countenance, thus said unto him. "Your words (mighty Prince) were unfit either for me to hear, or you to speak: but yet the large testimony I see of your affection makes me willing to suppress a great number of errors. Only thus much I think good to say, that the same words in my Lady Philoclea's mouth, as from one woman to another (so as there were no other body by) might have had a better grace, and perchance have found a gentler receipt [reception]." ' Thus Pyrocles contrived a private interview with Philoclea, to whom Basilius immediately went and required her to declare his affection to Zelmane.

6–8 *and yet her fortune such . . . any contrary mean help her:* Her 'fortune' as a daughter obliges her to help her father; which could do her no harm, nor could any other course do her good, since a consequence of her being a *daughter* is that she can never marry Zelmane.

22–25 *A love more clear . . . a world of fire within me:* The 'clearness' of his love seems to be its purity, the 'coldness' its apparent impossibility of success. The antithesis of 'clear' and 'night', 'cold' and 'fire', is rather decorative than explanatory.

42 *But in the sand my pains foretold I find:* his love is as fruitless as words written in sand are impermanent.

102–3 *neglect his country . . . forsake to be Pyrocles:* Pyrocles is now repeating Musidorus's charges (see p. 81), to show Philoclea how far love has transformed him from his real self.

104 *a ship:* alluding to his supposed death at sea, Musidorus having told Pamela (the better to conceal his friend's disguised identity) that he was the only survivor. Pyrocles then develops an extended metaphor.

134 *honour:* in the special sense of strict sexual propriety; cf. *Astrophel and Stella*, Eighth Song, l. 95: 'Tyrant honour doth thus use thee.' It is likened to a mere candle in comparison with the sun of Philoclea's natural virtue.

162–3 *lay marble colours over my ruinous thoughts:* disguise cracks in a plastered surface by painting them to look like the veins in marble: an interesting sidelight on Elizabethan interior decoration.

168–9 *my passions . . . to be desired:* my feelings were those of a lover rather than of one beloved: active, not passive.

191 *commanded the contrary:* This is not the end of the chapter, in
  which, at Philoclea's desire, Pyrocles now resumes the history
  of himself and Musidorus.

BOOK III, CHAPTER 2

When Pyrocles had declared himself to Philoclea, and had told her
the rest of his adventures, he was called on to perform a fresh deed
of courage in defending Basilius's lodge against an angry rebellious
mob (suborned for the purpose by Cecropia), and of wisdom in
pacifying them with an eloquent speech. Musidorus, who had
arrived in time to second Pyrocles's defence, thereby gained Pamela's
favour; but he lost it again by rashly attempting to kiss her soon
afterwards, whereupon she banished him from her sight. In despair
he left her a long letter in classical elegiac metre, 'as fittest for
mourning'.

16 *impossible granting:* of Basilius's suit. *dangerous refusing:* of
  Gynecia's.

39 *the face of the foremost of them, in excellency fair:* This was
  Artesia (whose beauty Phalantus had boastfully asserted at the
  tournament) in disguise. When Phalantus was defeated she
  quarrelled with him and returned to the castle of Cecropia, who
  had brought her up (being the orphan daughter of her late
  husband's friend) in her own selfish principles. For her reward
  see p. 187 and note.

70 *busied in weightier affairs:* Philanax, the regent, had come to
  inquire into the late rebellion.

86–87 *who disgraced weeping with her countenance:* Sidney inverts a
  conventional idea (of spoiling a beautiful face with weeping) in
  order to ridicule Mopsa's ugliness.

111 *with a gag in her mouth:* poetic justice; Miso is a shrewish wife,
  and her conversation 'noisome', p. 137.

185 *my husband's virtue:* 'virtù' very much in the Italian contem-
  porary sense, meaning 'strength of mind', 'firmness of purpose'.
  Cecropia is the type of the Elizabethan 'Machiavellian': she
  employs any means to secure her selfish ends, and makes use
  of 'policy' or scheming.

BOOK III, CHAPTER 3

1–22 *pictured the two passions of fear and desire:* Amphialus's
  costume is a striking instance of Elizabethan symbolism. When

Sidney was readmitted to Queen Elizabeth's favour after offending her with his dissuasion from marriage his New Year's present to her (1581) was a whip garnished with small diamonds, in token of submission. Compare also the Knight of the Tomb, p. 173.

BOOK III, CHAPTER 6

While Amphialus prepared to resist Basilius and his army, Cecropia ('stirred with no other pity, but for her son') visited Philoclea and urged her to marry Amphialus, promising her not only liberty but also power if she did so, recommending the joys of a husband and children, and praising Amphialus for his beauty, his rank, his wealth, and above all his love. To this Philoclea (who thought only of Pyrocles) replied that she would never yield under the pressure of imprisonment.

34–35 *tedious clogs of a thralled obligation:* irksome encumbrances, enforcing a constrained gratitude: a clog is a heavy object attached to a prisoner's chain.

38–39 *only construing . . . right bitter servitude:* she interpreting her servitude only in its true nature, and judging it a true and a very bitter servitude.

107–8 *all her senses . . . her inward motions:* all her outward actions merely suggesting her inner feelings, which were too sublime to be adequately expressed.

BOOK III, CHAPTER 16

Basilius's army now arrived, and fighting began. The king was supported by Philanax (the regent, and commander of the army), and by an unknown knight in black armour (Musidorus). Besides the general skirmishing there were formal single combats, Amphialus challenging his adversaries to meet him within sight of Philoclea's window, hoping (though vainly) that his courage might win her heart. All comers were overthrown by him. At last Basilius summoned Argalus to accept Amphialus's challenge. Argalus was living in his castle in perfect happiness and love with his recently married wife Parthenia: the summons distressed them both, but he could not neglect the call of duty. They took a sad farewell, Argalus trying to persuade Parthenia that he would return ('I shall live, doubt not: for so great a blessing as you are was not given unto me, so soon to be deprived of it.'), in spite of his misgivings. Argalus and

Amphialus encountered, and Argalus was slain, dying in the arms of Parthenia, who had followed him.

Amphialus's party was now reinforced by his proud friend Anaxius; while the king's party received aid from the black knight once more, accompanied by two other knights, equally unknown, one in white and the other in green armour.

63 *missed his rest:* the 'rest' is the hollow in the tilting-saddle, into which the lance was placed to hold it the more steady.

135 *Atropos:* the third of the Fates; her office was to cut the thread of each human life.

157 *have her heart's desire:* by which they understood revenge, but she meant death.

BOOK III, CHAPTER 20

The unknown Musidorus, using the title of the Forsaken Knight, and still wearing his black armour, challenged Amphialus; who encountered him also in black armour (symbolizing his sorrow for Parthenia's death, and his grief at Philoclea's continued refusal to love him), wearing as his only crest Philoclea's knives. Their combat was particularly hard and long, the contestants being most equally matched in strength, skill, and eagerness; and at last, both being badly wounded, they were carried off by their several supporters.

While Amphialus lay senseless in his bed, his wicked mother used such means as she dared not use when he was well: by threatening to cut off the heads of Basilius's daughters and Zelmane, she got the king to withdraw his army.

5 *Zoilus and Lycurgus:* brothers of Amphialus's friend Anaxius, who was also wounded in the recent fighting.

63 *still swelling the more she was stopped:* The image is that of a toad, then supposed full of poison: cf. ll. 67–68, 'with a countenance empoisoned with malice'.

71–72 *like a Fury . . . Diana's temple:* Diana's temple at Ephesus was burned by Herostratus: it was a notorious act of arson. Philoclea's body, virgin and untouched, suggests Diana's temple; Cecropia's rod, which would be a bundle of twigs tied together at one end, is likened to a faggot; and Cecropia herself, deformed with anger and cruelty, is compared with a Fury who tormented the souls in Hades.

77–78 *Virtue rarely found . . . oppression of that day:* Compare *The Defence of Poesy*, p. 34, where Sidney says that the historian is 'captived to the truth of a foolish world', and, whereas the poet can show virtue rewarded, must sometimes show virtue oppressed.

120 *that imperious power:* what is today called telepathy.

134 *the fruit:* their consent to marry her son.

165–6 *the case wherein . . . shepherd:* his despair at the disfavour which had greeted his attempt to kiss her.

BOOK III, CHAPTER 23

Finding her cruelty useless, Cecropia devised a stratagem. To show Philoclea that she was in earnest, she forced her to look from a window into the great hall of the castle, and there, upon a scaffold covered with crimson velvet, see a blindfolded lady beheaded. Pyrocles was likewise shown this execution from another window, and both he and Philoclea were assured by the lady's apparel that it was Pamela. Then Cecropia arranged an interview between Philoclea and Pyrocles (still supposed to be Zelmane by all but Philoclea), whose fear for Philoclea's life made him urge her to save herself by pretending love to Amphialus. But she refused; and in a few days Pyrocles, hearing some noise in the hall, saw from his window the scaffold bearing Philoclea's head in a golden basin. The sight filled him with despairing grief.

114–15 *the soul of Philoclea:* Pyrocles is incapable of the idea that Philoclea is alive. He takes his visitor first for an angel which has assumed Philoclea's form, and then for the soul of Philoclea.

115 *her double falsehood:* Artesia had betrayed Cecropia as well as the Princesses. Cecropia had made her think that by enticing them to her castle she would procure their deaths and afterwards be married to Amphialus, whom she loved. Finding this untrue, Artesia joined with the treacherous steward Clinias (he whom Cecropia had employed to raise the countrymen's rebellion) in a plot to smuggle in armour and weapons for Pyrocles (Zelmane) and to contrive the Princesses' escape. But they overreached themselves in planning also to poison Amphialus, since Philoclea's kindness and Pamela's uprightness alike abhorred such treachery; and while trying to persuade Pamela, Artesia was overheard and detected by Cecropia.

120–1 *bringing me down under the scaffold:* The trick here described
was an illusion performed by jugglers at fairs and used as a
stage device in the theatre. Among the properties at Henslowe's
theatre, the Rose, in 1598 was 'a frame for the heading [be-
heading]'. This trick platform, enabling a performer 'to cut off
one's head, and to lay it in a platter', is reproduced from
Reginald Scot's *The Discovery of Witchcraft* in C. Walter Hod-
ges's book *The Globe Restored* (1953), p. 74. Scot's book was
published in 1584, and we may assume that Sidney learned the
trick from it, and that therefore he wrote this part of the revised
Arcadia not long before his death.

203–6 *procure him liberty . . . promise to himself:* for, once free, he
assures himself that his courage, strengthened and motivated
by his love, will be capable of her rescue.

BOOK III, CHAPTER 24

28 *poor gentleman:* a phrase used more than once by Sidney of
Amphialus.

36 *thy godly mother:* strong irony (stronger than Philoclea's 'the
good woman Cecropia', p. 188), for Cecropia, like a true
'Machiavellian', is an atheist, as she has shown in her arguments
to Pamela in Book III, Chapter 10 ('The aunt's atheism refuted
by the niece's divinity', as the heading puts it).

44 *unkindness of his wrong:* resentment of the wrongs done her
(though indirectly) by him.

50 *by threatening torture:* thus showing the unaccustomed violence
of his feelings, and presaging his next deeds.

91 *Philoxenus:* a young lord of Corinth. His story is told in Book I,
Chapter 11. Amphialus was brought up with Philoxenus by
the latter's father Timotheus, having been sent there by
Cecropia when Gynecia had borne the two Princesses, she
'either disdaining or fearing that her son should live under the
power of Basilius'. The two young men became close friends.
Philoxenus, falling in love with Queen Helen of Corinth, employed his friend to speak for him, which Amphialus sincerely
did, but with this result, that she fell in love with the spokesman.
Amphialus decided to leave the country therefore, but was
overtaken and challenged by his enraged friend, and unluckily
killed him; and Timotheus, at that moment coming up (having

followed his son in hopes of calming him), was overwhelmed with grief and fell down dead.

In Book III, Chapter 25 (the chapter following Amphialus's tragedy), Queen Helen arrives 'to carry away Amphialus with her to the excellentest surgeon then known, whom she had in her country, but so old as not able to travel'. Perhaps Sidney, having brought him 'to the senseless gate of death', nevertheless meant to rescue him, and preserve him for fortunes more fitting his deserts.

95 *Ismenus:* Amphialus's squire, brother of Artesia. In the first battle with Basilius's forces (Book III, Chapter 8), when Amphialus's horse was killed under him, Ismenus remounted him on his own horse, 'asking no advice of no thought but of faithfulness and courage', and in the ensuing hand-to-hand fighting was killed by Philanax.

97 *unknown knight:* Musidorus, who struck him down in the course of their undecided combat.

118 *Charon's boat:* to ferry him to the Underworld.

121 *Philoclea's knives:* their frequent mention since her imprisonment has prepared the reader for this symbolic climax to Amphialus's tragedy.

127 *kindness and unkindness:* love and hate: love of Philoclea and hatred of himself.

MISCELLANEOUS POEMS

I. From the Old *Arcadia*. Musidorus, planning his elopement with Pamela, sends Dametas and his wife and daughter on various wild-goose chases. Dametas is set to dig for hidden treasure, Mopsa to climb a magic tree and get her choice of a husband, and Miso to surprise her husband in the arms of a young woman whom Musidorus declared he had heard singing this song to Dametas. The occasion is comic, but the lyric (really a sonnet arranged as two stanzas) is pretty, and has won its independence from its context. Its opening line is perhaps the best-known line of Sidney's poetry.

7 *He loves my heart for once it was his own:* The symmetry of the statements requires this ambiguous line to be interpreted as the converse of the next: that is, 'He loves the heart in his bosom (my heart) because once it was his own'.

II. From the Old *Arcadia*. Pamela, eloping with Musidorus, sleeps in a wood, while he speaks these verses, a sonnet on two rhymes.

III. A satire on love, originally included in the First Eclogues of the Old *Arcadia* and recited by the shepherd Dicus in explanation of a satirical picture he brought with him. In the revised *Arcadia* it is recited by Dametas's wife Miso.

10 *How is he young, that tam'd old Phoebus' youth?:* Cupid made Phoebus in love (with Daphne); therefore, if he is as old as the sun, Cupid is as old as creation.

11–12 *But arrows two . . . horny head:* Besides the arrows which encourage and discourage love, Cupid is satirically given a third, which causes adultery and makes cuckolds; cf. *Astrophel and Stella*, LXXVIII, l. 14.

14, 16 *Argus:* Jupiter changed Io into a heifer to conceal from Juno his courtship of her. Juno, however, set the hundred-eyed Argus to guard her, but at length he was charmed asleep by Mercury and so slain. The parentage of Cupid is, of course, satirical invention, to explain his physical characteristics in ll. 25–30.

IV. An epithalamium, or marriage song: later well-known examples are by Spenser and Donne. Sung in the Third Eclogues of the Old *Arcadia* to celebrate the marriage of Lalus and Kala, a shepherd and shepherdess. The stanza is modelled upon that of a Spanish poem.

24–25 *And, like . . . do endure:* grammatically confused, but meaning 'and be like lilies pure, which' etc.; cf. ll. 33–35.

V. First included in the 1593 edition of *Arcadia*. The structure is like that of the preceding poem, a stanza being given to each object in turn, with a final recapitulation. The stanza is modelled upon that of an Italian poem.

1 *Philisides:* Sidney's name for himself, under which he plays a very minor part in *Arcadia*. In this poem he is an English shepherd lamenting the absence of his beloved Mira, who is supposed to be somewhere in the West, beyond the hills; ll. 96, 105–9, 125–6.

78 *bae-waymenting:* (text: 'bea-waymenting.') The Northern 'bae' comes nearer to the Elizabethan pronunciation than the standard 'baa'.

79–81 The turtle is here supposed to have a living mate, but was 'a widow' in l. 6, there serving as an object of pathos.

105–13 This short stanza is the 'envoy' in which Philisides consigns his song to Mira. It is linked to the preceding stanza by the rhyme of its second line.

113 *willow's bark:* The willow was the symbol of forlorn lovers (cf. Desdemona's willow song in *Othello*), and here, like the rest of the imagery, expresses the speaker's mood.

114–26 This stanza, the last, is distinguished from the rest by being written entirely in feminine rhymes.

VI. From the Old *Arcadia* (Fourth Eclogues). This, like the preceding poem, is a lamentation of the beloved's absence. Strephon and Klaius are gentlemen who have become shepherds through love of Urania, supposedly a shepherd's daughter. Sidney introduced other references to their story in the revised *Arcadia*, and no doubt would have brought Urania's true birth to light if he had finished the revision.

Their lament takes the form of a double sestina. In a sestina the lines of each stanza end with the same six words, systematically interchanged, each stanza using the endings of its predecessor in the order 615243, until at the end of the sixth stanza the complete change has been rung. As this is a *double* sestina, the whole process is then repeated. A three-line conclusion introduces the six words in their original order.

The sestina form is an evident test of a poet's technique, but there is more than technique in Sidney's poem. He not only sustains the interest by introducing fresh ideas but also produces an impression 'most musical, most melancholy' by his versification: notice in particular the plangency of 'Is gone, is gone' (l. 71), which is the climax of the lament.

VII. First printed in 1598 as one of the *Certain Sonnets* (i.e., lyrical poems, including some sonnets in the strict sense of the word) appended to *Arcadia* (see Chronology).

The nightingale traditionally sings with her breast against a thorn (l. 4, and refrain): she was originally Philomela, and was turned into a nightingale after Tereus had ravished her and cut out her tongue. Sidney alludes to this legend with some surprising touches of humour (ll. 16, 20), which, however, are not out of harmony with the prevailing mood of a lover's self-pity. It is a delicate and graceful lyric.

VIII. From *Certain Sonnets*. Sidney ingeniously works out the conceit of Love's death and burial as the vehicle for an attack on women's disdain; but the last stanza is a recantation. The refrain is modelled on the petitions in the Litany, from which the phrase 'Good Lord, deliver us' comes.

15 *false-seeming holy:* hypocritical virtue. Faux-Semblant, in the *Roman de la Rose* (the most famous medieval allegory of Love), is hypocrisy. Why Sidney calls this Love's 'will' is not clear.

IX. From *Certain Sonnets*.

X. From *Certain Sonnets*. The Latin postscript means 'I bid a long farewell to splendid trifles.'

1 Sometimes printed without the comma after 'Love'; this distinguishes earthly love from heavenly love, but spoils the surprise of the end, where it is revealed that devotion to God is also 'love', and not transient but eternal.

3 *that which never taketh rust:* i.e., treasure in heaven; cf. Matthew VI, 19–20.

6 *that sweet yoke where lasting freedoms be:* cf. the second collect at Morning Prayer: 'the author of peace and lover of concord, in knowledge of whom standeth our eternal life, whose service is perfect freedom'.

Short Bibliography

WORKS BY SIR PHILIP SIDNEY

The Complete Works of Sir Philip Sidney, edited by E. Feuillerat, 4 vols., 1912–26. (Cambridge English Classics.) Reissued, with minor corrections, 1962.

The Poems of Sir Philip Sidney, edited by William A. Ringler, Jr, 1962. (Oxford English Texts.)

The Defence of Poesy (or *An Apology for Poetry*), edited by Evelyn S. Shuckburgh, 1891 (revised 1896); edited by J. Churton Collins, 1907.

Astrophel and Stella, edited by A. W. Pollard, 1888; edited by Mona Wilson, 1931; edited, with French translation, by M. Poirier, 1957.

Arcadia, edited by E. A. Baker, 1907.

OTHER WORKS

Baker, Ernest A. *The History of the English Novel: Vol. II: The Elizabethan Age and After*, 1929.

Boas, F. S. *Sir Philip Sidney, representative Elizabethan: his Life and Writings*, 1955.

Buxton, John. *Elizabethan Taste*, 1963. (Chapters on *Astrophel and Stella* and *Arcadia*.)

Danby, J. F. *Poets on Fortune's Hill*, 1952. (On the relationship of *Arcadia* to other Elizabethan and Jacobean literature.)

Greaves, Margaret. *The Blazon of Honour: a Study in Renaissance Magnanimity*, 1964. (Chapter on Sidney.)

Greville, Fulke (Baron Brooke). *The Life of the Renowned Sir Philip Sidney*, 1652 (written c. 1612); edited by Nowell Smith, 1907.

Jusserand, J. J. *The English Novel in the Time of Shakespeare*, 1887; English translation, 1890.

Lamb, Charles. *Last Essays of Elia*, 1833. ('Some Sonnets of Sir Philip Sydney.')

Legouis, E. (and Cazamian, P.). *A History of English Literature*, 1926; English translation, 1930.

Lewis, C. S. *English Literature in the Sixteenth Century, excluding Drama*, 1954.

Muir, K. *Sir Philip Sidney* ('Writers and their Work' series), 1960.

Myrick, K. O. *Sir Philip Sidney as a Literary Craftsman*, 1935.

Poirier, M. *Sir Philip Sidney, le chevalier poète élizabéthain*, 1948; not yet published in translation.

Smith, Hallett. *Elizabethan Poetry: a Study in Conventions, Meaning and Expression*, 1952.

Spencer, T. 'The Poetry of Sidney', *ELH (Journal of English Literary History)*, Vol. XII, 1945.

Wallace, M. W. *The Life of Sir Philip Sidney*, 1915.

Wilson, Mona. *Sir Philip Sidney*, 1931.

Woolf, Virginia. *The Second Common Reader*, 1932. ('The Countess of Pembroke's Arcadia.')

Zandvoort, R. W. *Sidney's 'Arcadia': a Comparison between the Two Versions*, 1929.

Index to First Lines